HE WAS ALWAYS WITH ME

"What a captivating read! The book takes you on an incredible journey. Robert Hornak's life story is replete with both hilarious and dangerous adventures that leave you on the edge of your seat. Taking in the highs and lows makes you appreciate the capacity of the human soul to endure suffering and heartache. Between the laughter and the tears, you will be deeply moved by the love the Lord Jesus has for His people, and the great lengths God goes to woo the hearts of His children."

Jahan Berns
Founder & CEO-Triumph of Hope
Author of *Stories and Prayers to Ignite Your Heart*

"Faith is a journey that happens in community. Robert Hornak's story is a lifetime of growing in grace, whether he knew it or not at the time. Saved by Jesus and the love of his family, each chapter is punctuated by Scripture to reveal God's hand in each of our stories. Read and be honest, read and be blessed."

The Reverend Richmond R. Webster
Rector, Saint Luke's Episcopal Church
Birmingham, Alabama

"I have had the privilege of knowing Robert and Bentley Hornak for many years, and I've watched their incredible children grow from young kids into Christ-filled adults. Robert has always been the kind of man people look up to—an alpha, a man's man, a collegiate athlete with a successful career, a strong marriage, and a beautiful family. From the outside, he seemed to carry it all with ease. But *He Was Always with Me* reveals a deeper truth: even the strongest among us are incomplete without Jesus.

Robert had accumulated an impressive amount of worldly success, but his treasure was being stored outside the Kingdom of God.

Through the unwavering faith, love, and strength of his amazing wife Bentley—and through God's persistent pursuit—Robert surrendered his life to Jesus. He stopped living merely *for* his family and began living *for* God and leading His family toward Him. That decision transformed them from a great family into a Godly one, and opened the door for God to use Robert, Bentley, and their children for His divine purposes and glory.

This book is a powerful word of encouragement to men who believe they 'have it all' yet feel that something is missing. Without a relationship with Jesus, we have nothing. He alone is our great advocate, our peace, and our purpose. Our lives are not our own, and the choice to follow Jesus shapes not only our present but the legacy we leave for generations. I urge every reader—especially every husband, father, and leader—to choose the narrow path, surrender to Christ, and call on the Holy Spirit to guide your heart and your home. Robert's story is raw, honest, and filled with hope. I wholeheartedly recommend *He Was Always with Me* to anyone seeking transformation through the One who never stops pursuing us."

Brad Hassig, DC
Chiropractic Physician & Functional Health Provider
Host of the *Second Chance at Health* Podcast

HE WAS ALWAYS WITH ME

*A True Story of God's Persistence
in My Chaotic Life*

ROBERT HORNAK

Stonebrook Publishing
Saint Louis, Missouri

A STONEBROOK PUBLISHING BOOK

©2025 Robert C. C. Hornak
This book was guided in development and
edited by Nancy L. Erickson, The Book Professor®
TheBookProfessor.com

Scripture taken from the New King James Version®,
Copyright © 1982 by Thomas Nelson. Used by permission. All rights reserved.

Scriptures taken from the Holy Bible, New International Version®, NIV®.
Copyright © 1973, 1978, 1984, 2011 by Biblica, Inc.™
Used by permission of Zondervan.

Holy Bible New Living Translation, copyright © 1996, 2004, 2015
by Tyndale House Foundation. Used by permission of Tyndale House Publishers,
Carol Stream, Illinois 60188, USA. All rights reserved.

Library of Congress Control Number: 2025918816
Softcover ISBN: 978-1-955711-43-2
Hardcover ISBN: 978-1-955711-44-9
eBook ISBN: 978-1-955711-45-6

www.stonebrookpublishing.net
PRINTED IN THE UNITED STATES OF AMERICA

For Jesus, the One Who saved me!

CONTENTS

FOREWORD

Robert called me one day and asked if I would write a foreword for his book. I was truthfully a little baffled but felt honored that he asked. I asked why he wanted me to do this, and he just said, "You will know as you read the book."

In the book, he wrote that he had met me at a Braves Fantasy baseball week in Orlando, Florida, and I thought, *Is this why he wanted me to write a foreword?* As I read further, I realized why he had asked me, and I was honored.

Robert often uses movie titles to make his points. So, I'm going to throw a movie title at you to describe my sentiments about his book. My movie title for his book would be *The Good, the Bad, and the Ugly*, but by the time I reached the end of the book, I wanted to add another word to the list—*Beautiful*.

As I read through this book, I initially wondered what it had to do with Christianity. Robert describes a pretty wild and adventurous lifestyle. Before and after his marriage to Bentley, I was a bit jealous of how they lived their lives. They traveled more and did more than most people could do in two lifetimes. And, at the end of every chapter, Robert wrote a Bible verse. With each chapter, I'd think, *How does this have anything to do with Christianity and living your life for Jesus Christ?* I was baffled. That was the good part of the good, the bad, and the ugly.

The bad part was Robert's lifestyle and all the things he did that were illegal, wild, and unhealthy—but again, at the end of every chapter, I found another Bible verse.

The ugly was all that Bentley had to go through in her life and their struggle to keep things together. I felt sympathy for her with every surgery and every recovery she went through, but Robert and Bentley did it together. And he educated me throughout the book about the procedures she had to undergo. He was in surgical equipment sales, and he brought me along with all of Bentley's operations that she endured.

Now, to the beautiful part. Through all the good, bad, and ugly, Jesus Christ was doing something beautiful. He was bringing both Robert and Bentley closer to seeing the goodness of God—something that all of us need to understand. No matter what we've done, Jesus Christ is still standing there with open arms, waiting for us to come to Him and surrender. Robert's family did that. Now they walk with the love of Christ in their hearts, and they share that with others.

I was reminded of the parable where Jesus speaks about the shepherd losing one of His sheep. While He still had ninety-nine, He was so concerned about losing that one sheep that He left them all to go find the one. Well, in this case, it was not just one, but an entire family.

While reading this book, you might find yourself saying, *Are you kidding me?* throughout it, but in the end, the final pieces of the puzzle will be put into place. It is where God and His Son, Jesus, want all of us to come. Remember, His arms are always wide open and waiting for each of you to say, "I need You, Jesus."

Thank you, Robert, for allowing me to read this book. I am thankful, in the end, that you are a child of the King. Keep going and finish the race God has put before you!

—Sid Bream,
Former MLB player, motivational speaker,
but better yet, a Christ follower

"What we do in life echoes in eternity."
—Russell Crowe as Maximus in *Gladiator*

PROLOGUE

"I shall be telling this with a sigh
Somewhere ages and ages hence:
Two roads diverged in a wood, and I—
I took the one less traveled by,
And that has made all the difference."

—Robert Frost

Robert Frost wrote the poem "The Road Not Taken" in 1915, more or less as a joke for fellow poet and friend Edward Thomas, chronicling the question of which path to take when they both went walking together. But those five lines became my mantra for almost thirty-six years. Whether or not they fueled me to lean into difficult life choices or allowed me to take on and overcome a variety of obstacles, I had confidence in Frost's sage words. So, when it came time to select a college, I chose The Citadel, the Military College of South Carolina. In fact, it was the only school where I applied.

I selected The Citadel for a multitude of reasons: to please my dad, to honor my statement under oath to a Charleston judge, to differentiate myself from everyone in my high school, and to perhaps stubbornly push back on all the people who told me I'd never make it. Instead of going to Auburn, Florida, or Virginia to party and run from a myriad of problems, I decided to show them all and walk straight into the fire. I took the road less traveled. I knew it made all the difference.

You could see that difference in my life, in my work, and in the way I lived. I'd succeeded when others had failed because The Citadel taught me how to persevere. I married a beautiful, Southern California beach girl, we reared three amazing kids together, and I had an incredible decades-long career in the medical field. My fingerprints were on everything I touched. In my world, no one made decisions without me—at least not without my input. I was in control. I was an island.

However, something more devastating was lurking out there. Something I never saw coming—a Mike Tyson right uppercut that hit me so hard it would change my life forever. A cataclysmic series of life-altering events that reached a devastating crescendo four and a half years later when I answered my cell phone and heard the words, "We can't do this over the phone. We must meet in person."

The world as I knew it, as I lived it, as I ran it, was crumbling all around me.

I thought I had a plan. Shoot, *I* was the plan. I was the captain of a massive battleship, and I kept it running without fail until one day, when I was humbled in a way that brought me to my knees. And once I processed the five stages of grief, I realized that perhaps the road less traveled wasn't about choosing military school as I'd thought my entire adult life, but rather, and more importantly, a walk with Jesus.

"Enter through the narrow gate. For wide is the gate and broad is the road
that leads to destruction, and many enter through it.
But small is the gate and narrow the road that leads to life,
and only a few find it."

—Matthew 7:13-14 NIV

1

LATE CHECKOUT

"Welcome to The Rock."

—Sean Connery as John Patrick Mason in The Rock

I lived in a hotel for two years of my life. For most of my middle school years, the Charleston Riverview Hotel, a fourteen-story, round Holiday Inn located in Charleston, South Carolina, that towered over the city and marina, was my home. The hotel stood nestled between two drawbridges. The westbound span was the Ashley River Memorial Bridge, and the eastbound span was the T. Allen Legare Bridge.

I'd never even seen a round hotel before, and this one came with a rooftop bar and restaurant with the best view of Charleston you could find anywhere. My sad feelings about leaving Atlanta and my two good friends behind earlier that morning were quickly exchanged by the prospect of infinite possibilities. Over the next week, I was going to see our new house, pick my room, visit my new school, and start football practice. In the meantime, I'd enjoy room service, swim in the pool, and play *Pac-Man* in the rooftop lounge. But what seemed like a dream week-long vacation would turn into a two-year prison sentence.

"Everything will be better."

At least that's what my dad told me as we finished loading up the family Oldsmobile Cutlass Custom Cruiser on that July 1980 day in the sweltering 105-degree Atlanta heat. Our classic American station wagon, still fresh with that new car smell, was packed to the gills. We had so many bags tied to the roof rack that the weight strained the rear shocks. My mom's car was a cross between navy and royal blue, and it came fully loaded with an enormous amount of dark wood paneling. If you've seen the movie *Vacation* with Chevy Chase, you know what I'm talking about. We squeezed into the wagon, waved goodbye to our Dunwoody, Georgia, house, and began the five-hour drive to South Carolina, presumably to a new start.

My dad drove that day, which was a bit of a surprise since he'd moved himself to Texas around 1977 to start a new career. He was rarely around. We'd see him for a week at Christmas, on an occasional weekend or at a big event, but any other time was a crapshoot. My mom sat shotgun in the car, and the night before, she'd made us a spaghetti dinner to commemorate our last night in Atlanta. That was unusual, too, because it's my only memory of us eating a meal in the dining room of our old house.

My little sister, Emily, and I grabbed our customary spots in the back seat. We weren't allowed to bring our cat, Jakey, or her kittens with us. My dad didn't like cats because his mom didn't like cats, so our family cat had to go. As well as the kittens. Fortunately, our next-door neighbor took Jakey in, and the pet store found a home for all her babies. I was thirteen, my sister was ten, and we were being driven to our new life by the man who had very little to do with ours.

We'd been driving for well over two hours, so we took a lunch break and pit stop in Augusta, Georgia, before continuing to Charleston. While traveling east on I-26, about fifteen minutes outside the city, I shouted, "Who ripped one? That's terrible! Hold it, what's that smell?"

I thought someone had passed gas, but it turned garlicky and, in mere seconds, evolved into the worst rotten-eggs odor I'd ever smelled. That sickening emanation latched itself onto the back of my throat before I knew what was happening. And while I didn't know it that evening, that stench would illicit an instant reaction and a flood of memories every time I approached The Holy City from the north.

While Charleston might be best known for its antebellum homes, cobblestone streets, picturesque views overlooking the Ashley River, and Old South charm, the city is thought to have derived its nickname (The Holy City) from its religious tolerance. The skyline boasts approximately four hundred church steeples that span a multitude of denominations. On the flip side, Charleston is also a city still trying to recover from its past involvement and profit in the slave trade. It's estimated that over one-third of all enslaved Africans coming to North America passed through the port of Charleston.

Adding to the history of the city, many scholars also believe that Citadel cadets fired the first shots of the Civil War on the merchant steamship the *Star of the West* as it was heading to Fort Sumter with reinforcements and supplies. After the war ended, with the region reeling, scientists and chemists discovered that the Charleston area was rich with phosphate "stink rocks" that could be used to produce modern-day fertilizers.

So, ten miles outside the city, somewhere around Ashley Phosphate Road, I got a whiff of that putrid odor. On some days, if the winds coming off the Atlantic were robust enough, that rotten stench could carry all the way downtown or much further north. If you blindfolded me and I parachuted into one hundred cities around the world, I'd know the second I landed in Charleston.

From the moment we exited I-26 onto Meeting Street, I still had the remnants of the phosphate stuck to the back of my throat. As we drove past Francis Marion Square, my eyes quickly noticed all the historical buildings and countless churches. So many of these structures predated the Civil War. After we parked on Market Street, my ears could hear the clip-clopping of horse hooves pulling tourist carriages up and down the street in this bygone era of transportation. I'd never seen a real horse before and wanted to pet one, but my nose was inundated with a new collection of smells. First, the powerful stench of ammonia from massive amounts of urine followed right behind, literally, with the heavy smell of manure that hung over and permeated the entire outdoor market. It's noteworthy that in 2024, the city used GPS trackers to mark defecation locations, but way back in 1980, there was no such technology, so it took considerable time for cleanup crews to find and remove all the horse whizz and feces from the roads.

It was impossible to enjoy my ice cream cone while a one-thousand-pound horse released quarts of urine and unloaded six or seven pounds of solid waste in between the cobblestones or onto the heavily traveled roads. As we walked from the market to The Battery, I was introduced to another kind of rotten egg odor: pluff mud at low tide. Equally rancid, that foul stench also left a bad taste in my mouth. These were just some of the many unmistakable sights, sounds, and smells of downtown Charleston. We definitely weren't in Atlanta anymore.

That July evening, we did a little sightseeing, had dinner in a beautifully restored Victorian-house-turned-restaurant on Queen Street, then called it a night. We packed into our 324-square-foot room at the round Holiday Inn.

Day two started with peak anticipation. My dad had bought a historic, four-story double tenement home built by local merchant James Matthews around 1740. This home on Tradd Street was built more than 120 years before the first shot of the Civil War was fired. For approximately two hundred years, it remained a tenement home, but in the mid-nineteenth century, it was converted into a single-family residence when contractors pierced the interior walls and joined the two houses together.

It rested about 13 feet above sea level and needed extensive repairs. My dad saw this as a savvy investment, but to maintain its historical status, it needed time-consuming and expensive repairs to comply with a multitude of city bylaws, ordinances, rules and regulations. My sister and I walked through the house, picked our new bedrooms, and got a sense of what life would be like living on the peninsula. To say that this house, street, and city were different from my life in Atlanta would be an understatement. Everything about living in Charleston was different.

After walking The Battery, a local landmark and defensive seawall, we drove through The College of Charleston and across the Ashley River to see my new school. After a quick tour of the grounds, my mom and dad took us to Ye Old Fashioned, an ice cream cafe and sandwich shop. It became one of my favorite places to pass the time, eating grilled cheese sandwiches and French fries, drinking mint chocolate chip milkshakes, and playing hours of *Pac-Man, Donkey Kong,* and the coolest game ever, *Dragon's Lair.*

As we ate dinner, my dad informed us that work on the house was taking longer than expected and that it might be more like a month or two and less like a couple of weeks. I was totally fine with that. More room service, swimming, and video games in a hotel sounded perfect to me. We dropped him off at the airport that Sunday night, and he went back to his life in Texas. I had no idea when I'd see him again.

While I'd never played football, my dad had signed me up for the seventh-grade team at Porter-Gaud, a former all-boys Episcopal military school that had gone co-ed a few years earlier. I'd only played church league basketball and soccer in Atlanta, so I was way out of my element trying to learn this new game, as well as the names of all my new teammates. Classes started a couple of weeks later, and I had no idea what was about to hit me. As a student, I had to wear a coat and tie or a full suit with dress shoes every day. While I was comfortable taking English, math, and science, I was also enrolled in Latin, philosophy, government and world affairs, and art history. I'd been a decent student at my public grade school in Atlanta, but now I was completely out of my element only one week into the new year. My classmates had been in this environment since first grade, maybe even earlier, and I'd never heard of Latin or GAWA, and I'd never seen a famous painting.

I later learned that I'd tested two to three years behind my classmates. Academically, I should have been going into fourth or fifth grade, but the decision makers decided to place me in seventh grade. Maybe it was too close to the new year, but I didn't have to go to summer school, and I sure didn't have a tutor. I wasn't struggling. I was drowning.

There were a couple of kids I talked to at school, but make no mistake, I was an outsider—an awkward teenager born in Milwaukee and plunked into one of the snobbiest Old South cities that still clung to old ways of thinking. Northerners didn't belong, especially those who thought they could encroach on the generations of charmed history that was one of the only things that defined some of these families.

My granddad had immigrated from Slovakia, my dad was living in Texas, and I still resided in the round hotel between the twin drawbridges. I was miserable in school, I hated football (or at least getting hit), and every night, I was crammed into that tiny hotel room with my mom and sister for hours on end. Even if I wanted to take my classes seriously, there was no place to study. I physically couldn't stay in the room with them for extended periods of time. My only options were to head to the lobby, sit by the pool, or head up to the rooftop lounge.

The bar became my refuge. Before the dinner rush or hotel guests came up for drinks, I grabbed a bite to eat and charged it to the room, took a nap in a corner booth by the dance floor, or got in a few games of *Pac-Man*. If I'd completed all three of those tasks to my satisfaction, then I might crack a book. But by that time, while the staff was setting up, I might be having a conversation with the bartender or, more likely, I was trying to get the high score on the only video game in the place. One quarter could last me an hour on that tabletop machine, so most nights, I never tried to study. Not one lick. How did I manage to learn Latin? I didn't. When the bar got full or loud or someone asked why a kid was in there, I headed back to the room and sat in my cell. I told my mom that I'd done all my work, and she never checked to see if I was telling the truth. I slipped through the cracks socially and academically so quickly and had no idea how I would ever get out of the hole I'd dug.

I needed to find a way to fit in. I had football and a decent ability to make most folks laugh, but it was a charade. My terrible grades were piling up, and I panicked on the inside. We had Chapel every Wednesday, which I saw as an opportunity to grab a quick power nap in the pew. I can't recall one moment in those two years when I was impacted by any of the services. If God was speaking to me back then, I tuned Him out or simply didn't hear Him.

However, at some point during my seventh-grade year, I discovered the game of Slaughterball. I have no idea if our class invented it that year or if it had been played at Porter Military Academy for fifty years, but it was beyond exhilarating. It got me through that first year and would elevate my social standing from being an outcast to a likable outsider. There was only one match a day, which started just minutes after we finished lunch and lasted until the school bell rang for the first afternoon class. The faster we ate, the more time we had to play.

Slaughterball should have been a gladiator sport in the Colosseum. Imagine two basketball goals on a dirt and grass field the size of a tennis court, surrounded by marsh and rows of trees on three sides. Now picture fifteen or so young men dressed in suits, coats, and ties, wearing slippery dress shoes on the field of battle. The game was sort of like basketball. You could make unlimited passes, had to dribble the ball every three to four steps in a wide-open run, and could finally shoot a basket at the opposite end to score two points. Everyone got unlimited fouls. There was an occasional jump shot, but the three-point line hadn't been invented yet, and there was no such thing as an easy layup.

Every drive came at a price. It might be grass stains on your pants or a ripped collar or shirt, but it could also mean a torn sleeve on your suit jacket or even a bloody nose. Every drive was contested. We had no title on the line, just bragging rights heading into fourth period.

That's when I got to know Maje. He was a former Marine infantry-man who fought in the Battles of Guadalcanal, New Guinea, and New Britain. He received a Purple Heart while fighting in Guadalcanal, which Japanese soldiers described as the "Island of Death." After the war, he became a teacher, coach, and principal at Porter Military Academy and then at Porter-Gaud, where we met. I was often in his office, wondering what kind of punishment he'd deliver. He was always compassionate and kind and had the most amazing stories to tell. He never berated me, chastised me, or made me feel less than I already felt—even when I was caught cheating in Latin class or forging the letters he sent home for my parents to sign. I don't remember if I told him about our hotel life or what he knew about me that first year, but he did all he could to keep me afloat.

Our two months in the hotel had turned into ten. I spent the summer after seventh grade lounging by the pool, listening to my boombox, and making mixtapes. Incredibly, I didn't have to go to summer school, so I presume that my system of cheating worked well enough because I sure didn't know the course material. My dad's credit card was on file at the hotel, so I could order lunch and skip the cus-tomary argumentative meeting and request for money back in Room 210. If it was raining or I was sick of the pool, I'd hang out in the rooftop bar. After living there for so long, I knew everyone, and no one ever kicked me out—not even the managers. The hotel employ-ees were my friends, and our age differences were irrelevant. I'd have breakfast in the lounge or sit in the lobby each morning reading the newspaper with all the businessmen. Every page, article, and box score. And how I never drank a single cup of coffee back then or during my life is beyond me. I'd just turned fourteen, had no car, and was sur-rounded by highways, drawbridges, and marshland. I couldn't see a way off this rock.

We tried moving out of the Holiday Inn Riverview a couple of times, but the ongoing work at our house on Tradd Street made it impossible to have any sense of normalcy. I recall a contractor mentioning that they'd stripped over twenty coats of paint from the family room walls, which likely dated back hundreds of years. The house was caked in lead paint, and once damaged by moisture, it produced lead dust. If inhaled, it could cause a series of major health complications in as little as a few months, except none of us knew that back then.

We briefly moved into the Tradd Street house, which unveiled a whole new world. I began playing pick-up basketball a few blocks away, started running daily, rode my bike through the streets of Charleston, and formed some new friendships. What I didn't have was money. My parents took care of my basic needs, but they never gave me an allowance, so I began stealing some basic, low-value items that I wanted. A candy bar, maybe some packs of *Star Wars* or baseball cards, a can of soda, but nothing too crazy. The problem was that none of these things put any money in my pocket, and the appearance of new cards in my room would be a problem if my mom had noticed. And if I were starving after a long day of hoops, I couldn't simply go into the Market Gourmetisserie and swipe a bowl of pepper steak from the Chinese restaurant. I had to evolve.

I started stealing things I could sell. Local Charleston tourist maps were the easiest to pilfer, and every single out-of-town visitor needed one. I could lift three or four at a time from a Quick Mart, walk two blocks to the market, and sell them for a few dollars each in a matter of minutes. And inventory was everywhere. Half of the downtown businesses sold maps, so I never had to hit the same store during the same weekend.

The Market was my honey hole. The open-air sheds took up four city blocks. The property had been given to the city in 1788 so the land could be used for a public marketplace. This was the part of town for tourists to visit and find some of the best Charleston souvenirs, like the hideous city T-shirts, easy-to-move magnets, saltwater taffy, or artwork from a cross-section of talented local artists.

Maybe the most famous items produced in Charleston were the hand-crafted sweetgrass baskets. The basket-making tradition came to

Charleston during the slave trade and dates back to the seventeenth century. Hundreds of people sold their goods in the market every day, and many children helped their parents, so a young kid like me hocking $1 magnets or $3 maps didn't stand out at all. I could make enough money in an hour to last me the whole weekend.

We hadn't been in the Tradd Street house long when my mom started feeling sick. While I don't think she was ever officially diagnosed, my dad thought it might be from all the lead dust and fumes from the related paint work that was still being completed in a few of the rooms. So, we went back to the hotel. I'd felt like I was out on parole and living my best life when, without any notice, I was taken back to prison. One toilet and one sink. I'd been young and dumb those first ten months, but now I'd awakened to the hustle, bustle, and opportunities that were across the river. My connection to the peninsula had been severed; I lost access to inventory and customers and went back to sleeping in that cramped room with my mom and sister. Locked up again, I asked myself, *How can I possibly bust out of this tower?*

Then I had an idea. In late summer of 1981, football was about to start up again. I couldn't stand the idea of playing another season, so I either just stopped going to practice or quit the team altogether. I honestly don't remember. Each day, my mom dropped me off at the practice field and waved goodbye. Then, I would throw my gear by the tree line at the end of the school property and jog along the train tracks from Albemarle Road down to South Windermere Plaza. It was about a mile and a half drive with a lot of stop signs and stoplights but only a ten-minute run down the tracks. I'd hump it at a decent clip, trying not to get too sweaty, and when I got to the shopping plaza, I'd head to the drug store to look at magazines or hit Ye Old Fashioned to play video games.

There were no tourists in the West Ashley area, so I couldn't sell anything. It was time for me to evolve again. There was a hierarchy to playing the video games, which was very similar to pick-up basketball.

I'd place a quarter on the right side of the slightly angled glass screen and wait for my turn. And like in basketball, once I got on the court, I didn't want to lose. If I won, I kept playing. Lose, and it was the back of the line. Since I'd studied all the patterns of *Pac-Man*, it was impossible for me to lose. Other kids wanted to play, and they might give me $1 to let them take a turn or give me $1 if I'd enter their three initials into the high scores list. If someone didn't know me, they might bet $1 that they could beat me. No matter what the situation was, I knew I could make seventy-five cents for every quarter I put in the machine.

When the brand-new games like *Centipede, Donkey Kong,* or *Defender* came out, they added a bit of variability to my winnings. I was good but not great, and I didn't win every time. So, *Pac-Man* was my go-to game and a sure-fire winner. I'd play for ninety minutes or so, pocket a few dollars, sprint back down the train tracks to school, get a good sweat going, and make it back just in time to meet my mom.

Eighth grade started, and it was even worse than seventh. I was failing everything, had no desire to study or even go to school, and started skipping classes after lunch at least once or twice per week. I was supposed to be on the football team, but my parents never asked about going to a game. And to this day, I have no idea when or if my parents ever knew I'd quit.

I was so underwater at this point that it didn't matter what I did. If the school sent home an official letter or a bad report card, I'd forge my dad's signature. His handwriting was terrible and easy to master. In fact, I still sign my name a lot like his. But my mom's signature was super clean, and the school might call her if I tried to sign her name. I couldn't take that chance.

If the school wanted to reach my dad, they had to use an 800 number and call his company in Texas, go through the main operator, then his personal secretary, and even then, he'd most likely be in a meeting, so he'd have to call them back. I was certain he wouldn't bother to return their call and that our administrators would lose interest in me the way I'd lost interest in their school and teachers, except for Maje.

He still talked to me, told me stories about his past life and experiences, and tried to help me get a breath of air as I bobbed unmercifully in the water. I know he genuinely cared for me and wanted to see me succeed, but there was only so much he could do.

Getting booted from Porter-Gaud was inevitable and long overdue. I can't recall the exact infraction that sealed my fate, but there was a litany to choose from. I guess my dad made some calls and found a place that was sympathetic to whatever story he told them, and I changed schools. I never quite fit in at that school either, especially because my classmates had been together and built relationships for the past seven or eight years. It was hard to break into those social circles, and I know it was the same for my sister.

"To you, LORD, I call;
You are my Rock,
do not turn a deaf ear to me.
For if you remain silent,
I will be like those who go down to the pit."

—Psalms 28:1 NIV

2

MISPLACED CHILDHOOD

"What one loves in childhood stays in the heart forever."

—*Mary Jo Putney*

M y earliest, most vivid childhood memory is from when we lived in Georgia. I was sitting by myself in a dollar theater watching *Star Wars* when I was around ten years old. My mom and sister dropped me off at a strip mall on Buford Highway, just a couple of stoplights north of I-285 in Doraville, Georgia. My mom handed me a $5 bill, which gave me $1 to buy a ticket and $4 for candy, popcorn, and a drink. That was supposed to last the entire day because I'd be there for three or four showings of the same movie.

In between screenings, I hid out in the bathroom while the workers cleaned the theater. When the coast was clear, I sneaked back in and watched *Star Wars* again. And again. And again. Later in the evening, my mom and sister would pick me up, and we'd grab a bite to eat at Arby's, Long John Silver's, Dairy Queen, or some other fast-food joint near the house and head home for the night.

What was at home for me? To this day, I don't remember anything I did before turning nine. As I got older, on rare occasions, I'd bum myself out by thinking about possible repressed events, but then I quickly reminded myself of the tagline from the movie *Memento*: "Some memories are best forgotten."

My dad had the ultimate Type-A personality. He was a Jesuit Catholic from Milwaukee, Wisconsin, played collegiate basketball at Marquette University, and was the MVP of the team that finished third in the 1962-1963 National Invitational Tournament (NIT) at Madison Square Garden. The NIT was the premier college basketball tournament in the country at the time. He went on to serve as an Army Ranger, fought and was wounded in action during a ground patrol outside Pleiku, Vietnam, made a full recovery, and then spent time as a Ranger Instructor at Fort Benning before he retired.

He met my mom during Ranger School. She was a Southern Methodist from Hurtsboro, Alabama. Her hometown was tiny, and I mean tiny—maybe three hundred people, one blinking light, and a city grill that was the center of the universe for its citizens. She was a flight attendant for Eastern Airlines when she met my dad on a blind date. They got engaged a few months later, he shipped off to Vietnam, and she joined him in Japan while he recovered after being shot. Soon thereafter, they got married, he retired from the Army, and they moved to Milwaukee, where I was born. Their religious upbringings and social differences clashed early in their marriage and were ultimately major factors in their relationship failure.

While my parents never divorced, everything went into a freefall in 1977-1978. My sister, Emily, was six or seven, and I was nine or ten when my dad left Atlanta and our family for his new job and life in Freeport, Texas. I asked to go with him, but he said it was only temporary, and since he'd be traveling all the time, there wouldn't be anyone there to take care of me. His job was going to be so good that he could fly home every other weekend to see us. However, good visits twice a month turned into once-a-month drop-ins, and they usually ended with my parents yelling at each other. After a while, his trips home and time with us became shorter, more sporadic, and always argumentative.

If Emily or I wanted to hang out with our dad on one of those so-called weekends, we joined him at the local Waffle House for breakfast before he left to play golf, watched him hit balls at the driving range, or rode our bikes to the local elementary school where he played basketball with the guys. That was a typical Saturday with him in town. If all emotions were in check on Saturday and we had peace in the house, we might go to Wieuca Baptist, Dunwoody Baptist, or the Cathedral of Saint Philip on Sunday morning, grab a bite of lunch together, then drop him off at the airport on our way home. I never knew when I'd see him again. I felt alone.

Star Wars had been released in 1977, but in those days, it wasn't uncommon for movies to have long theatrical runs, and *Star Wars* had a run of 135 weeks, second only to *The Sound of Music*. That meant it was in theaters slightly more than two years and seven months, with official re-releases in 1978 and 1979. There were no VHS tapes, no streaming services, and the movie wasn't available for home viewing until 1982, when it was finally released on pay-per-view, a full five years after it first hit theaters. The only way to see it was in the theaters, and I went a lot.

At that point, my maternal grandmother moved in with us—right across the hall from me. Our family arrangement wasn't working for anyone, and I think my mom wanted me out of the house as much as I wanted to be anywhere else besides home. My mom dropped me off again at the dimly lit, musty dollar theater, handed me my $5 bill, while Han, Chewie, Luke, Leia, C-3PO, and R2-D2 kept me occupied and out of trouble for the day. It wasn't every day, but that's how I spent two or three days a week for the entire summers in 1978 and 1979. After a while, I knew most of the workers, no longer had to hide, and could roam freely between the theater, snack counter, and bathroom. Now, when people ask me how many times I've seen *Star*

Wars in a theater, they're shocked to hear that it's somewhere north of five hundred.

When we lived in Atlanta, I had two neighborhood friends, Luke and Alex. Luke was my best friend, and we both loved *Star Wars*. In fact, we'd make stop-motion movies together with an 8 mm camera that we were allowed to use without parental interference. One of our most ambitious projects was a re-creation of the Battle of Hoth from *The Empire Strikes Back*. We got a massive piece of plywood, set it on two sawhorses, built papier-mâché mountains, painted it white, and added flour to make it look like snow. We built plastic models that we blew up with firecrackers and made our first three-minute reel-to-reel movie. We shot a bunch of different films in those days, but the sheer production effort put into the snow battle still makes me smile to this day.

My other friend was Alex. He lived across the street, and when we hung out, we lived a little more dangerously. We skateboarded together, beginning high on our street and picking up speed as we headed into the blind curve. If we were going too fast, we zoomed straight through the stop sign, crossed over the side street, hit the gutter, and launched ourselves into the neighbor's yard. Every weekend, we rode our bikes to an enormous gully a couple of miles from our neighborhood and played at an empty construction site. We both had BB guns that looked like air rifles, and we battled it out by shooting at each other from our yards with trees and a large boulder as cover.

That exhilarating game of potshot came to a screeching halt when a couple of rounds hit the front window of my house. My seventy-something grandmother came out to see what was going on. Alex squeezed off one more round, which was meant for me, but came oh-so-close to her, and that put the game on ice forever. Punishments were usually doled out by my dad, but since I never knew when he'd be home again, my actions rarely had consequences unless I did something to completely unhinge my mom. This was one of those times, and that almost always meant the belt.

I was becoming more introverted and pulling further away. I leaned into everything *Star Wars*, ship designs, and making three-minute shorts on 8 mm film. Much of my Christmas wish list was action figures, starships, and playsets from the movie, and my mom was pretty good about buying me one new figure when we went grocery shopping. But I wanted to film bigger scenes, so I needed more actors. What I needed was an army of Stormtroopers. My parents didn't understand why I needed so many of the same things and said that what I had was more than enough. But it wasn't. You can't realistically film an Imperial Army scene with a half squad of troopers.

Tagging along on my mom's next grocery run, I decided the only way to build my platoon of soldiers was to steal them one by one. Each figure was encased in a transparent plastic cover that was heat-sealed onto a thin piece of cardboard backing. It took me more time to find the figure I wanted than it did to rip open the blister pack and stuff the newest recruit in my pocket. Every Saturday, I built upon my squads of Stormtroopers and Rebel Soldiers and my tribes of Tusken Raiders and Jawas. I understood I was stealing, and I'm sure I knew it was wrong, but I couldn't see any other way to get what I needed. I was an aspiring filmmaker, and I had a vision. And while this was my first memory of ripping off things, it wasn't the last.

DID I SAY WE MOVED AROUND A LOT? I was born in Milwaukee and baptized in the Catholic Church. My dad's job took us from Milwaukee back to Atlanta, where my sister Emily was born. We then moved to Brentwood, Tennessee, and a year later wound up in McLean, Virginia. Another move took us back to Atlanta in 1976. I don't remember any of this—where I lived, where I went to school, or if I had any friends. My memories come from a cross-section of family members, what I've seen in a handful of home videos, and an assortment of old family photo albums. I only know I was there because I was in the pictures. I've seen myself in front of an old house, in a class photo, on a sports team, and even in front of a grizzly bear, but I can't tell you a single thing beyond what's in the photograph.

The safest or most reasonable answer I've heard for my childhood mind-wipe was because I had a major concussion. When I was eight, I was competing in a swim meet in Atlanta. While racing freestyle with my eyes closed (I didn't like opening my eyes underwater), I swam straight into the wall instead of making the flip. I drove my head into the concrete and knocked myself unconscious. A lifeguard pulled me out of the pool, and I heard that my flaccid, lifeless body freaked everybody out that day. I don't remember any of it.

Apparently, I played in a few sports leagues, but I only know that because I've seen the team photos—basketball mostly, but some soccer, too. I really liked sports growing up, and I remember my dad took me to Hawks or Flames games at the Omni and a few Braves games with a bunch of my cousins at Atlanta-Fulton County Stadium. My childhood—at least what I remember—can be summed up in movies, sports, and getting ice cream at Baskin-Robbins on my birthday.

On May 21, 1980, *The Empire Strikes Back* was released. It is unequivocally my favorite movie of all time and will never be displaced. Why? For starters, I was twelve years old when it came out. The original release was the most monumental event in my life, and I couldn't wait to find out what happened to all my favorite characters. I'd waited three years to see the next chapter.

That morning, my dad and I drove over to the Phipps Plaza mall near Buckhead, Georgia. It was about 11:00 a.m., and our plan was to get lunch in the food court and then catch the afternoon show. The only problem was that the rest of downtown Atlanta had decided to do the same thing. The line went on forever and snaked back and forth in front of all the stores. Thousands of people were waiting for the same movie. They eventually started letting folks in for the 1:00 p.m. screening, and the line began to inch forward. Painfully slow. Like we'd never reach the ticket window. And we didn't. The movie had sold out, and everyone in this long, torturous line had to sit back down on the cold tile floor and wait more than two hours until the first group finished watching the film.

When that initial screening ended, hundreds of people poured out of the theater, and some tried to tell us what they'd just seen. People in our line yelled for them to shut up, and all around us, everyone was getting angry while some other jerks tried to cut in line during the confusion. The bodies of men, women, and children were pressed up on each other like a mob about to storm a Black Friday sale. Again, we shuffled toward the ticket window like a leaky faucet. Drip. Drip. Drip. Drip.

My dad and I were so close. But when we were fifty people away, the manager came out and said they'd sold out again. It was torture. I was beside myself.

"We'll never get in!" I shouted at my dad.

People in line yelled and cussed. The cinema staff tried to calm us down, but the frustration had peaked. As the dust settled and reality set in, we were all hungry and wanted something to eat while we waited. One group went to get pizzas, and another went for drinks. And instantly, we bonded—perfect strangers eating, drinking, and sharing stories. This was the day I fell in love with the *Star Wars* community.

When the theater doors burst open again two hours later and a flood of people came out, I heard one guy shout, "Darth Vader is Luke's father!"

No one was buying that. We laughed and yelled back at him and said he'd have to do better than that. We weren't morons, after all.

What a loser, I thought.

We finally made it in for the 7:00 p.m. screening, and we high-fived our new friends and settled into our seats. I couldn't believe we'd sat on the floor of Phipps Plaza with total strangers for eight hours. It's one of my fondest memories, spending time with my dad, and I'd like to think he felt the same way.

With my dad living in Texas, my mom decided to move us to Charleston, South Carolina. My parents never divorced, but I know they weren't happy together either. I believed they really loved each other early on, but once my dad moved out of the house, I'd have to guess the void became insurmountable, and the relationship was effectively over.

As a family, we were borderline dysfunctional, and I saw passive-aggressive behavior on both sides. My dad used money as a weapon, and my mom started to hoard everything she could get her hands on. I lived in my fantasy world, and I think Emily was caught in the crossfire.

Whatever my childhood was, or the little bit that I remember, it's all in the past, and that's where I want to leave it—except for all the Stormtroopers I stole from the grocery store. I need to make amends for that.

"And he said:
'Truly I tell you, unless you change and become like little children,
You will never enter the kingdom of heaven.'"

—Matthew 18:3 NIV

3

SUMMERTIME ROLLS

"Do not follow where the path may lead,
go instead where there is no path and make a trail."

—*Ralph Waldo Emerson*

"You're going to love it." When my dad uttered those five words, I knew I had no way out. The decision had been made, but it wasn't mine. He was sending me to the mountains of North Carolina, where I'd participate in a summer-long program focused on basic military survival skills, like sourcing food and water, starting fires, building shelter, navigation, and mental resilience. When my dad decided something was good for me, it was better to say, "Yes, sir" than try to fight it.

I was fifteen years old, and I think my dad knew that I wasn't 100 percent on board with his latest mandate. So, he called his brother-in-law, C.D., who offered to send his fifth son on the same forced adventure. James was my first cousin, one year older, and we'd spent a fair amount of time together when we lived in Georgia. I don't know what he thought when he got the news of our summer plans, but I'm sure he was even less excited than I was.

We picked up James at his house and drove three and a half hours to North Carolina. The last two miles took about ten minutes as we made our way up a long, narrow, winding dirt road that dumped us into a clearing cut right out of the forest. This was HQ, our base camp. It had a large cabin to the right and a giant lake in front of us. On the left, I saw a much smaller wooden structure and could barely make out another large cabin further up the mountain. We got out of the car, and a tall man who wore an olive-green ("OG") utility uniform and had a buzz cut ordered James and me to swim to the far side of the lake and back. He said it was the first step of our check-in process. James and I were both strong swimmers, so we peeled off our shirts, leapt off the dock, and started for the other shore.

I'd never been in a lake before, and it got surprisingly cold very quickly, which made it hard for me to swim. My body tightened, and I struggled to maintain my breathing. I was cold but kept moving at a brisk pace. I could see that my dad was standing on the shoreline with his arms crossed and watching every stroke—the same guy who'd trained as a winter Ranger and, after being shot in Vietnam, had become an instructor for the same elite military unit at Fort Benning. Being cold or showing signs of weakness was not an option.

I made quick work of the swim, pulled myself out of the frigid water, and was toweling off when I saw James struggling. The cold had affected him far more than it had me, and after twenty-five minutes in the mountain lake water, it was clear he wasn't going to make it back to the shore without help. My dad saw James's early signs of hypothermia (uncontrolled shivering and loss of coordination) and knew there was no way he could finish the swim. Two counselors and I jumped into the lake and pulled him to safety. I think he was shocked and a little embarrassed by what happened, but this was only the first hour of our "summer break." We looked at each other and wondered what we were doing here.

Over the next few weeks, we learned how to canoe, rock climb, rappel, and hike. And boy, did we hike a lot. We spent time on some well-marked local trails, hiked along parts of the Appalachian Trail, and did our fair share of bushwhacking, which required us to travel through dense tree lines or uncultivated country, and it usually involved the frequent use of a machete. Something felt very primal about hiking and clearing an unmarked path through the Blue Ridge Mountains with a sword in your hand.

I developed a real sense for how to travel and what to carry. When we went out in a group, we discussed how many days we'd be gone, what kind of terrain and distance we'd have to cover, and how much food to carry. Our leaders were only seventeen or eighteen, but they had anywhere from one to five summers of experience under their belts, so we first-timers listened intently to their advice. We split the group's food weight evenly amongst us, and the only way to reduce your pack weight was to leave other essentials behind. While many guys opted for larger, heavier tents, I chose a lightweight hammock, parachute cord, and a poncho.

That week, James and I went with a group of six guys on a bushwhacking expedition, which would involve shorter but more time-consuming and exhaustive distances. In a ten-hour day, and taking only short breaks for water or lunch, we could travel only five or six miles. By comparison, if we hiked the Appalachian Trail in good weather, we could cover twenty-five-plus miles in a single day, depending on the elevation. So, as the sun set on the day, we picked a moderately flat area below the ridge to make camp for the night.

We were tired from the frustratingly long and arduous hike, but we still had to collect wood, build a fire, set up camp, and cook dinner. And all these tasks needed to be completed before it got dark. My setup was easy. I found a pair of suitable trees spaced about 8 feet apart, tied my hammock between them, ran the parachute cord—a lightweight nylon rope—above my securely suspended bed, and tossed my poncho over the top cord. The last task was to hang my pack in a tree about 50 feet away to keep the animals at bay. I could knock all this out in a matter of ten minutes, five if I was pressed for time.

The other guys liked their tents. They were certainly bigger and more comfortable, but it took them much longer to set up and tear down, and they were always restricted to the ground. I absolutely feared and hated every kind of snake, so it was mentally impossible for me to sleep if I knew one of those slimy creatures lurked outside my tent at night. I was more than happy to sleep in my elevated but cramped bed all summer.

We ate a hearty meal, shared stories about our lives back home, and settled in for the night when I heard the muffled thumping of earthy rain hitting my taut poncho. It was soothing at first, like a modern-day sound machine on its forest setting. Drup, drup, drup. It quickly picked up in intensity. Without warning, we found ourselves in the middle of a severe rainstorm with thunder and lightning pounding all around camp. I generally felt safe, but the high winds slung the rain in on me from the large openings at my head and feet. I had to just lie there and take it, and I felt a twinge of regret for not bringing a tent. But that paled compared to what my companions would soon endure. Rivers of water poured down the side of the mountain and into our camp. As I lay in my hammock and looked up at my poncho, I heard the rush of water below me and thought, *James.*

We all had a rough night, but James and the guys on the ground had been unmercifully drenched. Their packs, clothes, and food were soaked. We tried to find dry wood and some kindling to make a fire, but it was impossible. There's nothing worse than hiking all day in wet socks and underwear because jungle rot will take over and ruin your week. We made it back to HQ a few days later—tired, wet, and hungry—and vowed to never set up camp in a gully again.

After hiking in the mountains for a week, we spent a few days in Asheville, North Carolina, to train with some experienced mountain climbers. It was nice to get off the trail and develop another skill. It was my fourth day climbing, and I loved the heart-pounding exhilaration of scaling and summiting a steep rock face. But that day, I climbed faster than my belay could keep up, and with slack still in the line, I lost my handhold, fell about 10 feet to the ledge below, and broke my left arm. My instructors eventually got me off the mountain and took me to the hospital, where I had my arm X-rayed, set, and cast. I was sure this would be my ticket home, but the camp director talked with my dad, who told him I wouldn't be leaving camp under any condition.

Geez! James had almost drowned on the first day, and I'd slipped off the side of a mountain and broken my arm. We wondered what it would take to get out of this place. We got our answer soon enough. The next morning, I was assigned to a group that was leaving on a five-day elevation hike. The guys on my team felt sorry for me, so they filled my rucksack with bread, bananas, and trail mix to make things a little lighter and easier for me. We set off on day one of our hike.

With my newly cast arm, I was slower than usual over the rough terrain and had fallen to the back of the pack. It had rained overnight, so everything was slippery. As I was traversing my way across a sloped rock face, I leaned out a little too far, slipped right off the ledge, and bellyflopped on the ground below, striking my head in the process. When the guys came back looking for me, I was face down and unconscious. They rolled me over and saw blood gushing from the split in my forehead.

When I came to, I heard one of them say, "Look, he's alive."

"There's so much blood," said another.

"Sorry I squished the bread," I said.

We were in the middle of the Blue Ridge Mountains, and only one man knew our approximate location. So, I had to get up, shake it off, and keep moving forward. I wouldn't see an adult until we arrived at our pick-up zone four days later, and that's when I was finally taken to the hospital for the second time that week. They took more X-rays, re-casted my arm, and confirmed that I'd suffered a concussion. And you guessed it. No one came to pick me up. A few weeks later, James and I completed our summer adventures together and went back to our lives.

A couple of weeks before school started, my dad invited me to visit him in Texas for a few days. This was the first such invite I'd received since he left us in Atlanta six years earlier, and I couldn't help but wonder why he invited me now. He picked me up at the Houston Hobby Airport, and we drove south to the small Gulf town of Freeport. We caught up about my summer with James, his near-drowning, and my two trips to the emergency room. Deep down, I think my dad relished the fact that it had been hard on me and that I might have learned something about myself and my inner drive. For me, there was no epiphany; I was tired and only wanted to relax for a while.

As we got closer to our destination, he told me about a new restaurant in Lake Jackson called The Trough. It was a Texas-sized, all-you-can-eat chili bar, and he promised it would be different from any place I'd ever eaten before.

"What's so special about this place?" I asked.

"For starters, when you walk in, someone will take your measurements," he said.

"Measurements for what?" I asked.

"For your chili suit," he said.

"What are you talking about?" I asked. "What's a chili suit?"

"It's like a yellow rain jacket and pants. It's waterproof," he said.

"Why do I need a waterproof jacket to eat dinner?" I asked.

"It's so you don't get chili all over your clothes. And they'll give you a pair of latex gloves, too," he said.

"Hold it. Why do I need gloves?" I asked, more confused than ever.

"For scooping the chili from the trough," he said. "It's all you can eat."

"You can't be serious," I said.

"Very serious. It's the only one in Texas. The line's always out the door," he chuckled.

He was joking with me, but I bought it hook, line, and sinker, and we both had a good laugh over how disgusting such a place would be.

My dad always shared crazy or funny stories with me, and I couldn't wait to tell this tall tale to my classmates when I got home.

We grabbed a bite of dinner, and I ate catfish for the first time. My dad drove me to see some of the sights around town, and then we went to his apartment, which had been his primary residence since he left us in Atlanta. It was a dark, musty two-bedroom apartment with not a single picture on the wood-paneled walls. The electricity occasionally flickered in the living room. It felt like he lived in a long-ago abandoned apartment. I couldn't understand it back then, and I still find it hard to believe that he would leave his family for this alternate life. Was the work that good? Would he rather spend his free time with friends instead of his wife and kids? Was it something else entirely?

For the next two summers, he sent me back to the camp in North Carolina. I went on multiple group hikes that spanned one to two weeks and covered large swaths of the Appalachian Trail. I led small teams and knocked out most trails in the Nantahala National Forest, including the Standing Indian and Yellow Mountain Trails and the incredibly picturesque Art Loeb Trail in the Pisgah National Forest. I enjoyed incredible climbs with my friends at Looking Glass Rock, Cedar Rock, and Laurel Knob and spent many days on the natural water slide called Sliding Rock. A few years later, filmmaker Michael Mann came to the same region and filmed his masterpiece *The Last of the Mohicans*.

James never went back, but the memories from our first summer together are something I'll never forget. During my third summer, when I was seventeen, I completed an eleven-day solo hike. The only hiccup was that I ran out of food and ate some pesticide-riddled tomatoes. I haven't eaten a tomato since. I met amazing strangers while walking along the Appalachian Trail and pushed my body to limits I didn't know were possible. The experience I had wanted no part of—that had been forced on me by my overzealous dad—turned out to be the most adventurous and picturesque time of my life, and it changed me forever.

> "Trust in the LORD with all your heart,
> And lean not on your own understanding;
> In all your ways acknowledge Him,
> And He shall direct your paths."
>
> —Proverbs 3:5-6 NKJV

4

HEY YOU!!!

"If I'm going to get busted, it is not going to be by a guy like that."
—*Matthew Broderick as Ferris Bueller in* Ferris Bueller's Day Off

"Hey, you!" A wave of instantaneous dread rushed over me in those first few seconds. I didn't want to turn around because I already knew what was going to happen. I was two months shy of turning eighteen, was walking out of a Kroger store a few miles north of Charleston, and my life was about to change.

I was a hustler and had always looked for ways to make money. My ability to do so depended on where I was living, and we'd lived in a bunch of different places. We still owned the Tradd Street home south of Broad, but we hadn't lived there in a while, and my mom always made excuses not to go inside it. This or that wasn't right, it was too dirty, or too old, or her allergies were acting up. Or it had ghosts. I'd heard stories of it being haunted, but I never believed them. And I never saw anything to suggest such a thing, but my dad must have given in to my mom, and we bounced from rental house to rental house all over the city or on adjacent islands. We'd live in someone's carriage house for a few months, and then we'd abruptly pack up one weekend and go to a new place. My mom saved everything, and I mean everything, so we always had to move her "stuff" too. And as we moved from place to place, I moved from school to school. It was tough to settle in anywhere because we had no stability.

I had a roof over my head, food to eat, and hadn't needed a ton of money. I'd stolen candy bars, magnets, maps, and trading cards for years and had enough loose change to play video games, but that wasn't enough to cover the big-ticket items I wanted. I loved music and wanted a new Panasonic boombox, the one with a dual cassette deck, AM/FM radio, and two integrated loudspeakers. And if I had that, I'd need cassette tapes to play. My dad had bought me an Apple computer, and I needed programs to run on it. The bottom line was that stealing maps for three bucks a pop didn't cut it anymore.

I loved Van Halen, Foreigner, and The Police, but without a boombox, I was at the mercy of whatever the local disc jockeys played on the radio. And then there were all the ads. The five or six minutes of ads at the top and bottom of every hour were terrible, and since the radio stations rarely played a great song, I started stealing cassette tapes to play in the car.

Anytime my mom went shopping, I went with her. There were three major malls in the Charleston area, and each one had at least one and sometimes two record stores. There was no such thing as security in those days, and because cassettes were so small, I could easily fit one in each of my pockets. That meant I could snag up to four tapes every time I went to the mall. And the stores made it too easy to steal. They built these perfect little cubbies that held hundreds of cassettes, and I could walk right up, grab the latest release from The Cars, and slide it into my pocket. It was as easy as walking past a counter and grabbing a cookie.

After a few weeks, I had all the music I wanted. But much of what I listened to couldn't be played during car rides to school. My mom was certain to ask questions if I popped in a Billy Idol, The Clash, or Talking Heads cassette. It was time to get a portable Sony Walkman, but I needed cash for that, so I started selling my gently used cassettes at school, around the neighborhood, or at the basketball courts for $3 to $5 each. I had a backpack full of tapes and priced them to move. The going rate for a brand new, still sealed album was right at ten bucks, and mine were selling for more than half off.

If I sold something I really liked, I knew I could replace it over the weekend. If there was a hot new release like Duran Duran's *Rio*, I'd swipe two or three, knowing I could move them the following week. Then, one day, my business took a giant leap forward. My customers started placing orders and paying me in advance. This seismic shift completely changed the game and removed all the guesswork concerning customer preferences and trends.

Regularly, I walked into the mall with my mom and sister, got treated to an Orange Julius, and told them I was going to play video games. As soon as they went around the corner, I hit the record store with those easy-to-access cubbies. I carefully scanned the store and snagged four tapes, but if it was a big order week, I might double up and put two cassettes in my back pockets. I couldn't put two of them up front because it looked like an iPhone 14XL jammed into a pair of skinny jeans. And this was way before the iPhone.

Each trip to the mall would typically net me about $25 cash, so I was pulling in about $100 to $150 a month. Eventually, stand-alone record stores popped up, and soon after, grocery stores started to sell music, albeit with a much smaller collection. With these new entrants, I didn't need to be as brazen anymore. I could grab two or three tapes here or there, depending on where my mom took me. It was a good hustle, and I never saw a downside.

Eventually, all these stores implemented some bare-bones security measures, and the cassettes were placed in a longer, plastic protective cage. The clerks had a key to open them, but a short, flathead screwdriver or dull dinner knife could pop the plastic lock off just as easily. It felt like the stores had placed a one-foot hurdle in front of me, but it never slowed me down. And it never dawned on me that I'd left all those empty plastic cages behind as evidence. It was eerily similar to all those *Star Wars* card backs I left littered in the grocery store toy aisle back in Dunwoody.

Then, in 1984, the compact disc hit the market. This new, sleek invention promised incredible improvements over the cassette. I didn't have to press and hold a fast-forward or rewind button to hear a song. I could click a number and skip right to my favorite track. The songs sounded better, and the technology blew my mind, but it came at a price. I needed a new player and new media, and each CD cost just under $20. These new discs were larger, harder to hide, but also easier to get out of the packaging. With a quick cut of a razor blade, I could slice the poly sleeve wrapping on the long box and slip the CD right out. Most of the people I'd sold cassettes to didn't have a CD player yet, so I went back to stealing for myself and building my personal collection.

IN THE FALL OF MY JUNIOR YEAR, our soccer team was solid. We thought we could make some noise in our conference or at the regional level. But one rainy night in Georgetown, South Carolina, I was running to make a slide tackle on the ball and planted my right foot into a decent-sized divot in the field. I was in terrible pain—not the worst pain I would ever feel, but enough to know something was wrong. I was helped off the field and dropped on the sideline near the end of the bench. Some random man came up with an ice-cold can of soda, told me to hold it on my knee, and then wrapped it with an ACE bandage. I lay there for another hour while my team finished the game and was finally loaded onto the school bus. Everyone wanted McDonald's, so we stopped to eat and then finally started the ninety-minute drive back to Charleston. My parents weren't at the game, and no one offered to drive me home or to a hospital. The pain hadn't gone away, and it had been about three hours since my injury.

My mom and sister were at the school when we arrived. My coach told them I might be hurt and that they should take me to the ER. It took another thirty minutes to drive to Roper Hospital and another hour to be seen. While waiting in the emergency room, my mom called my dad in Texas. She told him what the coach had told her and then handed me the phone.

"What happened?" he asked.

"I think I hurt my leg," I quietly replied.

"This better be good," he snapped back.

"What do you mean?" I answered nervously.

"You'd better have a real injury if you're going to drag your mother and sister down to the hospital this late," he firmly stated.

"I have no idea what's wrong. It just hurts so much," I said.

"I'm going to tell you again, this better be good!" Then he said he wanted to talk to my mom.

I had a non-displaced fracture of my fibula and a Grade 2 tear of my lateral collateral ligament—a thin band of tissue that helps stabilize the knee joint and prevents it from buckling outward. They put me in a full leg immobilizer, and I was out of commission for the next three months. My quadricep muscle atrophied terribly, so I had to go to physical rehabilitation, ironically enough, at The Citadel.

We moved out to Kiawah Island for the fall, a small island about twenty miles outside Charleston, famous for hosting the Ryder Cup in 1991. To me, it was just another place to live for a short period of time. But Kiawah was a new twist to our housing situation. We were far enough outside the city, and the only way in or out was via a long, winding two-lane road from downtown onto James Island and eventually out to Kiawah Island. There was nothing to do except ride bikes, and maybe that was the point. My dad was still gone for extended periods of time, I never saw my mom engage in a single adult conversation outside her immediate family, and I had absolutely nothing to do on this island. It was just another round Holiday Inn.

The isolation started to creep in. I had no friends, no sports, and nowhere to go. There was one general store at the entrance to the island, and the resort had golf and tennis, but I played neither. I'd missed the rest of soccer that year, as well as the entire basketball season, so I was desperate to do something—anything. Even if it meant I had to entertain myself.

I listened to music, went to rehab, and started to program on my Apple IIc. Nothing fancy at first, but I worked hand in hand with my computer science teacher and learned how to program in a couple of languages. I started building 8-bit full-screen images and using a lot of "if…then" statements. Pretty soon, I got into some world-building and story writing. It was similar to, but cruder than, the Oregon Trail game by MECC, with prompts on each page that guided the player. My hero could move left, right, forward, and backward and was confronted with obstacles or creatures along his journey. Some encounters might help the player, while others might set them back, but each screen allowed the participant to perform multiple tasks or complete a specific quest.

It took a few months to design and work out the kinks, but I eventually finished the game. I designed a cool cover, packaged it, and gave a demo to my dad the next time he came home. I made ten copies, packaged them as best I could, and told my dad that a computer program like this would probably sell for $20 in a retail store. Mine was nowhere near as good as a store-bought game, but he didn't need to know that. I imagined him roaming the office like any other dad selling Thin Mints on behalf of his daughter and her Girl Scout troop.

I assumed that one of two things would happen. First, he was the boss, and his employees felt obligated to buy my game from him. Or second, and more likely, he threw the copies in the trash can at the Charleston airport and handed me the $200 he'd "collected" the next time he came home.

My rehabilitation was going well, and I was building strength in my right leg again, but I still used the immobilizer for support. In fact, I didn't mind wearing it since it became my partner in crime for my music-stealing business. Stores had upped the ante and had cracked down on stealing by adding electronic security towers to their exits at the front of the store. If I walked out with a stolen item, the alarm would go off. Except I had metal on both sides of my immobilizer, and the alarm went off every time I walked in or out of a store. So, it seemed logical to put that to work for me.

I could stuff five or six tapes or two to three CDs into the top part of my immobilizer near my quadricep. There was so much padding in those days that you couldn't see a thing. I would dig through the $1.99 bargain bin, chat it up with the clerk, pay for my cassette, and head to the exit. When the security scanner lit up, I'd hold up my bag and receipt and point to my knee.

"It's probably the brace," I would say.

"No problem," the clerk would reply. "Get better. See you next time."

I knew what I was doing was wrong. I'd been stealing a little here and a little there for about eight years, and it had become a habit.

By March of my junior year, I was running every day to get back in shape for track season. I was eager to compete. My wide-open sprint times were still lacking, but I knew I still had a couple of months before the state championships. My coach suggested that I get into hurdling and work to become technically proficient at both the 110m high and the 300m intermediate hurdles. The logic was that if I could get the technique down and cleanly clear the hurdles, it would substitute for whatever I lacked in pure speed. And there was also a big gap in the number of entrants for the sprints versus the hurdles. The 100m, 200m, and 400m races were always packed with speedsters, while only a handful of head cases wanted to attack eight or ten hurdles every single race. I'd found my niche.

I was winning all the Charleston area meets, and that excited me. However, my school didn't travel very far to compete, so I was running against many of the same local guys twice a week. I put in the time on the track and got stronger every day and felt more confident than ever that my two new events would get me to state. Throw in the 4x100m and 4x400m relays, and I knew I'd already secured a stack of blue ribbons.

I'd won every race in the 300m hurdles during the regular season but had one crummy night in the 110m hurdles in Walterboro, South Carolina. It was raining, the track was slick, my stride shortened, and I tried to bully my way through the fourth hurdle. That collision took me straight to the ground like I'd been hit by a sniper, which ended my hope of a perfect season in that event. Everyone at every level of hurdling falls at some point, and I was happy it hadn't happened on a big stage. The fall didn't mentally scar me, so I chalked it up to a wet track on a miserable Tuesday night. A couple of weeks later, I went on to win both the 110m and 300m hurdle races at the Lower State meet.

In May 1985, I was getting loose for the South Carolina State Track and Field Championships in Columbia, South Carolina. It was 90 degrees that Saturday afternoon, and I was about halfway through my warm-ups when my coach approached me.

"How are you feeling?" Coach asked.

"Really good. Ready to go. Did you get my lane assignment?" I asked.

"I did. You're in lane five," he replied.

"Five? What are you talking about?" I pressed.

My coach told me that I'd been seeded second in both my hurdle events. Apparently, there was a kid from upstate who was just a little bit faster than me, and in those days, the runner with the fastest time was always assigned lane four. The second fastest got lane five, the third fastest went to lane three, etc. My rock-solid confidence had just been doused with ice-cold water. What I believed would be a simple walk in the park was shaping up to be a legitimate race for the title.

The 110m high hurdles was first. I had a confident exuberance and wanted to send a message early in the day that the kid from Charleston was the real deal. But I trailed at the first hurdle and wasn't within striking distance of the guy who won that final. I got third place.

"That sucked, but no big deal. I've got three more to go," I mumbled.

Next up was the 4x100m relay. We took fourth place. Two shaky handoffs doomed our team. Frankly, it was over halfway through the race and cost us the podium.

The third race of the day was my premier event. The 300m intermediate hurdles. This race separated the men from the boys. I was in lane
five, and the upper state champion was setting up about 23 feet behind
me in lane four. The time sheet and seedings don't lie, so this was going
to be a two-man race since no one else had a time that could compete.
But being in lane five was different than being in lane four, and I had to
race from the front. I couldn't see what my opponent was doing, how he
was running, or if he hit a hurdle. I was blind to everything that tacti-
cally mattered and would be hunted for the next forty seconds.

I stood behind the blocks when I heard the starter say, "On your
mark." The track was so hot that I'd poured ice-cold Gatorade on the
starting line, just to put my fingers down on the rubber surface. I
kicked out my legs one by one and placed them both into the blocks.
I don't remember that kid's name or the school he represented, but I
remember my mouth went instantly dry when I heard, "Set." I raised
up, locked my body into position, and waited for the gun to go off.

Most high school kids don't have a plan for this race, and that
stems from either bad coaching or a lack of coaching. I had a decent
coach, but he wasn't a hurdler, so I looked up to Edwin Moses, a
400m hurdler who won Olympic gold medals in Montreal in 1976
and then again in Los Angeles in 1984. He surely would have won in
1980, but those games were held in Moscow, and the United States,
along with sixty-five other countries, boycotted the games due to the
Soviet-Afghan War. He was the most dominant hurdler from 1977
until 1987. Edwin was my ABC television coach, and I tried to model
my race plan after his. I developed a decent technique, and my leg and
knee had healed enough for me to be confident in my abilities. But my
endurance was lacking, and I knew it.

The gun went off. I came out of the blocks and went into full
sprint mode. My plan was usually simple. Be the first guy to the first
hurdle—but this race was different. The fastest guy on the track that
day was behind me, so I had to attack that first barrier like my life
depended on it. I can't remember how many steps I took to the first

hurdle, but that's what I'd practiced ten times a day every day during the 1985 season. There's no better feeling than perfect steps to the first jump, and I skimmed over the top and was now running tall and accelerating to full speed. This was key heading down the backstretch approaching the second and third hurdles.

A clean jump over the third barrier meant two things. I was into the curve and had less than 200m to go. But here's where my technique was bad. Because of my injuries, my right leg was still a little suspect. Most good hurdlers would plant with their right leg and lead with their left leg over hurdles three, four, and five. But I didn't feel confident pushing off with all my body weight on my right leg, so I purposely led with the wrong leg. By doing that, I wasn't looking and leaning into the curve or taking the optimal path. I was drifting a little to the middle or outside of my lane, so to use a Formula 1 analogy, my lines were off.

Coming off the fifth hurdle and into the homestretch is both euphoric and humbling. With about 80m to go, all the staggers had been made up, I was leading and could see the finish line. Standing in my way were the final three barriers, and my legs were getting heavy. I'd already run two other races that afternoon, but I felt good, cleared number six without any problems and was still in the lead. Between six and seven is when the gorilla jumped on my back. My quads were screaming, my technique was fading, and I focused on driving my arms to help keep my legs moving. It was the "fast hands" that were going to get me through this race. I brushed over seven and knew my tank was almost empty. I was still in the lead, but now it felt like I was running in quicksand. There was one more hurdle to go and then a short dash to the finish line.

Eight. I think eight reached up and grabbed me, or that's what it felt like. My right lead leg got over the bar, but as I brought my left trail leg over, I topped the hurdle with my knee. It was all slow-motion after that. My left leg came down to the track with such a jarring thud that I struggled to keep my balance. I took one or two more hard, heavy steps, and out of the corner of my eye, I saw my state championship cruise right by me in lane four. He'd been in my blind spot off my left shoulder, and with only ten meters to go, my stumble allowed him to take the title.

The last race of the day was the 4x400m relay. It was my only chance to win a state championship. I'd blown it in the 300m hurdles and was now zero for three coming into this race, and my season was ending in thirty minutes. My coach told me to forget the three other races, but that's a hard thing to do when you're seventeen years old and still licking your wounds. Even though the rest of the team remained positive, I already knew we were doomed. While I was warming up for the last race, I saw one of my teammates smoking a couple of cigarettes near the back row of the stands. Michael usually smoked before and after each race, so this was nothing new, but now my season depended on him running his absolute best race. We finished third.

Junior year ended, and I told my mom and dad that there was no way I could stay at that school for one more year. I disliked a lot of the kids, the environment, the drive, and pretty much everything about it. There were a few teachers, two coaches, and a handful of kids I really enjoyed hanging out with, but I needed something different. They said they would try their best to find someplace else for me.

The summer of 1985 wasn't much different than the previous two. As soon as school ended, I was shipped back to camp in the Blue Ridge Mountains for continued survival and wilderness training. I went back for my third year as a counselor, and after I spent a decent amount of time in the mountains of North Carolina, I'd earned the right to come home. I spent the last two weeks of summer running, playing basketball, and stealing music.

That August, my sole request had been granted, and I transferred to a new school. But the first day was awkward. I'd lived in Charleston for more than four years, but I didn't recognize a single person. In fact, I don't remember knowing a soul in the entire school. But sports were always the great equalizer, and we had our first soccer practice that afternoon. I got to know a few guys from the team, but the first couple of months were about me keeping to myself and trying to get through each day. I fit in OK, but most of my classmates had known each other for years, and I was an outsider yet again.

Before Christmas break, we learned that our school was going to close by the end of the school year. The seniors would finish and graduate, but there was some heavy pressure on the parents of non-seniors to proactively transfer mid-year, so they'd be assured a spot in their new school going forward. If they waited until the end of the year, other area schools might not have a place for them, so the administrators leveraged this fear against the parents. As a result, more kids in the lower grades vanished every week. The hallways became a veritable ghost town, and school became a slog.

The basketball team was predominantly made up of seniors. We put a team on the floor, but we looked a lot like the boys from Hickory in the movie *Hoosiers*. Well, not that similar. We didn't have a Jimmy Chitwood that could shoot lights out, and we never came close to a state title. But I liked all the guys on the team, and I think we all made the best out of a really bad situation. We may have been knocked out in the first round of the playoffs, or maybe we just lost our last regular-season game. Either way, I can't remember our inglorious ending.

The bad news kept coming. With the school closing its doors, there was no money for a track coach, so the principal decided to shut down the program. I wanted to be a collegiate athlete. How could I possibly be scouted by college coaches if I didn't get to run my senior year? So, I hatched a plan and challenged the leadership to rethink their decision.

I pitched an alternative solution to the headmaster that would require the school to do nothing but stay out of my way. I would recruit a team, find a coach, and raise the money for uniforms. Any level of failure would be on me. He agreed, likely assuming I was on a fool's errand, but perhaps secretly hoping I could pull it off and help him finish the year on a high note.

I pulled together about a dozen kids from our nearly empty halls who said they would run, and then I set my sights on finding a coach. Since I'd done all my rehabbing at The Citadel, I drove over to meet with the athletic director. I shared my story with Coach Nadzak, told him our school was shutting down, and asked if he could help me find a coach. I hadn't raised enough money for uniforms, we didn't have a home track to run on, and the senior cadet who got the job would have to work for free, but I guaranteed that I'd have everything taken care of by the first day of practice. His response? He gave me two coaches: Ray Rivers and Tom Fagan. They helped change my life forever.

I placed calls to every public and private school in a fifteen-mile radius and finally found a sympathetic principal in Mount Pleasant. He connected me with their head coach, and they gave me permission to use their track free of charge. And not only did they guarantee practice times, but their coach also slotted us in for six home meets. With our high school activated and on the city-wide calendar, I called my old coach at Porter-Gaud, and he gave us three more dates. I rounded out our season schedule with multiple meets at James Island and Saint Andrew's schools by pretending to be our head coach.

Uniforms were another story. I had a three-tier approach to raising money. My most profitable legal venture was selling Krispy Kreme doughnuts. I bought them by the dozen, but at a reduced school fundraising rate. They were about $2 or $3 a box, and I could sell them for a minimum of $5, and even up to $10 each if I found a generous customer. Teachers, parents, and neighbors knew our story and were eager to help. Another program on the up-and-up involved my sister and her friends, who sold candy bars and drinks at other school sporting events. Emily and company could make $1 or $2 off each Snickers bar, bag of M&M's, or soft drink sold. On the shadier side, I diverted some funds from my thriving weekend music business.

Track season started, and almost everything had come together perfectly—everything but the athletes. I felt good about my recruitment efforts and that at least fifteen decent runners would begin the season. But with the school closing in a few months and apathy setting in, only about ten showed up for the first practice. And of the two Citadel cadets assigned to our team, Ray was a contract Marine, and his coaching style was reflective of his vocational choice. They expected everyone to practice and perform to the best of their abilities, and they didn't allow anyone to slack off. As a result, before our first meet, ten athletes were cut down to four. I lamented the fact that I'd spent all that time and energy raising money for fifteen uniforms. And then I wondered why my dad didn't just write a check or make some calls to help me out.

I shared with the coaches my experiences from the junior season, including the knee and leg injury, the disappointment of being blanked at the state championships, and the frustration I felt with my new school. I said that all I wanted was to win the 300m hurdles title and that they could train me however they thought best. I was running six days a week, with at least three of those days consisting of full workouts on the track, training with hurdles. With only three guys on our team, there was no opportunity to win a relay title. It would all come down to my individual events.

Ray and Tom came up with a plan that would get me in the best shape of my life. There were several meets where an athlete could participate in four events, but at some schools, we were allowed to enter up to six. On those days, I would run the 110m hurdles, 100m dash, 400m dash, which was immediately followed by the 300m hurdles, and then the 200m dash. For my sixth event, I would either do the long, triple, or high jump, depending on my ability to score points in one of those events. The biggest challenge for me would be running the 400m dash, one of the most grueling races for a sprinter, and then immediately following that up with the 300m hurdles. It was a grueling double, but both coaches felt that the back-to-back nature of competing in these two races would allow me to win the state championship in my main event. We agreed on the plan, and it was time to execute.

I went grocery shopping a couple of times a week with my mom, but mostly to check out the new music and snag a CD or two. One night after track practice, she had to grab a few things at the store, so I started thumbing through their racks of music looking for Prince's latest release, *Around the World in a Day*. The store didn't have that one, but they did have UB40's *Labour of Love*. There was one song that stuck in my head called "Red, Red Wine," which was a number one hit, so I went for that instead. Since I'd just come from practice, I didn't have my normal cutting tool on me and had to break the plastic cage with my fingers. I remember it took longer to get open, but I was hidden away in a corner of the store and confident no one saw anything. I finally busted it out of the packaging, tucked it in the band of my running shorts, and went deeper into the store to find my mom and sister.

They were wandering the aisles, and I told them it was time to go. I never liked to linger in a store, especially after I'd lifted an item and had it on my person. Slipping out of the store quickly was my modus operandi, but I was on someone else's schedule that night, and my normal routine was broken. We made it to the checkout counter, and I was nervously standing in line wearing running shorts and a tee. I knew it was obvious that I had something under my shirt. We checked out. I grabbed our bags to help conceal my contraband and headed toward the exit. With freedom just feet away, I heard those heart-stopping words: "Hey, you!"

The security guard had spotted me on one of the store's surveillance cameras and had already called the police. Because we'd lingered around the store for so long, a real police officer had arrived and stopped me as I was walking out. He grabbed my left arm right as I was about to step on the mat in front of the electric door. He took me upstairs to the manager's office, where I was asked to produce what I'd stolen. I reached into my shorts and pulled out that stupid CD with that ridiculous song.

The officer let me leave with my mom that night, but I had to appear in court later that month. I was only a few weeks shy of my eighteenth birthday, and everyone told me how lucky I was to get caught before I turned eighteen. Otherwise, I would have been arrested right then and taken to jail. I felt like I'd weaseled out of this situation. But my dad would see all this very differently. My day of reckoning was coming.

I made my big appearance at the Charleston County Courthouse. My dad flew in for my hearing and landed in a foul mood. He'd hired a well-known local attorney to represent me, and frankly, it seemed like a lot of hubbub over one CD. I stood up when my name was called and listened to the prosecutor and my attorney banter back and forth. After a few minutes, the judge turned and looked straight at me.

"Anything you would like to add, son?" he pointedly asked.

"Yes, sir. I'm so very sorry. I've never done anything like this before, but some kids at practice dared me to steal something that night, so I tried to do it," I replied.

The judge kindly replied, "You say it was your first time?"

"Yes, sir. I didn't even know how to open the case and cut my fingers trying to get the CD out," I said as the judge nodded in affirmation. My confidence level shot from a three to an eight.

"Well, I can see you don't have a record. How are your grades, and where are you thinking about going to college?" he asked, now fully engaged in our conversation.

"I'm a pretty good student, but I play a lot of sports, so I don't get straight As like a lot of guys. My track coaches are Citadel seniors, and they're trying really hard to get me to go there, but maybe I'll go in the Army like my dad. I just hope this one CD won't wreck any of that, your honor," I said.

Nobody in that courtroom knew it at the time, but they were watching a salesman being born right in front of their eyes. As for me, I knew for sure I'd get out of this unscathed.

"We're not going to let that happen here," the judge said. "I think we can all agree that this young man has learned his lesson, and I don't see any need to escalate things further."

I was mere seconds away from having all charges dropped when my dad stood up and started slow clapping in the direction of the judge.

"Who are you, sir?" the judge asked sharply.

"I'm his dad, and that may be one of the biggest whoppers I've ever heard," he said.

"What do you mean?" asked the judge.

"If you think this was the first time he stole something or did something wrong, you've been fooled like the rest of the people in this courtroom. I want you to send him a message and punish him the same way you would any other repeat offender," my dad said. "Only you have the power to wake him up and make sure this never happens again."

What was he thinking? My dad was ordering a county judge to bring the hammer down on his son. Who does that to his own kid? How did he even know what I'd done in the past? I hadn't seen him since Christmas, so why would he come home and wreck my hearing?

Of course, my dad got his way, and I was sentenced to three months in a supervised juvenile diversion program. My mom, sister, and I were stunned. We left the courthouse and drove my dad back to the airport in silence.

It wasn't an overnight detention center, but there were classes I had to attend with ten-plus other at-risk youth. I had to appear two nights a week, and one of those nights was every Tuesday, which was the same night as half of my upcoming track meets. Depending on whether the meet was on time or running late, I had to leave to report to the detention center for my court-appointed group session. One such night, I was still participating in the long jump. I looked at my watch and knew I had to leave that second. I grabbed my bag, hightailed it to my car, and left the meet without telling a single person. Did any school officials wonder what happened to me? And what about my coaches or teammates? Was anyone concerned? After all, I was a seventeen-year-old kid who simply vanished from the meet before my fifth jump.

That program was very interesting. It was like my dad had sent me somewhere to learn how to be a better criminal and a worse kid. All kinds of delinquents were in there. Some had been busted for alcohol and drug offenses, trespassing, or vandalism. But others were in for burglary or weapons possession. And one of the girls I had the hots for was there for breaking and entering. I so wanted to get her to go out with me. Maybe it was the short shorts I was still wearing from my track meet, my terrible haircut, or the fact that I was still in high school, but I never mustered up the courage to ask her out.

In the two months leading up to my graduation, my dad and I would occasionally speak on the phone. I would inevitably give him grief about his outburst in court, what he was putting me through, but also what it was teaching me.

I'd turned eighteen, and track season was in full swing. I was winning a fair number of races, but that wasn't the goal. The mission was to be in the best shape of my life leading up to the 1986 State Championships and win my state title. I entered the 110m high hurdles, the 300m intermediate hurdles, and the 200m dash. I won both hurdle events at lower state and finished second or third in the 200m, which was good enough to advance to the finals. Two of my other teammates also qualified for state, but the third did not. The four of us had gotten very close by this point, having trained together five days a week for a few months. They were the closest friends I had during that most bizarre year.

In May, I was back in Columbia, South Carolina, for the state championships. The first race of the day was the 110m hurdles. I'd spent a lot of time on the track, focusing solely on hurdles, but not on that specific event. It wasn't my best race, and I didn't care if I won. I finished third. My white whale was up next. I'd recorded the fastest time in qualifiers and had the lane I wanted. This was my race to win.

The gun went off on that hot, humid Saturday afternoon, and I was trailing the kid in front of me by a step as we got to the first hurdle. My start was solid, and as I was running my race, I started thinking, *He's going out way too fast.* Nothing changed on the back-stretch or heading into the curve. Hurdles are a funny thing. Even though they're scattered all over the track, you can tell exactly who's in front or behind by watching the timing of each runner's jump. I was behind and started to press.

By the sixth hurdle, the staggers had been completely made up, and everyone in the stadium knew who was in the lead, and it wasn't me. I was behind by at least two good steps and did nothing to improve on my position as we jumped over number seven. He was still in the lead, and I had no way to make up the gap. I was destined for another second-place finish, but then a funny thing happened on the way to his title. I watched him clip the eighth hurdle, stumble just enough to give me an opening, and I sprinted in for my one and only South Carolina state title.

That victory was a culmination of a great many factors—hard work, perseverance, and sacrifice, but not just by me individually. I had a lot of help from my coaches, teammates, sister, and countless others who contributed to the success of that season. My mom and sister were there, and I'm sure my dad was, too, but I don't remember if we celebrated as a family or just drove home. It would be almost three months before I'd see my dad again.

"As obedient children, do not conform to the evil desires
you had when you lived in ignorance.
But just as he who called you is holy,
so be holy in all you do;
for it is written: 'Be holy, because I am holy.'"

—1 Peter 1:14-16 NIV

5

THE LONGEST DAY

"There aren't any grown-ups. We shall have to look after ourselves."
—William Golding, Lord of the Flies

I snapped awake in a cold sweat on August 18, 1986. I'd known for months that I'd be attending The Citadel, and my official acceptance letter emphasized two things. The first was to make sure I arrived in shape and could effectively complete the Army physical fitness test. The second was to study *The Guidon*, the book of knob knowledge published annually, which would be critical to my survival and overall well-being for the next nine months.

I was in fabulous physical shape. I'd just wrapped up my senior year of high-school track, capped it with a state championship, and had trained all summer preparing for NCAA competition. I even logged close to three hundred and fifty miles on the Appalachian Trail, starting at the Nantahala Outdoor Center in Bryson City, North Carolina, passing through a lengthy portion of Tennessee, and finishing in Damascus, Virginia. I covered between fifteen and twenty-five miles each day, depending on the elevation, terrain, and the distance needed to reach the best shelters on the trail. Since I'd lived in Charleston for the past six years, my body had adapted to the sweltering heat and humidity. So, I was well prepared for the physical. But that fourth-class book of knowledge—*The Guidon*—that was another story.

Books weren't my thing, and I never cracked a page. I probably had three or four months to read it with ample opportunities along the Appalachian Trail to learn the basics, such as campus building names or rank hierarchy. Alternatively, I could have spent a few hours cramming the week leading up to check-in, but I didn't do any of those things. I figured none of that really mattered. Seriously, did I need to know the name of the building that housed the School of Engineering, or was it more important to be able to crank out one hundred pushups?

My dad came into town the night before I reported to The Citadel. We lived in yet another rental property, a tiny two-bedroom house compared to the home we owned on Tradd Street. In fact, the rental property was only four blocks from our primary residence, which my mom considered "uninhabitable." No work was being done to the house, and therefore, I saw no sound reason to be in yet another rental home. Maybe my mom just didn't want to go back.

I didn't sleep much that night, so I got out of bed early, walked downstairs, and saw my dad sitting on the couch in the living room, reading my copy of *The Guidon*.

"Have you read this book, Robert? I see that knowing this material is the most important thing you can do before your arrival," he said, his comment a mixture of accusation and curiosity.

"I know most of it," I said, lying through my teeth.

"Excellent. If you're a Second Lieutenant and receive a promotion, you become a…" he quizzed.

"Oh, I don't think I know that one," I said. "I haven't studied all the ranks."

"Hmm. What building will you be taking your Army instruction in over the next four years?" he asked in a snarky tone.

"I think I might have skipped over that page somehow," I snapped back.

"Interesting. Where would you go to get snacks or a haircut, check your mail, play pool, or make a call home to your mom or me?" he asked.

I knew it was over. He had me, but I wasn't going to give in. "Clearly, I have no idea."

He thundered, "Have you even cracked this book? Did you even read a single page? Have you done anything to prepare?"

"Not a thing," I said in the most childish of ways.

I'd poked the bear, and he wasn't having any of it. His anger had been building with each additional question, and my flippant attitude had ignited the dynamite. I hadn't seen my dad since the state championships back in May. I was leaving for college in thirty minutes, and we picked this time to hurl insults and accusations back and forth like two prize fighters standing face-to-face. My mom and sister were upset, so we took it outside and kept arguing. In the grand scheme of things, this meant nothing, but it was supposed to be my big day. All four of us were together for the first time in a while, and it had turned into a typical angst-ridden screaming match. The tensions eventually subsided. My dad snapped a few awkward photos of the family to commemorate the day, and we loaded up the car and took off for my date with destiny.

The nervousness that had been building in me all week had turned to dread when I first woke up, but now, I had full-fledged nausea during the car ride. Even though I was only going into the abyss for the next nine months, that fifteen-minute drive packed an incredible gut punch. I had no idea what to expect, and my heart was beating a mile a minute. We made the three-mile trip in relative silence, and I was about to begin the longest day of my life.

It was a scorching ninety-plus degree day, the humidity was through the roof, and I could feel the heaviness of tension, anxiety, and fear that permeated around the Padgett-Thomas Barracks on the campus of The Citadel—the Military College of South Carolina. I glanced in all directions, taking in the mix of military tactical officers, cadre, families, and a few girlfriends who milled about between 1st and 2nd Battalions.

The cadre, those young men who were awarded the opportunity to train the incoming freshman, were stationed everywhere, and as we parked, a welcoming committee of three upper-class cadets came to greet my mom, dad, and sister like they were long lost relatives. They acted suspiciously courteous, even the corporal who directly approached me.

"Name and company?" he asked.

"I'm Robert Hornak, and I got a letter that said I'd be in Echo Company."

He looked at his clipboard and gave me my room number. Since females weren't allowed in the barracks, my dad jumped into action to help me unload.

Our station wagon was parked just outside the black, cast-iron side gate between F-Troop and Golf. It didn't take long to unpack. I had a small duffel bag full of white boxers, white T-shirts, white socks, and white towels. I had two sets of white twin sheets, some running shorts, and a few T-shirts. In a smaller bag, I'd packed a toothbrush, toothpaste, two bars of soap, and shampoo. I was also allowed to bring one box fan since there was no air conditioning. Moving into my dorm room was barely a one-person, one-trip operation. My dad and I each grabbed a bag and entered through the side sally port together.

Regimental Band took up the entire first floor, and four other companies rounded out my battalion. Each company occupied a corner quadrant and had rooms on the second, third, and fourth decks. In the middle of this open-air structure was a red and white checkered quadrangle. Golf was to my right, but we made a sharp left turn below F-Troop. We walked forward twenty paces to the corner alcove, turned right, and it was a straight shot into Echo Company and the giant black stairwell that would take us up to the fourth deck. We made a quick right at the top of the stairs, took in an incredible view of the quad below us, and then walked fifteen steps to my room on the left.

My roommate hadn't yet arrived, so I casually started to unpack my sparse belongings.

My dad asked me if I had any questions, and I slowly shook my head no. I'm sure he sensed my stress, and he shared a hilarious story about the day he reported to Ranger school. He told me that I'd have some bad days, and that if I ever got so low that I was contemplating quitting, I could call him day or night. If he were in a meeting, he would step out and take my call. He looked right at me and said that if I called him, it would signal the urgency of the situation, and he'd drop everything to get to the phone. He handed me a laminated piece of paper with his corporate 800 number written on it and said I could call for free from any pay phone on campus and that his secretary Linda would pick up.

"Just give her your name and tell her it's urgent."

His last words of advice were to never render a bad salute. He showed me a proper one and then manipulated my hand, wrist, and elbow into the correct positioning with the tips of my fingers of my right hand resting ever so gently on the edge of my right eyebrow. We repeated this drill for a few minutes until he felt I could snap off a good one every time.

Back outside the barracks, I said goodbye to my mom and sister. Everything was still calm and cordial, but my heart was pounding inside my chest.

"Don't worry, ma'am," said one of the cadre. "We'll take care of your boy."

My mom never met anyone she didn't like, so she started giving my soon-to-be Lieutenant a few nuggets about her only boy, Robert. She might as well have handed him a David Letterman Top Ten list of ways to torment me in the coming weeks. We all took turns with the hugs; I told them I loved them and walked back through the side gate over to the Echo Company sign-in desk.

"Name?!" The 1st Sergeant exclaimed.

"Robert… Hornak," I nervously responded, having already made my first mistake of the day.

"I'm not your friend," he coldly responded. "Last name first. First initial last."

"Hornak, R.," I tensely replied.

"Aren't you missing something?" he quipped back. I stood there unable to think of anything. "Like a middle initial?"

"Yes, I have two," I said, instantly aware of how that sounded to this odd-looking, bald man in front of me.

"Two middle names? You've got to be kidding me," he said, sounding put upon.

"No, sir. Not kidding," I replied, already aware that I'd fallen down a rabbit hole.

"Where are you from, Mr. Fancy Pants?" he toyed with me.

"Charleston," I proudly snapped back.

"What part of the city? What street did you grow up on?" the junior 1st Sergeant fired off.

"Downtown," I replied. I already sensed his tone and knew the next answer would hurt. "Tradd Street."

"So, we have a real-life S.O.B. (South of Broad) with two middle initials whose mommy and daddy drove him here today all the way from downtown who thinks he's going to make it through my knob year," he rattled off.

"No, sir," I began.

"That's Sir, no, Sir. And don't you ever forget it. Do you know how to properly salute, Hornak?"

Surrounding my 1st Sergeant and his table were a slew of his minions from the sophomore class. Cadets who, in theory, were well trained to effectively tear me down and build me up into a better version of myself. A group from all walks of life that would decide what I could and couldn't do for my entire freshman year. But they were actually just a bunch of nineteen-year-olds with little to no leadership training who'd just come off the worst year of their lives and were ready to inflict the same level of harassment and hazing—if not more—than they'd just endured. Fellow students who could do whatever they wanted without fear of repercussion because there weren't any adults around to provide oversight. Young men salivating to run me and everyone else who checked in at this dinky, little white table out of school. And the man who orchestrated it all, the man with the cleanly shaved, bald head, looked at me with such disdain and fired off the most puzzling question yet.

"Who taught you how to salute, cadet recruit?"

"My dad, sir," I proudly replied, improving my posture a bit more.

"What's so special about your daddy?" he mockingly asked.

"He was an Army Ranger and taught me how to salute. I know for a fact that this is a good one," I said.

My nervousness had turned to confidence mixed with a hint of anger, but clearly, I wasn't in control. This exchange had already become a top ten terrible moment for me, and I was only minutes into this hellish experience with no way out. I couldn't quit. It would destroy my dad and all his military friends. He had taken me to Fort Benning a couple of times to meet the guys, and those brief encounters had weighed heavily on me since the day I committed. My mom and sister had told everyone I would be attending The Citadel, and they couldn't wait to see me in a uniform. I was also the only one from my formerly decimated and now shuttered high school who chose this place. I had to make it for my family, my two high-school track coaches, and my old teacher, Mage, over at Porter-Gaud. I wasn't going to give anyone the satisfaction of saying, "We thought you wouldn't make it."

"Your dad can't save you in here. And he didn't even teach you how to properly salute. It's embarrassing. You're embarrassing. Hornak, you won't last the week."

Apparently, my inability to give him one good salute outweighed the check-in process for my new company mates standing in line behind me. I had saluted like my dad showed me, but these jokers weren't letting me off that easily. My mind started to wander. *Where was all the yelling? I expected more yelling.* This was more like an incredibly condescending conversation, but eerily relaxed. My dad and I had been screaming at each other toe-to-toe just an hour ago, so this felt surprisingly tame.

"Do you know how to sign your name?" he taunted.

"Of course," I said.

"That's Sir, yes, Sir or Sir, no, Sir," he clapped back.

"Sir, yes, Sir," I said.

"Just stand on the line and sign your name on the piece of paper, Hornak."

I toed the line and leaned toward the table to grab the pen in my left hand, but it was slightly out of reach. I caught myself on the corner of the table with my right hand.

"Don't touch my table!" the sergeant blurted out.

I reset and toed the line again, knowing that grabbing the pen was going to require a little work. I took a second glance at the table. *Did they lower that thing just a little bit,* I wondered to myself. I leaned in again, but this time I rose a hair on my toes to get that extra inch of reach I so desperately needed. I lost my balance and fell forward into the table.

"Wrong again. Don't ever touch my table," he challenged again.

How long was this game going to go on? What was the point? Was everyone getting this treatment, or had my mom's conversation with these guys rubbed someone the wrong way? What could she have said? Why did I choose this place? *I've made a terrible decision. I should have gone to Chapel Hill or, better yet, Gainesville. There would be so many beautiful girls at those places. There aren't any girls here—just jerks.* The thoughts swirled in my mind.

"Sign in. I don't have all day," he ordered.

But they did, and I hadn't learned that yet. I slowly inched my shoes as close as possible to the line, rose up onto the very tips of my toes, and slowly leaned in. My calves started to ache as I tilted forward centimeter by centimeter. The pen was so close. I reached out with my left hand and tried to stretch my index and middle fingers out as far as they would go. The collection of table brutes was intently watching and waiting for the screwup. *Almost there,* I thought as the sweat beads that had built up since my first salute were now in free flow. My index finger was stretched out as far as it could go, and the closer I got to the pen, the more I started shaking. I finally touched it, flicked it back a few millimeters, picked it up with my left hand, careful not to touch any part of the table, and signed in.

"Next!" the 1st Sergeant shouted as I was whisked off to stand in formation with all the other suckers assigned to Cell Block E.

There was no right way to complete that task. It was always going to be his way, and it was a constantly moving target. The point was that there was no point, and that was true for me, the guys that signed into Echo Company, and the 653 cadet recruits who began their quest to become members of the Class of 1990 that day.

Thirty-eight of us checked into Echo Company on that hot, muggy August morning to begin our journey together. I knew my roommate's first name, but I wouldn't know how to properly say his last name for weeks since all the upperclassmen pronounced it wrong. I knew a few last names because that's all they called us, but everyone blended in together.

We all wore the same uniforms, had the same buzz cut, and didn't dare look left or right for fear of repercussion. They called us knobs, a term derived for us because our bald heads resembled doorknobs. A plastic "idiot bag" was strung around our necks, stuffed with our most vital information, and we carried our book of knob knowledge everywhere we went. Our names were on the front of our screen doors, so I might have an idea who lived a couple of doors down from me or might hear a cadre corporal yelling out a last name one floor below, but there was no way to match a name with a face.

NOTHING CRAZY HAD HAPPENED YET, AND EVERYTHING FELT ROUTINE—physical training runs, countless formations, rifle drill, academic orientation, marches all over campus, military training, and three square meals a day. Some of the Echo Company knobs weren't used to the heat and struggled on the runs, but that was the easiest part of my day. We jogged at a medium pace with everyone packed into a large formation. The cadre ran in front, behind, and around our company of recruits with our 1st Sergeant chanting jody calls, a time-honored tradition. I'm not sure what percent of my day was spent running, but I never got winded. The same couldn't be said for some of the other guys. I wondered, *Did they even train for this?*

Whenever we stopped marching, we snapped to attention as the sophomore leaders swarmed around to see if we'd studied our handbook. The questions came word-for-word right out of *The Guidon*. Whether we were inside the barracks, in front of a building, or smack dab in the middle of the road surrounding the parade deck, they asked questions. The biggest shock in my first few days was how I'd grossly miscalculated the ratio of preparation between being in shape and reading the cadet manual. I was completely wrong to prioritize only my physical preparation, and my poor decision was exposed at every stop.

That first week was tough, but it wasn't awful. Once I realized I wasn't making decisions for myself anymore, coping became easier. Be in the right uniform, arrive on time, and avoid saying anything stupid. Go where they tell you, march in step, and try to blend in.

On a late afternoon a few days in, the entire freshman class was herded to Mark Clark Hall to the large auditorium on the second floor. Sitting down for a few minutes in an air-conditioned room was a welcome relief. The upperclassmen had left us alone, and we started to relax. I looked around, got the first name and hometown from the guy on my left and right, and we shared a couple of stories about our first few days. Some nearby cadet recruits had already started checking their eyelids for cracks when in walked Major General James A. Grimsley, our commandant, to congratulate us on an incredible start to our journey. He said that our freshman class aptitude and physical performance were the best in a decade and that we'd earned ourselves a well-deserved night off from training. Shortly after dinner, we could all call it a night and catch up on some sleep, but he reminded us to be ready to go for PT the next morning.

And that's when the real fun began.

The abrupt, violent banging on trash cans and the slamming of screen doors woke me up instantly. As I tried to focus my senses, I heard a consistent, elevated yelling and general chaos. It didn't matter that I couldn't pinpoint it because it was everywhere, and it was getting closer to my room by the second. Our creaky screen door opened outward, and the heavy wooden door to our room was kicked open by two of our cadre leaders. They ordered us downstairs immediately. I launched off the top bunk, and my roommate, Rich, and I frantically threw on our PT uniforms. We put on our standard-issued blue short shorts, white T-shirts with blue collars and cuffs, white socks, and tennis shoes, and we sprinted to get into formation on the bottom deck. The battalion lights were on, which was unusual since it was after 10:30 p.m. The chaos was palpable, and it was evident that something had changed. We'd heard mumblings and whispers about this being *the night*, but now that we'd been yanked out of bed and forced downstairs, it was clear that the earlier pep talk from General Grimsley was a charade.

All of us knobs made it downstairs in various intervals over the course of ninety seconds. As we took that last fateful step off the stairs and onto the main deck, a member of the cadre grabbed us by the arm and positioned us on a corner edge of either a red or white square slab of the quadrangle surface that faced our company letter. I stared at a giant block "E" twenty feet in front of me that was painted on the bottom quarter of our stairwell in The Citadel's traditional Infantry and Flag Blue color pattern. It faced out at an acute angle from our corner of the battalion, and one by one, my classmates were placed into position. Approximately three or four rows of ten or so recruits stood equally spaced apart, front to back and left to right, and we were ordered to stand perfectly still. The yelling had died down, no one moved, and they killed the lights. Pitch black, the midnight heat was unbearable, and the mosquitoes landed on our arms, legs, and necks. We stood still.

It was so dark that I could barely make out the silhouettes of my classmates in front of me. No one dared to look left or right for fear of who might be watching. We couldn't see our tormentors, and maybe they couldn't see us, but it wasn't worth the risk. I tried moving my eyes as far to the left and right as I could without moving my head, but I only saw shapes and shadows. And the multitude of bug bites was simply overwhelming. I didn't see anyone else trying to squash the bugs, so I stood motionless and let them feast. The silence was deafening. I could hear soft whispers but couldn't make out any words. I kept thinking to myself, *I know they're there. What are they waiting for?* But our cadre had all the time in the world, so we stood there being slowly devoured by the bugs.

Just before the dozens of welts on our bodies had become unbearable, somebody yelled an order, and the cadre began stomping around the company. Throughout the entire battalion, each company's cadre marched in unison. I had no idea how long we'd waited for something to happen because time literally stood still. Suddenly, a faceless voice sounded off directly in front of us. He explained the uniqueness of this moment in time and that we were to explicitly follow orders, respect our training cadre, and perform all tasks to the highest possible standards during our training cycle. Still standing in complete darkness, the staff was introduced one by one, and this is when we were all taught how to "brace." Instructions were simple. Let our arms hang straight down, place our cupped hands along the side of our pants, and suck in our stomachs while simultaneously rolling our shoulders back and down until they couldn't possibly go any further. And lastly, drive our chin through our chest.

It was dark and quiet again, but the silence was interrupted when the battalion-wide sound system turned on. We were serenaded with the song "Home Sweet Home" played on a harmonica. The last bar of the song faded into the night, and next up on the slow road to pain was when they closed the two gates in the front sally port of Padgett-Thomas Barracks. The creaking of the gates, in desperate need of some WD-40, echoed through the thick night air. Slowly, they came together at what seemed like a centimeter per second. My heart quickened as the gates slammed shut, and a voice came over the loudspeaker.

"Members of the Class of 1990, the 4th class system is now in effect."

All the floodlights snapped on and thrust me into a temporary state of blindness. Where I thought no one was standing in the dark only seconds ago, the light revealed a cadre member only inches from me, and I knew the misery was about to begin. I was bombarded with yelling, cussing, and spitting. Clearly, some of our trainers had been dreaming of this moment ever since they'd applied for this duty, but they had no business being in a leadership position because they simply wanted their pound of flesh. Others had real aspirations for a military career or saw this as a steppingstone to a more senior role in the Corps of Cadets. All of them wanted to haze some knobs that night.

The sheer physicality of their demands dragged on for what seemed like hours. When my arms gave out from doing pushups, I was ordered to get on my back and do sit-ups until my stomach muscles started shaking and I couldn't lift my shoulder blades off the concrete surface. Sit-ups turned into high knees or mountain climbers, and many of us were relocated to the stairwell to give piggyback rides up to the fourth deck. And when my body was exhausted, instead of getting a second to rest, a cadet corporal pushed a single pointy index finger into my chin and told me to "rack it in." Or my platoon sergeant snuck up behind me and ran the outside portion of his hand up and down my spine to get me into a brace position. Or finally, that one member of the cadre with the massive Napoleon complex (the one who liked to tell me he was going to make my life utterly miserable until I quit) stopped and yelled and told me to do pushups until I couldn't do any more. Then he stood me up, put a finger in my chest, and said, "Attrition is my mission, Hornak, and you're next." *OK,* I thought to myself, but what I really wanted to tell him was that he'd already said the same thing three times. Instead, I kept quiet and wondered how much more we'd have to endure.

And like all good or bad things, it eventually came to an end. Maybe there was a time limit, maybe they got sick of hazing us, or maybe they got someone to quit and had satisfied some seemingly unquenchable thirst for exploiting weakness. Whatever the catalyst, we formed back up, sprinted to our rooms, and tried to fall asleep. My roommate ran in after me, and I was glad to see him, glad that he'd made it back upstairs. Neither of us knew about the other thirty-six guys. Did anyone quit? Did anyone come close? We honestly had no idea. Shoot, we didn't even know the names of at least ten guys in our company.

In the coming weeks, knobs from every company began leaving. Maybe it was the physical aspect, maybe the mental, or perhaps another reason altogether. We witnessed a few of those breakdowns in real time, and those stories won't be shared. Most of the time, we knew his last name, and sometimes we even knew his first name. But in those early days after Hell Night, I might not have even known that an Echo Company classmate ever existed.

One hot August evening, one of us—or more likely a few of us—had messed up in such a major way that it required corrective action. Other times, the cadet cadre didn't need an excuse and just wanted to have some fun. Either way, word came down from top brass that we were going to have a "Sweat Party." We were already in our duty uniforms, but we were told to put on our neck-to-floor heavy-duty raincoats and meet in the second-floor alcove. Most rooms at The Citadel held two cadets, two bunk beds, two desks, two full presses for hanging clothes, and two half presses for your perfectly folded T-shirts, underwear, etc. An alcove room could hold three or, more typically, four cadets, as well as four of everything else I described above. There was one alcove on each floor and in each corner, making a total of sixteen of these rooms in each battalion. And alcove-room gatherings could only mean one thing: group hazing.

When we were all lined up in the hallway, they shuffled us into the large corner room. Whoever lived in this room had already cleared out, so it was thirty or so freshman cadets and a handful of cadre. We sweated profusely. After all, it was late August in South Carolina. We were wearing long pants, grey short-sleeve shirts, and raincoats, which made our sweat glands open up right away. The room was built to house four people, but I counted at least forty in there that night. With no air conditioning, it got hotter by the second. The cadre were standing toe to toe with the guys on the front line, who were yelling at us for being pure garbage and simultaneously pushing us backward toward the closed window with the radiator just below. The heat was turned up full blast, and we were roasting in this tiny corner of the room. The yelling got louder, but it wasn't directed at anyone in particular. At least not yet.

"Who wants to quit?" one cadre corporal asked.

We stayed strong and offered no response. They pushed us closer to the wall, packing us in tighter. Sweat ran down my body.

"Who's ready to go home? You can call your mommy from my phone, and she can pick you up in the morning. Maybe even tonight for the local knobs," said one of the senior officers.

Nobody moved—not even an inch. Nobody spoke or even dared to think. The cadre corporals pushed their fingers into the chins of the four guys in the front row and forced them to inch back, but there was nowhere to go. The wall unit was belching out unbearable heat, and we were right up on it. Someone was going to touch it for sure; the question was who would it be? My entire body was drenched, my pants were sopping wet, and I had no saliva in my mouth. They pressed closer, we fell back into one of the knobs, and he was forced back onto the steaming hot radiator.

"Aggghhhh!" he pitifully yelped, trying his best not to make any noise.

"WHO MADE THAT NOISE?!" a corporal shouted.

"Arrrrrrgggggghhhh!" he more painfully let out.

One of the sergeants pierced through our barrier of soaked bodies and got right up in his face and shouted, "What's your problem, knob?"

"Sir, it's hot, Sir. I'm burning, and I think my shoes are melting," he said in a high-pitched voice.

In fact, the wax on his freshly shined, leather shoes was liquefying and dripping onto the floor. It provided us a second of levity, but we didn't dare laugh for fear of reprisal. Hutch was one of nineteen guys in Echo Company who made it through that first year. His jovial attitude often made me—and the other guys—smile during those first few weeks, and boy did we need that.

I'd been living in this prison for a few weeks and hadn't seen or spoken with my parents since I'd checked in. I'd already lost a massive amount of body weight, wasn't getting quality sleep, and certainly wasn't focused on school. Desperate for sleep of any kind, I resorted to taking naps in my classes, one of only a few places on campus that was free from harassment. I was so hungry, starving in fact, that I joined the Fellowship of Christian Athletes and the Cadet Choir because it meant two things: one, I could get out of my room and the barracks without fear of persecution, and two, they always had a plate of chocolate brownies or cookies and cans of soda for members of either organization.

I would love to tell you that I found God or learned a meaningful scripture in one of those meetings or that I had a voice like an angel and led the worship team on Sunday mornings, but none of those things are true. I was desperate for calories of any kind, and I didn't care where they came from.

Parents' Weekend marked the end of our cadre training period. We were minutes away from being thrown to the wolves that made up the entire Corps of Cadets. For six weeks, we'd been under the protection of our guards, but we were about to be moved into this prison's general population—a place where basic rules existed, but few upperclassmen seemed to follow them.

Many freshmen in Echo Company had already quit, and it was visibly obvious. I couldn't remember the names of the first few guys to leave, but the more recent departures had hurt because we'd experienced some bad days together and had become close friends in the process. I looked to my left and right and knew this group could all make it seven more months.

All our meals were served family style in a giant mess hall. During those early days of training, only knobs and cadre ate together. One long table was split down the middle, and each side sat up to seven people. The highest-ranking cadet sat at the head of the table with the second-highest in one of the two seats next to him. At that time, I usually sat with my squad sergeant at the end of the table and my squad corporal next to him. Five of us knobs filled the rest of our side. The same was true for the other end of the table, which looked like a mirror image of us.

However, once we were integrated into the rest of the Corps, all bets were off. I might have a really laid-back senior private who wanted to be left alone to talk to his buddies and would let me eat in relative peace, or I could get an over-the-top junior jockeying for a regimental staff position who wanted to show everyone how tough he could be. Or, like many days, I'd get someone who wanted to have some fun and make my dining experience as miserable as possible.

Meals with the entire Corps became routine. We said grace, and everyone sat down. Knobs waited until the upperclassmen were seated, and then we could quickly sit down. We had to take drink orders and fill everyone's glasses with water or tea. Food was passed around family style, and occasionally we had to serve our mess carver and staff, but once everyone else had been taken care of, we could fix our plates. At some point during this process, the head of the table asked us three questions, almost always taken right out of that pesky *Guidon* that I still hadn't read. Other times, we might have to research a subject and bring that information back to the table for the next meal. When all our tasks were completed, including additional drink refills, we could eat. Many times, the horn would sound to indicate the end of the meal before I'd completed all my tasks, so I was dismissed without ever eating a bite. There was a rule that forbade this kind of behavior, but did anyone really check?

One day, after everyone was served and I'd spouted off all my knob facts, I made the most colossal blunder in dining hall history—a mistake that I paid for dearly until my indoor track season started. As the food was passed down to me, I said, "No, thank you," to a serving of broccoli.

"Don't you like broccoli, Hornak?" my mess carver asked.

"Sir, no, Sir," I replied. I hated it. Both the smell and the taste. And I'd just cracked open a door to a whole new form of torture.

"Well, you haven't tried this broccoli. Nobody makes it better than the cooks here," the sophomore next to me said.

He picked up the family-style bowl and poured the rest right onto my plate, splashing broccoli juice onto my duty gray shirt and leaving a stream of the foul greenish liquid running off the side of the table and onto my trousers. I wanted to vomit from the smell.

"Eat," said an upperclassman.

"Now!" shouted another.

I slowly picked up my fork. There was no way out of this. My gag reflex was already warmed up. Everyone at the table stared at me. I had to take a bite. As I brought the fork toward my mouth, I glanced down and sized up my water glass. There was only one or two fluid ounces remaining, and I knew it wasn't enough to wash it down. The first piece went in my mouth, and I did some fake chewing, took what was the only swig of water left in my glass, and swallowed it whole. I didn't ralph and was so proud of myself.

"More!" my mess carver demanded.

No one else was eating. They were all watching me and waiting for the train wreck. I drove my fork through the smallest stalk, moved as slowly as humanly possible, and took a second bite. I fake-chewed again, but the whole table was onto me.

"Chew it!" they yelled in unison.

I had no water left. I was covered in broccoli juice. I knew in the deepest crevices of my mind that if I bit into this broccoli, I would throw up all over the table. I swallowed that piece whole and started to gag. And instead of a normal reflex gag, I decided my only way out of this situation was to ratchet up the volume. I made horrible gagging noises and forced my body to shake as I sat on the end of my chair in the brace position. Probably fearful that I might hurl all over their table, the senior in charge dismissed me. I grabbed my hat and booked it out of the mess hall. As soon as I got outside, I threw up.

This is what they do. They find a weakness, any weakness, and they exploit it. At each meal for the next two months, they made me try every single item on the table to see how I would respond. I wasn't a very picky eater when I entered The Citadel, but since those days, I've stopped eating about 90 percent of all vegetables and many of the basic food groups. I can't see something on a plate without being whisked back to being force-fed cooked broccoli, spinach, squash, or any of the other unnatural veggies. I didn't care what they did to me in the barracks, but I did pray to eat in peace. Finally, later that fall, I got my wish. I was moved to Corps Squad mess, which meant I would eat the rest of my meals with all my track teammates and the rest of the athletes.

Being from Charleston would serve me well in many capacities over those four years, but none was more important than my ability to ask for a date during my freshman year. Asking didn't guarantee anything, but I had better odds of success than almost all my out-of-state classmates.

There was an abundance of single girls at The College of Charleston, but in my anemic state and with my shaved head, I didn't stand a chance of meeting anyone new. Since I'd attended three different high schools since moving to the Holy City, I'd gotten to know a handful of girls I enjoyed hanging out with and felt comfortable calling.

Our first major event of the year was an on-campus Hop, known to the rest of the world as a dance. My first call was to my friend, Kim, to see if she would go with me, and also to ask if she could bring a friend for one of my out-of-town Echo brothers. She said yes, but since we weren't allowed to drive as freshmen, Kim and her friend would have to come to us. And since we were a dry campus, there would be no drinking, and I can only imagine what she must have thought after seeing me for the first time in months with my freshly shaved head, excessive weight loss, and sunken eyes. But she was sweet and never said a word about my appearance. I imagine my lethargic state and Guantanamo-Bay-prisoner-vibe was a little jarring compared to the guy she used to know, but I loved spending that time with her and having some normalcy, even if it was only for a couple of hours.

While my first semester trudged along and classes were in full swing, I'd made no progress at all on the dating front. It was time to take a big shot, so I called up Nicole, the girl I had a crush on in my juvenile correctional program. She was from West Ashley, lived a little harder, and was more worldly than the typical downtown girls I might normally meet, but Nikki had her own car and could pick me up. It didn't hurt that she was very attractive and would probably help me earn some much-needed brownie points with the upperclassmen.

A typical Friday at this early stage of the year consisted of multiple formations, classes, and meals, all bang, bang, bang. The Corps' schedule didn't allow for much downtime, so we were always moving and performing tasks. After my lone afternoon class, I headed back to the barracks to prepare for our weekly afternoon parade. This meant shining my shoes and brass, making sure my uniform looked tip-top, and ensuring my rifle was cleaned, or at a minimum, presentable.

At 1545 hours sharp, the entire Corps of Cadets marched onto Summerall Field for retreat, a traditional military custom that gave friends, family, and many out-of-town tourists an opportunity to witness a ceremony that dated back to the American Revolutionary War. This spectacle signaled the end of the official duty day and honored our nation's flag. The field is 1,060 feet long by 450 feet wide and spans about twelve acres in total. The Friday afternoon ritual was always open to the public. And at its conclusion, it signaled the beginning of the weekend for most cadets—at least those not restricted due to confinements or tours.

There were typically a lot of visitors in front of the battalion who milled about in the hour or so after a parade—a swarm of local girls, College of Charleston co-eds looking for their boyfriends, parents looking for their sons, or cadets going out on an afternoon run. The entrance to the Padgett-Thomas Barracks at this point in the afternoon always reminded me of a bus terminal in a medium-sized city. For a knob like me looking to escape the confines of my prison, this was the exact time to leave, under the cover of two hundred sets of civilian eyes.

Nikki didn't make the parade, and I didn't expect her to be there. She wasn't girlfriend material per se, and we weren't dating, but she was hot, we had juvie in common, and she was someone fun I could hang out with tonight. And she had a car. She hadn't seen me since I got to The Citadel, so I was equally excited and a tad bit anxious.

I didn't know the exact time she would arrive since I didn't have a phone in my room. I called her earlier that week from a pay phone, and we tentatively agreed that she would pick me up around 6:00 p.m. This meant she had to park outside the battalion, walk up to the sally port, and ask the guard to tell me she was here. But because of the time she was supposed to arrive, my civilian safety net was long gone.

There are a lot of moving parts here, and I'll do my best to explain. Guard duty on a Friday night is one of the worst assignments a cadet can have—at least for normal cadets. It's not the worst job, but it's close. Any kind of weekend duty was reason enough to begin the shift in a foul mood. On top of that, a seductive girl approached that guard and asked him to run and get me, a lowly, scum-of-the-earth knob.

None of this would sit well with anyone who patrolled the sally port or sat in the adjacent guardroom. So instead of doing the cool thing, which would be to send a runner up to knock on my door, he decided to announce Nikki's arrival to anyone within earshot.

"HORNAK! ECHO COMPANY! YOUR DATE IS HERE!" he belted out.

I heard it loud and clear, but so did the rest of my company and perhaps the entire battalion. My heart rate instantly doubled, and I knew I had to get out and fast. I ran to my full press, grabbed my garrison cap, and flew out the door. On a good day, I could make it to that front gate in under thirty seconds. That meant I had a clear running lane and didn't encounter any human obstacles. I took two steps out my door, made the sharp right-hand turn to head to the stairwell, and immediately saw a problem.

"Where's the fire, Hornak?" my platoon leader calmly asked.

"Sir, no fire, sir. Apparently, I have a visitor downstairs." I was careful to minimize the situation.

"Apparently? Hmmm. You sure got dressed super quick for an 'apparently,' and the way you came blasting out of that door... Drop and give me fifteen, Hornak."

I instantly dropped to the deck and, on my way down, removed my garrison cap and placed it on my lower back where it needed to remain balanced. Push-ups were a time-honored tradition at The Citadel, and I could crank them out. I knew this would be a skill I had to have to survive, so after I was accepted, I practiced every day all summer long. And I'd already done thousands and thousands of them since my August arrival, so I knew this would only slow me down for a few seconds.

"Begin."

"Sir, one, sir. Sir, two, sir. Sir, three, sir," I started counting out. "Sir, fifteen, sir. Sir, one for Echo Company, sir, and sir, one for the Class of 1990, sir."

Once I'd rattled off my fifteen, all the knobs were required to do a sixteenth pushup for our company and then a seventeenth for our class year. When finished, I stayed in the leaning rest position until I was told to recover. That was a mandatory requirement. On most days, the order to rise was given instantly, and I could have kept making forward progress. However, I quickly realized that today was not a normal day. I remained in position.

"So, who's the girl, Hornak?" he casually asked.

"Girl, sir?" I quizzed back.

"You heard me. Girl. Who's the girl? Everyone in this company knows you've got a date. Man, I can smell that Drakkar on you from here."

I reflected on his comments for a nanosecond. The announcement had just come over the loudspeaker. How could everyone know? And I certainly couldn't say how I'd met her. I'd been trying to keep my juvenile delinquency under wraps ever since I was sentenced. I had to come up with something quick.

"Just a girl I know from town. Hoping we might hook up tonight," I said, already uneasy about the answer.

"Looking for some action, heh?" he knowingly replied. "I get it."

That was a relief because I needed to get going. But I had to have permission to stand up first. We had that entire conversation while I was still holding in leaning rest, and he was standing over me drinking a soda. I wasn't uncomfortable in this position, but I couldn't get up until he gave the command.

"On your feet," he ordered.

As I sprang to my feet, I reached back and grabbed my cap off my lower back and placed it squarely on my head in one nice, fluid process. The by-the-book rule about doing pushups was that you could only be asked to do fifteen at a time. This language was inserted into the training manual to help cut down on hazing. The extra two push-ups for company and class were added in for camaraderie building, I suppose. But the upperclassmen had developed a workaround to that pesky rule since the number of times you could drop for fifteen had never been established.

"So where are you taking this girl?" he asked, like I was a high school football teammate who was taking out his sister.

As I was about to start my answer, he interrupted and said, "Drop."

I dropped to the ground again and began the next set while offering him a few details about my plans for the evening. He quickly brought me to my feet and then sent me right back down for another fifteen. This went on two or three more times, and then we both heard the shouting from the quad.

"HORNAK! YOUR DATE IS WAITING! GET YOUR BUTT DOWN HERE!"

There was nothing I could do until he released me. I'd done five or six sets of pushups during our little encounter, but it was enough to get the sweat going. If I wanted to stay presentable for the date, I'd need this to stop now.

"Sounds like she's waiting. You'd better get going, Hornak."

"Sir, yes, sir." I happily responded and made the six-step run to the top of the fourth-floor stairwell.

There were some basic rules about running up and down stairs for us freshmen. I came to a complete stop at the stairwell, looked to see if anyone was there, and if not, I was free to go unencumbered. If an upperclassman was present, I had to ask their specific permission to drive the stairs. This meant to ask them by name and perhaps throw a please in for good measure. Problems always arose in the early days when you didn't know someone's name. That type of misstep always brought the jackals out, but today was not that day. I glanced down from the top step and saw a senior I liked, one who'd never given me any trouble. His last name was Roof. *Lucky for me*, I thought.

"Sir, Mr. Roof, sir, Cadet Private Hornak, R.C.C., requesting permission to drive your stairs," I exclaimed.

"Permission granted," he lazily responded, seemingly unaware that I had a lady waiting for me downstairs.

I took a hard left and booked it down the stairs, passing him on his way up.

"Be careful," Mr. Roof casually said.

What did that mean? Be careful. What on earth was he talking about? As soon as I stepped onto the third deck and made my sharp right turn, I saw what waited for me. A slew of sophomore and junior rank holders were gathered by the corner alcove. It would only take one to stop me, and I'd be done for, but for one second, I thought maybe I could slip past them all.

I spent the next block of time doing pushups for the group, and I'd probably knocked out around three hundred by that point. My arms started to feel like spaghetti. Each time I began a new set, my upper body started to shake around the tenth one, so they stood me up and made me do high knees for a while. I was pouring sweat, and my shirt was soaked. I was only 100 feet from my room, and my tank was getting low.

Those guys finally cut me loose, and I made the short run to the top step on the third deck. I looked down and saw our company clerk standing there. He wasn't walking up or down. He was just standing there, and that only meant one thing: he wanted to play, too. I don't remember how many times I started and stopped doing pushups for him, but I'd been obliterated. He knew it, and I knew it. And my uniform looked terrible. It was drenched in sweat, and at any point, he could have sent me all the way back to the top to change and start over, but he didn't.

"Get out of here, Hornak. You disgust me," he said, and I hustled down to the first deck and the safety of Band Company. Nobody down there ever messed with an Echo knob, so I had safe passage over the last hundred feet.

I got to the interior entrance of the sally port and made a sharp right turn. Nikki was just outside the gate, and she looked great. I felt like I'd been in a sauna for hours and was sweating profusely. I had no concept of time or how long it had taken me to cover the few hundred feet from my room to where I was now, but she was right there. I was just seconds from getting out of this nightmare when the Officer of the Day, the man who'd alerted everyone in Echo Company about her arrival, stepped between us.

"This lovely lady has been standing here for a long time, and it's extremely rude of you to keep her waiting, Cadet Private Hornak. Do you have anything you want to say?" he toyed with me.

"I'm very sorry, Nikki. It took longer than I expected to get dressed and downstairs." I could see a slight smirk on her face.

"I don't know if I would accept that answer, Miss," he quipped as he looked back and forth between her and me. "I tell you what, why don't you drop and give me fifteen quick pushups, and I'll let you love-birds go on your date."

I think it took me close to thirty minutes to get downstairs, and I may have done or tried to crank out close to four hundred pushups. And when you're an athlete, you know your body, and I knew for a fact that I couldn't do fifteen more in front of Nikki. I wasn't even sure I could do five.

"Let's go, Hornak. Fifteen and you can go."

I slowly went to the ground and could barely get into leaning rest. My arms were toast and were already shaking. I unlocked my elbows and just dropped, my hands and chest completely flat on the ground. I tried to lift myself up, but I had zero strength.

"Your date's right here, knob. Haven't you learned how to do a push-up?"

"Sir, yes, sir," I said, lying completely prostrate on the ground.

"Then give me ten, Hornak."

I tried to push off the ground again. My adrenaline alone lifted me up four or five inches, but I knew I wasn't going any farther. My arms shook so violently, and the sheer embarrassment of this encounter washed over me. I didn't want to look up at Nikki, so I stared at a spot on the concrete.

"Can you do one, Hornak—one single pushup?" he mocked. "Just do one for your lady," he taunted. "Your lady just wants to see you do one."

Nikki and I had been through a few tough months together earlier that year. Parental punishment, condescending instructors, and we'd both tried to cover up what we had done. We both had secrets, we trusted each other, and she'd known a very different me before witnessing that debacle in the sally port. The OD let us go, and we had a quiet dinner downtown with a lot of talking between friends. We shared a good laugh about what I endured to go out with her and kept cracking up over the line, "Do one for your lady." We walked around the market after dinner and talked for hours. Around 11:30 p.m., Nikki drove me back to school. I never saw her again.

The Citadel had massive open-air latrines on each floor. In Echo Company, we had three of these large bathrooms, one on each deck, and as I ran in with the thirty-eight other knobs that first night, I did a quick scan of the room. There were about twenty bathroom stalls on the left side that ran the length of the wall, but none had a door. Not one single door. I assumed it was only for our training period, but I was wrong. It was like that all four years. And the toilet paper rolls were placed overhead on one long metal pipe that ran the entire length of the wall. For some reason, there was a padlock on the end of that pipe. If you needed TP, you had to ask a neighbor a few seats down to slide a roll your way.

To the right side of the room was a porcelain-tiled shower bank with twenty nozzles. During the first few weeks of training, all knobs were hustled in for one of two reasons: first, the mandatory ten-second shower that may or may not involve soap but might help get the stink off, or second, a little hot-cold action. The cadre would turn on all the shower heads, alternating between scalding hot and ice-cold, and then rotate us through like some outlandish game of musical chairs.

Birthdays? To this day, no one at The Citadel knows my birthday. I can't tell you what happened to guys once their actual birth date was discovered because knowing someone's birthday set off a series of events that the celebrant wanted no part of. Let's just say it involved hiding, hunting, capture, a bottle of black leather heel and sole edge dressing, partial nudity, and no cake. I'm proud to say that my birthday remained a campus secret my entire four years.

Haircuts were always over in Mark Clark Hall and were usually uneventful. I wasn't a big fan of the buzz cut, but I always enjoyed it when the barber would lather up my neck with warm shaving cream and use a long, straightedged razor to give me the closest shave possible. I usually dropped in on a Friday to get a fresh cut in preparation for our Saturday Morning Inspections. Late one evening, Rampy, one of the barbers, was touching me up with his straight razor and sliced the right side of my neck. Did I move, or did he miss? It doesn't really matter. But instead of getting me a towel or applying a Band-Aid, he grabbed his "air duster" and blew off all the blood, which spattered all over my neck, cheek, and onto my duty uniform.

Other times, Mark Clark Hall was my sanctuary. If I didn't get to eat at lunch in the mess hall, I'd make my way over to the canteen and order a grilled cheese, a large order of fries, and a chocolate milkshake. I had about twenty minutes to eat in complete solitude and decompress, to just stare out into space. Thirty-eight years later, I rate that canteen combo as my all-time favorite meal and could eat it every day for the rest of my life.

Then there was my coursework. I was falling asleep during lectures and failing multiple classes. The school had set up an evening study period for us each night. The rules required that knobs had to be left alone, but that was seldom the case. I tried to study a little, but most nights, I'd put my head on my desk for some shuteye. At the end of the study period, a few upper-class jokers would drop in and see how my roommate and I were doing. Those days moved painfully slow, and I started counting them down in my calendar.

One evening, while being harassed on the fourth deck by a member of the sophomore class, one of our Echo seniors stuck his head out of his screen door and ordered me into his room. That usually meant he had a job for me to do—what we fourth-class cadets referred to as "knob missions." I might have to shine his shoes, spout off some random knob knowledge, or hang by my arms from the full press until I gave out or they got bored and let me leave.

There were two seniors in the room. I was told to take a seat by the man to my right, but no second order was given, which created an unusually long, awkward pause. The senior who invited me in was Mr. Roof, and the senior to my left was Mr. Brown. They asked if I wanted anything to drink, but I thought to myself, *It's a trap.* I told them I was fine and stood at rigid attention, looking straight out the window directly in front of me.

They asked a bunch of questions about my life, where I grew up, and why I'd chosen The Citadel. I was bracing, sweating, and waiting for the hammer to drop, but they sat in their metal chairs with their feet up, like it was a normal conversation between three friends. They joked about all the times they heard my name being yelled, said they'd keep their eyes on my roommate, Rich, and me, and would intervene if they ever saw one of us being horribly mistreated. The last thing they said was to knock on their door if I ever needed anything.

They stood up, introduced themselves as Carl and Doug, shook my hand, and told me to get out of their room.

It was virtually impossible and usually not worth the effort to try to meet girls from the College of Charleston, especially during that first year. I stood out with my shaved head and withering body, and the girls that interested me didn't want anything to do with a freshman cadet. I didn't date much because every time I went out with a new girl, by the end of the night, I'd made up my mind about whether I had any kind of future with her. Sometimes it would take a couple of dates, but I knew very quickly if the relationship was going somewhere or not. So, I implemented a two-week rule with the basic understanding that I would break things off by the end of the second weekend if I didn't feel a connection. It made no sense to waste each other's time.

In fact, I'd rather spend my valuable free time on a Friday night with someone I already had a relationship with or had always wanted to ask out. So, I reached out to my friend Valerie. She was one of my track teammates in high school, and we'd spent a ton of time together at school and at practice, but more importantly, we genuinely enjoyed each other's company. I called her on a Sunday night and asked her out for dinner and a movie. While I wasn't surprised when she responded with a yes, I wasn't prepared for it to happen in five days. There was no way I'd let her pick me up at school, not after my previous debacle, so I said, "I'll pick you up Friday at 7:00 p.m."

Freshmen can't have a car or drive on campus, and I'm not even 100 percent sure what the rule was about driving around town. We all stood out like sore thumbs, so sneaking around anywhere was a recipe for disaster. I wasn't going to ask my mom to borrow her station wagon, and I was certain none of my classmates had access to a vehicle either. I only had a couple of days to figure it out because canceling my date was completely out of the question.

At practice on Monday, I asked my upper-class teammates if I could borrow a car, but none of them were willing to throw me a lifeline. They either had a car and were using it or didn't have wheels and rode with buddies. Strike one. During classes on Tuesday and Wednesday, I probed a few of my local friends to see who had access to a car, but they couldn't help. Strike two. Now it was Wednesday night, and I was in my room but unable to study. All I could think about was finding a way to get off campus to see Val. And then it hit me. I had one last shot.

I waited until our study period ended, grabbed my freshly shined shoes, told my roommate I'd be back in a bit, and shot out the door. Rich was shocked because most freshmen wouldn't willingly go out into the fertile company hunting grounds after study period. In fact, we were so scared to stray outside the confines of our room that most nights, it was easier to whizz in our sink rather than risk running into a wandering upperclassman on the way to the latrine. I made a right turn out the door and immediately ran into a roaming corporal looking for some action.

"Where are you headed, knob?" he fired off immediately.

"Sir, I just finished shining these shoes, and I'm taking them to Mr. Roof's room, sir," I said.

"Very good, Hornak. Make sure you're back before the horn sounds." And he walked off.

One of the greatest aspects of The Citadel experience is the honor code. It had a profound impact on my view of things when I arrived and led me to serious reflection on some of my past choices. It reads:

"A cadet does not lie, cheat, or steal, nor tolerate those who do."

I'd certainly given a truthful answer but left out some of the details, and I never lied. It's hard to imagine anyone at our school not developing this critical skillset. I continued the ten-second run to Carl and Doug's room. They didn't know I was coming, and I wasn't sure how to ask, but I'd already jumped off the deep end and needed to see this through. I approached their door, knocked twice, stepped back a few feet, and stood at attention.

"What?" Doug shouted.

"Sir, Cadet Private Hornak, R.C.C., requesting permission to enter your room, sir."

"Come in," Carl said.

Carl and Doug had offered me their friendship a couple of weeks earlier, but nothing unusually severe had happened to me or required a protective service intervention. And inside the company or around campus, there was no wink, pat on my rear end, or a "Good job, kid," as I hustled past them on my way to formation or class. And while they took it a little easier on me during lunch and dinner, they never asked how I was doing. This was a clandestine friendship, and it had to remain that way, but I was about to ask for an enormous favor.

"Somebody dumping on you?" Carl asked.

"Sir, no, sir," I replied.

"Don't call me sir. In this room, it's just Carl and Doug," he said.

"Yes, sir. Yes, Carl and Doug. Of course. Got it," I finally spat out.

"What are the shoes for, Rob?" Doug asked.

"Cover. I figured it might help me get here quicker," I explained.

"Smart. And it worked, I presume?" Doug continued.

"It did. Slipped right through," I proudly stated.

"So, what's up? Do you want to watch some TV?" Carl asked.

At that moment, I didn't know what was on the table with this new friendship, but were they saying that I could barge into their room and ask to watch TV? That was crazy, but I hadn't taken this leap of faith and risked complete exposure to watch an episode of *Moonlighting*.

"I have a crazy ask and…"

"What do you need?" both asked simultaneously, clearly curious.

"I need a car to go see a girl," I explained.

"You're sneaking out tonight at this hour!" Doug shouted. "The battalion will be…"

"No. For Friday night," I interrupted.

"Sure. You can take my car," Doug offered. "I'm restricted this weekend, so it's yours. Is she worth the risk?"

"For sure," I said, nodding my head.

"Can you drive a stick?" he asked.

"Piece of cake," I answered and ran back out into the thick night air.

I'd just solved my biggest problem, but I had no idea how to drive a manual transmission. I didn't even know what that meant, so I spent the better part of Thursday figuring out what I needed to do. There was no internet, no instructional video, and no class to take. One of my teammates, who had driven a stick shift, explained how to use the clutch and gear shifter during our track workout. It didn't sound incredibly difficult, and he never gave me a reason to doubt I could pull this off. How hard could it be?

Lunch rolled around on Friday, and Carl was my mess carver. Whenever he was in charge, I knew I'd have a relaxed meal. If I served everyone quickly and offered up three cool or unusual knob knowledge facts, I would get to eat whatever and however much I wanted, perhaps the single greatest perk in our newfound friendship. I'd shine one hundred pairs of shoes if it meant I could eat what I wanted and in peace. After the horn sounded that signaled the end of the meal, everyone stood up, but Carl looked at me and said, "Hornak, you aren't going anywhere."

A few of the other upperclassmen threw us a look, but it didn't seem to draw any unusual attention. With the two of us at the table, Carl explained that Doug had parked his car outside Hagood Gate on the right-hand side, heading toward the football stadium. He instructed me to casually walk out the side gate, as if I was heading to grab dinner at the Taco Bell down the street, and then quickly get in the car and take off. He said it was a blue Mazda and slipped me the key. The tough part, he explained, was that Doug needed me to drive it back on campus and leave it in his preassigned parking spot. Carl's parting piece of advice was that under no condition could I let anyone at the main gate stop me.

"You're going to have to be cool and hope it's not anyone who knows you," he said.

I was beyond nervous for the rest of the day, afraid that someone would find the key in my back pocket, that I'd be busted before I even got out of the battalion. I made it through our final formation and the Friday afternoon parade without incident. I hustled back to my room, changed into my Summer Leave uniform, and made the thirty-second run down to the sally port in fifteen and shot right out of the Padgett-Thomas Barracks. As I slid past the OD, I said under my breath, "Not today. Not today."

It was probably less than a mile walk from 2nd Battalion to the Hagood side gate. As freshmen, we had to walk in the gutter, always at a brisk pace. I was moving quickly, and my heart was beating faster than normal as I passed Bond Hall and took a sharp right onto Hagood Avenue. There it was. That tiny one-man gate that housed a sophomore corporal was only 500 feet away. All I needed to do was make it past this last layer of defense, and I was home free. I picked up my pace, kept my head down, never made eye contact, and walked right off campus.

Doug had parked the car about halfway down the block, right outside the gate. I couldn't jump straight into the car because I had no idea if the guard was watching me walk away, so I passed the car and walked up to the front door of a small home on the right side of the road. I glanced back toward the gatehouse and didn't see anyone following me, so I hustled back to the car, unlocked the driver's side door, and jumped in.

I'm not sure what I expected, but my five-minute conversation about driving a stick didn't prepare me for the next phase of my escape. I pushed in the clutch a couple of times, found first gear, and tried to start the car. Without giving it any gas, I took my foot off the clutch and lurched forward. I tried it again with the same result. *OK, that's not working*, I thought. *What am I missing?* I remembered the rule about the symbiotic balance between the two pedals and started to make some progress. My first success was getting the engine started and putting it in neutral. From there, I made multiple attempts to get it in first gear, but the learning curve was still steep. After all that effort, I'd only moved the Mazda forward a few feet, and now it rested just inches from the car in front of me.

I was already hot and couldn't figure out how to get Doug's car moving, much less find the air conditioner. I had no idea where reverse was because it wasn't displayed on the shifter. I put the car back in neutral, jumped out, put my left hand on the driver's side headlight and my right hand on the driver's side front panel, and pushed the car as far back as I could. With Doug's back bumper now touching the front bumper of the car behind me, it was time to try again. As I got ready to jump back in the car, I saw the guard straining to look in my direction. I wasn't wearing my garrison cap, so I think he thought I was an upperclassman, but then he took a few steps toward me, and I froze.

I was only a few hundred feet beyond that gate when he started to walk my way. I can only assume he'd heard all the engine starts, stops, and sputters, so maybe he thought he could help a fellow cadet. I was confident he'd be walking a lot faster if he knew I was a knob, so I jumped back into the driver's seat and frantically tried to get it started. Failure after failure. The approaching guard grew larger and larger in my side mirror, just like that T. rex in *Jurassic Park*. I knew I'd be busted, but with one last turn of the key, everything came together, and I put the car in motion. I turned the steering wheel as far left as I could and inched out into the street. I didn't dare do anything different with my feet for fear I'd jinx myself, conk out the engine, and get busted for who knows how many violations. The car was still in first gear when it finally leapt out of the parking spot and lurched down the road.

For the next ten minutes, I worked on my shifting skills at nearby Burke High School. I could get the car going without killing the engine about half the time. I had no idea how to downshift, so I just popped the shifter into neutral and rode the brakes when I needed to slow down or stop the car. I was mentally exhausted and pouring sweat, but I finally got the air conditioning working and went on my way to Val's.

My driving was terrible. I stalled out at lights and had a rough time keeping my feet in rhythm. I rolled through every intersection in neutral, knowing that if I stopped, I might not get the car going again. If Val was alarmed, she didn't show it. Every time I had trouble, I'd say, "I haven't driven stick in a while."

We planned to have dinner at Applebee's and then catch a movie. Somehow, we survived the drive from her house to the restaurant, and I could finally relax. We were in the middle of our dinner and having a great conversation, when in walked my company commander with his date. I recognized him immediately, and I was sure he'd seen me. The hostess seated him about ten tables away, and once he settled in, I gave him a wave. When he didn't wave back, I waved again. But he was just staring at me—a menacing stare. *I mean,* I thought, *he has to know who I am, right? He sees me every day. But clearly, I missed something in* The Guidon, *or did I?* While it wasn't written in the book of knob knowledge, apparently, there was never an acceptable time for a knob to fraternize with a senior officer, even if it occurred off campus. *Kind of like a Code Red*, I thought.

I paid the check and told Val that I wanted to introduce her to my commanding officer. Why not, right? It would be a perfect way to build a connection with him, and I thought that if his girlfriend knew what a nice guy I was, she might be able to convince him to take it easy on me back in the barracks.

"Hello, Colonel," I said. "I'd love to introduce you to my date, Valerie."

We left Applebee's, saw our movie, and I got Val back to her place in one piece. I drove back to campus, slipped in through the main gate undetected, and parked Doug's Mazda in his assigned spot.

On my walk back to the battalion, I kept thinking about Val and what a great time we had. That date was worth the entire ordeal, and I was hopeful we'd go out again. *And maybe,* I thought, *I made a new friend with the man in charge of Echo Company.*

However, in my zeal to be friendly, I'd made the worst mistake in a year of mounting miscalculations. I'd pulled the pin on a grenade at Applebee's that had a four-hour timer and had no idea it had already gone off when I ran through the front gate of 2nd Battalion.

The relentless onslaught directed at me following a single, kind-hearted wave to a senior officer was considerable, and it began the second I ran through the sally port and hit the first set of stairs in Echo Company. Word had spread like wildfire about the Applebee's wave, and a few upperclassmen, all restricted to campus for an assortment of violations, were more than happy to mess with me once I set foot inside the company. Reasonable weekend hazing was often expected if a knob came back too early and encountered a disgruntled sophomore cadet dealing with confinements or seniors coming off bad dates. But this felt different, went on longer than normal, and already had me thinking about what I'd done at the restaurant. What a boneheaded decision I'd made.

The torment lasted into the wee hours and picked right back up the next morning. It wasn't anything outrageous, but the protracted harassment was growing tiresome. When the rest of the upperclassmen returned from their weekend leave on Sunday evening, I'd already been under the microscope for thirty-six hours straight. I went to bed thinking they'd forget about me the next morning. They hadn't. Many guys who usually left me alone started making it a point to make me do pushups, shine their shoes, or harass me on the stairs. I'd become a mini celebrity, but for all the wrong reasons, and no one felt bad about exploiting my current situation.

Breakfast began like any ordinary day. I served the six upperclassmen at my table, spouted off three knob knowledge facts, and was ready to wolf down some sausage and eggs, but it wouldn't be that easy. My mess carver decided that I'd eat dry white toast. No butter, no jam, and no water. Just lots of toast. Where was Carl when I needed him? The first couple of slices went down easily, but after almost a dozen slices of dry bread and no water, my chewing labored, my mouth couldn't produce any saliva, and I struggled to swallow. I could think of a lot worse things to eat in bulk, but I realized I might be the only knob in the company on the radar, and at The Citadel, that was never a good thing.

The frequency and duration of the attacks escalated over the next two days. I was mentally wearing down but felt good that I could physically absorb all the body blows thrown at me. By Wednesday, I was fatigued, and by evening formation on Thursday, I was exhausted—mentally and physically. The pack of jackals had circled me all week, taking opportunistic bites along the way. I was at the end of my rope when I crawled into bed. If I'd had a phone in my room, I would have made the call.

I slept poorly that night, trying to play out the conversation I'd have with my dad the next day. He would push back hard, but he also had no idea what I'd endured the past week. I would explain the facts, see if I could swing him to my side, and if all went well, I'd transfer to UVA in January. Life would certainly be easier for me if I could get out of this place. The torment continued Friday as I navigated my way through morning formation, breakfast, three classes, lunch formation, and then what could very well have been my final meal on campus. All I had to do was walk over to the cadet activity building and call my dad.

I entered Mark Clark Hall through the main entrance. I took a quick left, passed the barber shop, hung a right into the post office, and approached the bank of pay phones tucked away in the back corner. I called the 800-number my dad had given me the day I checked in and waited nervously as the phone rang.

"Hello, Bob Hornak's office. This is Linda. How can I help you?"

"Hi, Linda, this is Robert. I'm Bob's son. Could I speak with my dad, please?" I asked.

"Well, hi, Robert. I've heard so much about you. How's everything going at school?" she said.

"That's kind of why I'm calling. Can I talk to him?" I asked.

"Let me see. Looks like he's in an important meeting right now. Can you call back in about thirty minutes? He should be out by then," Linda said.

"It's impossible for me to call him back. He said if it was extremely urgent to have you get him, no matter what. Please tell him it's urgent," I said.

"Hang on, Robert. I'll go speak with him," she said and placed me on hold.

The wait was agonizing. It was part anxiety because of what I wanted to tell my dad and part fear that some psychopathic upperclassmen would find me hiding in this cramped cubicle, calling for my freedom. I waited—and waited.

"I'm sorry, Robert, but your dad can't come to the phone right now. He asked if he could call you back."

"There is absolutely no way for him to call me back. Please get him," I begged.

"He told me not to interrupt him again, but I'd be happy to take a message for you," she offered.

"Tell him I can't believe he didn't pick up and that they're killing me. Did you write that down? They're killing me," I said.

"OK, sweetie, I'll let him know. You have a great weekend."

I slowly hung up the handset and sat in a stupor for about ten minutes. This wasn't how the plan was supposed to work. He said I could call anytime and that he'd pick up no matter what. Did Linda not explain the situation or even give him the message? I was caught off guard by this turn of events and tried to contemplate my next move, but I didn't have one.

Track practice would begin soon, so I headed over to the locker room, changed into my running gear, and lay down on the thinly carpeted floor. Eventually, some of the guys came in, and we started telling stories from the week. I shared the insanity of my current situation, and the guys shared a few of their more memorable moments. We joked about who had it worse. I gutted out the practice and looked forward to grabbing a bite to eat with a few classmates at Ryan's Steakhouse that evening. Expecting the punishment to continue when I got back, I ran in through the east gate, but no one was there to greet me. There wasn't a soul on the stairwell, and no one on the fourth deck was waiting to surprise me. I slipped into my room completely unmolested.

I'd fallen off the radar as fast as I'd gotten on. I can't remember if it was Gerald purposely wiping out the 1st Sergeant's shoes at mess, or perhaps it was Dan dumping water on our company commander. Maybe it was another one of my fellow Echo knobs who had acted colossally stupid or made an innocent slip-up, such as a friendly wave to the wrong person. We were learning that the upperclassmen didn't need a specific reason to target us. They simply went after the lowest-hanging fruit on any given day. I happened to be their target that week, and it would be someone else's turn the next. They worked you over until you demonstrated that you could weather the storm. And once they had their answer, they moved on to the next guy. Yes, guys were still quitting school, but those of us who remained forged a tighter bond every day. Our combined strength made it a lot tougher to railroad the next guy out.

I only had two morning classes that following Monday, so I stopped in the post office before lunch and called the 800-number for the second time. Linda picked up, said it was great to hear my voice, and connected me right through to my dad.

"RC! What's the latest?" he excitedly asked, using the nickname my Wisconsin family had given me.

"Um, why didn't you pick up on Friday? You said I could call any time and you'd pick up. Why did you blow me off?" I ranted.

"You were calling to quit, right?" he asked.

"I wasn't doing well. It was a terrible week," I said, but it now seemed so long ago.

"I figured. It was the first time you'd called my office, and Linda told me it was urgent. I already knew you were calling to get my permission to quit," he said.

"What if I was hurt?" I asked.

"You weren't. The school would have called if something bad had happened to you," he said.

I sat in stunned disbelief. "So, you weren't in a meeting?" I asked.

"Nope. I popped out of the office and was standing next to Linda's desk when she told me you were on the line. I heard everything you said and knew you were fine. Months ago, I told her you'd eventually call," his confession now complete. "You aren't calling to quit now, are you?"

"You know I'm not," I replied, rather annoyed by the whole situation. "I just called to chat."

And that was that. We laughed about all the events surrounding my date with Val and how that single wave had set off a firestorm of epic proportions that I hadn't seen coming. We talked about our numbers dwindling, my declining grades, and how track was going. It was one of our best conversations in recent memory, and he told me to give him a call any time I wanted to talk.

Quitting never crossed my mind again. Yes, there were plenty of bad days left to come, but now I was on a mission. I was going to make it to Recognition Day in May, no matter what they threw at me.

Thanksgiving would be our first real break from the insanity of The Citadel. I'd get a few days away to see family, catch up on sleep, and stuff my face. I attended a family wedding, watched some football, and slept a ton. The biggest takeaway was getting on the scale to weigh myself. I'd lost thirty pounds since my August check-in and was now sitting at an incredibly lean 150 pounds.

Our Sunday night formation at the end of Thanksgiving week was hard for all of us. We'd had a taste of home but hadn't been away long enough to get out of our routine. Plus, exams would start in a week, so it was a quick return to life in the barracks. I made it back to my room, changed uniforms, pulled my calendar out from my desk, and counted the days left until the end of the year and Recognition Day. I looked at my roommate and said, "Only 164 days and a wake-up."

Christmas was both a blessing and a curse. Our family gathered in Atlanta for the holiday, and my mom invited a big group of her extended family. It was a much longer break than Thanksgiving, and I was constantly eating and trying to stay in shape by playing basketball. It's amazing how lazy I got without the daily harassment and rituals that drove every second of my life.

I'd made it through that grievous first semester and was ready to go back and knock out the rest, but others in our class didn't feel the same. Some couldn't bear the idea of five more months in the big house, so they withdrew, but nobody else from our company did.

In early January, we reported back for the beginning of the second semester and the mandatory Sunday night muster. There weren't any welcome-back handshakes or hugs. It was a dreary and cold night. We changed into our duty uniforms for evening formation and prepared for the grind of the next four and a half months. But maybe the worst part, as we braced for the first time in weeks, was that we heard the repetitive taunts from the upperclassmen: "The party's over, knobs. The party's over."

The second half of the school year was a slog, and the routine of it all was so mundane. Our numbers held strong; I think as a direct result of us coming together as a company and constantly looking out for each other. We'd replaced our individual goals with the goal of group survival and success. My first semester grades had been terrible, so I had to repeat both Chemistry 101 and Statistics 101. Any passing grade I'd achieved was a direct result of absorbing enough information during labs and lectures to pass an exam, and even then, class time was still a chance to catch up on my sleep.

I stayed on Corps Squad mess for the outdoor track season so I could eat in peace with my teammates. While I was still in terrific shape, my body was much weaker, and my freshman times in the 400m were slower than what I'd run during my senior year of high school and the Junior Olympics that previous summer. It was yet another humbling, mentally and physically draining reminder of my self-inflicted wound of having enrolled at The Citadel.

Recognition Day began at the crack of dawn and was packed with intense physical activity and a ton of poking and screaming. While absolutely draining, it was the last day of being a knob for the Class of 1990. When the horn sounded that signaled the end of our knob year, we shook hands with our tormentors, exchanged first names, and were recognized as full members of the South Carolina Corps of Cadets. Thirty-eight of us began our Echo Company journey that fateful August day, but not everyone survived the rigors of that first year.

I preferred to think about the nineteen who suffered through those nine months in hell. We'd been complete strangers who were randomly selected and came together to endure the worst our company could throw at us, which included some of the most grueling, hilarious, and sometimes tragic experiences ever. The Citadel wasn't for everyone, and our total class attrition was a reminder of that. But it was worth it, even though I didn't know it then.

And maybe there was a spiritual influence during that time. Summerall Chapel is located on campus along the Avenue of Remembrance. It was named after The Citadel's tenth president, General Charles P. Summerall. And while my only church agenda each Sunday morning was to refuel with a cold soda and a couple of chocolate brownies, I passed underneath these words each time I walked into the chapel—words that I knew by heart and the first scripture I ever memorized, whether I realized it or not.

"Remember now thy Creator in the days of thy youth."

—Ecclesiastes 12:1 KJV

6

MY DANGEROUS SUMMER

"Nobody goes to bed in Madrid until they have killed the night."

—*Ernest Hemingway*

I finished my freshman year at The Citadel with a cumulative 1.70 GPA. The biggest blow to my average came from failing Chemistry 101 twice. I'd love to blame my results on the corpse-like teaching methods or the hours that upperclassmen toyed with me in the barracks, but that doesn't take my personal responsibility into consideration. It's true that I regularly slept in class, and it's also true that I didn't try to study—not once. I'd incorrectly assumed that my brain would absorb enough information to help me garner at least a C, but I probably took too many naps in class. However, I aced Chemistry Lab because it required active standing participation, Army ROTC, and computer science.

I was in a bind because the school and the NCAA required all athletes to have at least a 2.00 GPA to participate in competitive collegiate events. I wanted to run indoor track in the fall, so I had some time, but I needed to find a way to ace four classes and add twelve more credit hours to my totals. Near the end of the spring semester, I saw a flyer for the Spanish Club that announced its summer study abroad program in Madrid, Spain. I hadn't spent a summer at home since I was fourteen and had never been out of the country. The idea of traveling and partying in Europe was too juicy to ignore.

I called my dad, explained my pending academic and NCAA probation issues, proposed a solution, laid out all the costs, and assured him that my plan would guarantee him the desired outcome. It didn't matter if I was looking for him to make an investment, get a loan for a car, or request an all-expenses-paid trip to Madrid. I needed to speak clearly and quickly, ensure I had all my facts in order, and tie up all the loose ends so he wouldn't punch holes in my pitch. I think he latched on to the personal growth aspect and the savings it would offer him by eliminating my need for a fifth year.

I landed in Lisbon on a lengthy layover, which is where I met all the guys in the summer program. Eight of them were upperclassmen, while another guy and I had just finished our freshman year. But none of that Citadel nonsense factored in across the Atlantic. And frankly, I don't think they were the kind of guys who spent time hazing people. For the next two months, we were ten teenage guys looking to enjoy Spain and everything its capital city had to offer.

Not only did I have a roommate, Elliott, but I also had a host family. Elliott and I lived with Paloma, a single mom who took care of her family and supplemented her income by housing students from all over the world. We shared a room with twin beds, while groups of three to four girls would cycle through the house every one to two weeks the entire summer—young ladies who came to Spain from France, Germany, and the Netherlands. As soon as one group checked out, another batch arrived one or two days later. Paloma had it down to a science, but for us, it was a revolving door of amazing girls every single week.

Paloma was a lovely woman, and she watched over Elliott and me like we were her sons. Her oldest daughter was also named Paloma; she had a son named Javier and three younger daughters. It wasn't a big apartment, but with at least twelve of us in the home on any given night, it was busy but never felt cramped. The first week was a little awkward for everyone since Elliott and I spoke very little Spanish and absolutely no French. The four Parisian girls spoke a bit of Spanish and English, but it was easier those first few days to slip out quietly in the morning and head to school without attempting a conversation.

The Citadel had partnered with the Estudio International Sampere language school in the Salamanca neighborhood of Madrid. We had two young teachers who took turns teaching the morning and after-noon sessions. While we were stuck in class for the day, our European roommates spent their time canvassing the city. But in the evening, we all gathered back at the house, and Paloma served dinner for the group around 11:00 p.m. Paloma loved taking care of us and made everyone feel so welcome. I had more home-cooked meals that first week than I'd had since moving to Charleston six years earlier. It was the first time in a long time that I'd had any sense of normality in my daily life.

Paloma usually started to set the table around 10:00 p.m., and all her children, Elliott, the female travelers, and I would gather in the living room to hang out and share stories. As our Spanish improved, it became easier to engage in conversation, and dinnertime was a wel-come event. The meal could easily last an hour or more, and many times we didn't start clearing the table and washing dishes until well after midnight.

Around 1:00 a.m., Elliott and I would take off to meet up with our schoolmates or other new acquaintances. Some were local Spaniards, while others were exchange students just like us from Samford, The University of Alabama, or Virginia Tech. We all embraced the Spanish culture and tried to meet locals in bars or discothèques. For some of us, finding a young lady who wanted to hang out with us was difficult in the beginning. After a week of failed attempts, one of my classmates and I figured out that defenses came down faster if we said we were American fighter pilots who were assigned to a joint operation with the Spanish Air Force.

This cover story gave us all the wiggle room we needed. We had the proper knowledge from our military science classes, and our story explained our poor, yet improving Spanish, our closely shorn hair, and why we were only in town for a few days. That opening almost always led to drinks, dancing, and a conversation, but we were often limited by the language gap. If that first night in the disco went well, it could lead to an afternoon in the park, a Saturday at the city pool, or maybe even a dinner date. If we were less interested in the girls or our story developed cracks, we said that we were being recalled to our fighter squadron. It was the perfect alibi.

Many nights, we'd roll out of the club around 7:30 a.m., jump on the Metro, and head straight to our 8:00 a.m. class. We endured that first three-hour morning block and then took a break for lunch. Directly across the street from school was a café that served boca-dillo sandwiches, an eight-inch-long baguette sliced in half and filled with fried eggs. They made three or four different sandwich types, but I had that egg sandwich and a couple of Mahou cervezas every day for lunch. In the afternoon, our other teacher took over. We usually wrapped up class by 3:00 p.m.

By this point, we were dragging, so a bunch of us would head over to the Parque de El Retiro, drink a few beers, and take a siesta. Some days, we'd head to the public pool or walk the city and do some sightseeing. Other days, we spent time in the Prado or tried to meet up with our new Dutch housemates at a nearby café. We'd eventually head back to the house, take a siesta, and then begin a new day with dinner.

School, siestas, and sangria were a major part of our week, but so were the bars, discothèques, and bullfights at the Plaza de Toros. On weekends, we usually planned a touristy trip, jumped on a bus or train, and visited cities such as Segovia in the north, Seville, Málaga, and Toledo in the south, and Valencia on the east coast. One of our better excursions was when we gathered a tight-knit group of friends and spent a few days on the beaches of the southeastern Mediterranean port city of Alicante.

I also witnessed some history in Madrid at the Estadio de Vallehermoso. The city was hosting a major track and field event on June 4, 1987. Carl Lewis and my hurdling idol, Edwin Moses, were scheduled to run that day. Lewis burst onto the world stage when he won four gold medals at the 1984 Olympics and matched the record set by Jesse Owens in Berlin in 1936. Moses was riding a 122-consecutive wins streak and was the heavy favorite again that day.

Since nobody else wanted to spend the day at the track, I went solo and secured a front row seat on the third turn, which doubled as both the start of the 200m dash for Lewis and the fifth hurdle for Moses. Lewis won his race, but it was a different fate for Moses that day. He hadn't lost a race in almost ten years, owned the fastest time in the world, and had recorded the next ten fastest times, too. He was the dominant athlete in his sport, and I would be there in person to see him get number 123.

Danny Harris, a young hurdler from Iowa State University, had been chasing the world's best for the last three years. It was a tight race as they approached me on the back straightaway, and I snapped a single photo. Harris cleared the hurdle directly in front of me first and was in the lead by one or two steps. The race stayed tight through the curve and into the home stretch. It was impossible to see who was leading because it was dark, the stadium was poorly lit, and they were running away from me toward the finish line. I heard cheers go up from the crowd and chants of "Torero! Torero! Torero!" as Moses took his victory lap in front of twelve thousand fans.

I'd just witnessed history. My favorite track athlete and idol had extended his consecutive wins streak, and I saw it live. In fact, I could have reached out and touched him as he passed me. I rushed home to tell Javier what I'd seen, but before I could say a word, he asked how I was doing after the loss. I was so confused. The stadium had chanted for Moses and given him a standing ovation as he circled the track. But it hadn't been a victory lap, but rather a thank you to the fans as Edwin's streak of 122 consecutive wins had ended. That day, Moses lost to Harris by 0.13 seconds. The headline from *Sports Illustrated* read "The Reign Ended in Spain." I'd been a part of history, just not in the way I expected.

As the weeks wound down, I pursued Madrid's vivacious nightlife more aggressively. Bars and clubs, live music, outlandish entertainment, late-night tapas, and flamenco dancing were always available in Spain's capital, and I took advantage of everything the city had to offer. Excessive drinking was customary. Beers for breakfast, beers at lunch, beers at the park, wine with dinner, and finally drinking for hours in the nightclubs while trying to find a girlfriend. Many nights, I'd be so wasted leaving a discothèque that I wasn't sure how I got back to Paloma's house.

If the Metro were closed, I'd catch a cab with whoever was outside and get dropped off near the Alonso Martinez Metro stop in our neighborhood, then walk home from there. But cab rides in Spain were different because most cabbies didn't drive with their headlights on at night. They simply sped through the desolate city streets, and the driver flicked his high beams a couple of times when we entered and passed through an intersection. We could have been t-boned or plowed into another car a hundred different times. The night before my flight back to the States, the Metro was closed and I had only a few pesetas in my pocket. I walked out of the bar and fell asleep on a nearby park bench. I woke up the next morning, rode the Metro home, packed up my gear, and said goodbye to my Spanish family forever.

I had more experiences that summer in Spain than some have in their lifetime, and it changed me in almost every way imaginable. I stepped out of that sheltered, beaten-down knob body and experienced a rebirth into my innately confident, throw-caution-to-the-wind new self. Javier introduced me to styling mousse and forever changed my look. I hung out with beautiful girls from the US and many foreign countries, and I saw things that I didn't know existed. I made friends, experienced a new culture, and saw how much bigger the world really was. Elliott and I cooked a home-made fried chicken dinner for Paloma and her family, and I managed to come back to Charleston with four As, a 2.04 GPA, and a new lease on life. ¡Viva Madrid!

"When I was a child, I spoke like a child,
I thought like a child, I reasoned like a child.
When I became a man, I gave up childish ways."

—1 Corinthians 13:11 ESV

7

LONG GRAY LINE

*"You keep putting one foot in front of the other,
and then one day, you look back and you've climbed a mountain."*

—*Tom Hiddleston*

I didn't know anyone who could make me a fake ID, so I explained my dilemma to an "of age" buddy of mine, and without hesitation, he offered up his birth certificate, which I took to the DMV to get a new driver's license.

The plan made perfect sense. I memorized his personal information, walked into the SCDMV, handed the agent his birth certificate, and said that I'd lost my ID while traveling overseas. Fifteen minutes later, I walked out with my picture on a South Carolina driver's license, and at that moment, David Webb was born. Now I could walk, completely unfettered, into any bar or nightclub for the next two years. The plan was bulletproof.

I'd never needed a fake ID in Charleston because there were loads of places to hang out and grab a drink that didn't require a driver's license. Plus, plenty of my buddies had access to alcohol. But ever since I'd gotten back from Spain, a switch had flipped in my brain as well as in my entire worldview. I'd awakened to an entirely new wealth of opportunities, and I couldn't wait to grab them.

Sophomore year began in August 1987, and I found it to be infinitely easier. No one cared who I was or what I was doing. Due to my poor grades, I was ineligible for leadership positions or to hold rank. While the cadre was focused on training knobs, I was devoid of any real responsibilities and free to have a good time with my Class of '90 brothers. Cross country was in season, which meant I trained a few days a week and wasn't traveling with the team, so all that free time allowed me opportunities outside the gates.

On one of my first trips, I went to visit Mage, my old teacher, mentor, and disciplinarian at Porter-Gaud. After my unceremonious departure from that middle school, I never thought I'd go back to see anyone, but now that I'd made it through my knob year, I was proud and felt a bit more worthy. So, the first time I was allowed a weekday pass, I drove back across the Ashley River to see Maje. It had been more than five years, but it felt like not a day had passed.

We caught up and had some good laughs about my middle school experience, his desire to retire from teaching and move to Hawaii, and my decision—or better yet, a general lack of options—that landed me in military school just a few miles away. I told him about the insanity of my first year, only to learn many years later about his service for our country and the things he had endured.

Maje received a Purple Heart after being wounded in Guadalcanal, considered by many to be one of the Marine Corps' hardest won battles in history. He did get to retire to Waikiki, where he passed away in 2021. Corporal Theodore "Ted" Richardson, USMC, was laid to rest at The National Memorial Cemetery of the Pacific at the age of ninety-three. He was a great man, and I'll never forget how he helped me through one of the toughest periods in my life.

My second year at The Citadel was unmemorable by all accounts. Sure, we weren't knobs, but those of us who failed to earn rank didn't have a voice to do or say much of anything. I teetered just above the

2.00 minimum GPA required by the school and NCAA, so I decided to buckle down in the classroom. I'm not talking hours in the library every night, but enough to secure a couple of Bs and Cs that first semester to put myself in a position to lead a squad or even a platoon my junior year. By definition, leaders should seek to inspire and motivate, not coerce through fear, so based on recent real-life experience, I was unimpressed with many of my training cadre and the men who had selected them.

On a positive note, the dating scene was infinitely better, and I spent a ton of time with buddies carousing at The College of Charleston. My hair had grown out, mousse and cologne were in, and when coupled with my personal transformation in Madrid, I had a newfound self-assuredness everywhere I went. Girls were easier to talk to, taking risks didn't faze me at all, and I wasn't as fearful about violating the cadet code of conduct or being punished with demerits, confinements, or tours. As for track, I was officially done with the high hurdles and just focused on three 400m events: open, hurdles, and relays.

We loved tearing up the town. Some nights, my classmates and I wound up in a cramped dorm room at the College of Charleston; other times, we'd head to the Market area and catch a live band at Cumberlands or Myskyns Tavern, but quite frequently, we headed to a buddy's house in the Mount Pleasant, Sullivan's Island, or Isle of Palms area. Many times, those nights took on a life of their own, and way too much alcohol was consumed. One such night at The Windjammer, as I caught up with an old friend from high school, my buddy, Don, tapped me on the shoulder.

"Rob, we gotta go, man."

I looked at my watch. It was 0035 hours, and I said, "Wow! It's gonna be tight."

We downed our drinks, ran out the door, and prepared for the mad dash back to school. Yep, we still had a curfew. Freshmen had to be back in the barracks by midnight, but upperclassmen got an extra hour of leave. Every cadet had to be in the rack by 0100 hours for a final room check and lights out. Every night, every year, for four years, a cadet from all seventeen companies walked room to room, knocked on every door, and said, "All in?"

We always pushed the envelope and tried to squeeze every minute out of the evening. It was a thirteen-mile drive from the bar to the main gates of The Citadel, and without hiccups, it took about twenty-five minutes door to door. We had no wiggle room whatsoever. And that didn't include the extra five to eight minutes we needed to hit a fast-food joint for some midnight munchies, but there would be no Taco Bell for us tonight. I popped the trunk of my Audi 5000S; we grabbed our uniforms, jumped in the car, and peeled out of the parking lot to begin the sprint back to campus.

A quick dash down Ocean Boulevard got us out of the commercial district and onto 14th Avenue in a flash. I'd push it hard for 500 feet, and then we merged straight onto the Isle of Palms Connector, which spanned Little Goat Island. That four-mile stretch was nerve-racking because there were so many hidden spots for police checkpoints. That beach feeder road ran right into Highway 17, where I took a hard left and headed south toward Charleston. That's when I prayed for all green lights. Any delay on that roadway guaranteed a late arrival, which meant demerits, and enough of those meant confinements. Don was riding shotgun and had already started to change into his Summer Leave uniform, while I was picking up speed out of the turn and scanning the road ahead for cops.

High-speed maneuvering on the four-lane roads was critical through the city of Mount Pleasant, but once we passed the barbecue joint on our left, we had about fifteen seconds until we got to the foot of the Cooper River Bridge. There were two bridge pairs that spanned the river, and I always chose the "Grace" side on my way home because it was way more fun. It was a cantilever truss bridge, which the engineers and critics alike had nicknamed the "Rollercoaster Bridge" due to its 250-foot height, its two narrow, 10-foot-wide lanes, and a sharp curve and dip smack in the middle of the two anchor arms. Don finished buttoning his shirt as we zoomed past the historic aircraft carrier, USS Yorktown, on our left and started our attack run.

The Grace Bridge was only 2.7 miles long with high metal guardrails on both sides, but it represented two crucial aspects of our journey. First, there wasn't a single place for a cop to park, and second, it was the only part of the drive where I could safely change back into uniform. Speeds of 80 mph or faster were common, and on a rare night, I might find myself in a drag race with another cadet. I lifted my left foot off the floorboard, elevated my knee, and pressed it into the bottom of the steering wheel for stability. Aside from that dip and curve in the middle span, I had two reasonably straight stretches to change clothes. This high-speed magic act required a combination of speed and dexterity and was the key to making it back on time.

"Rob, do you want me to steer?" Don asked.

"That would be great," I said as I pushed down on the accelerator.

Don gripped the right side of the steering wheel with his left hand and helped center us between the two lanes. This meant that I could increase our speed, and we now traveled at just under 90 mph. I had a little less than two minutes to complete my quick change. I'd already flicked my shoes off before we got to the base of the expanse, and my shirt swap was easily completed on the first climb. Before cresting the first span, I took off my belt and unbuttoned my jeans. On the first downslope, I took my right foot off the gas, quickly kicked off my pants, and got my right foot through the right pant leg of my uniform and my foot back on the pedal. Taking that curve at high speed was a two-handed operation, so I took the wheel for about five seconds as we traveled through the dip.

Like a precision drill team, Don reached over to take the wheel again as we went into the second climb. With Drum Island just below us, I pulled up my leave pants to my waist. At the top of the second span, I straightened up my uniform and finished pulling myself together over the last mile back to campus. Looking good from the waist up, we passed through Lesesne Gate and made our way to the back part of campus. I pulled into my assigned parking spot and slipped on my shoes. We jumped out of the car, and I tucked in my shirt, zipped up my trousers, and buckled my brass. Don and I threw our civies in the trunk, and then our foot race started. We ran past McAlister Field House. He ducked into 1st Battalion heading to Bravo Company, and ten seconds later, I took a right into 2nd Battalion. Once I got back inside Padgett-Thomas Barracks, I made the hard left through Band Company and had a quick climb up the Echo stairwell to the second deck, hung a right, popped open my door, and dove into my bunk. Safe again. Nights like that pretty much summed up my sophomore year.

I LANDED IN CHARLESTON JUST A FEW DAYS before the start of my junior year. I'd spent the summer in the UK, this time at my mom's behest. Barbara and Harold, my aunt and uncle, were both professors at Samford University in Birmingham, Alabama, and they'd accepted a summer assignment to run the school's new residence center in South Kensington, London.

The five-story, historic Victorian townhouse was purchased by the school to serve as a living and learning space for students who studied abroad. They welcomed their first students in 1984, but occasionally a room or two was unoccupied. Such was the case that summer. My aunt said one of their students was a no-show for the semester and wondered if I wanted the room. My mom said yes, and my dad rubberstamped the plan and purchased my ticket. A week later, I boarded my Delta flight bound for Heathrow Airport.

The Daniel House was perfectly located in the heart of Central London, and only a short walk to Harrods, a luxury department store located on Brompton Road in Knightsbridge, and absolutely everything else the city had to offer. Royalty took center stage with landmarks like Buckingham Palace, Westminster Abbey, and the Tower of London, but there were hundreds of other things to see, including the National Gallery, the British Museum, Big Ben, and the Tower Bridge. Even with a massive population of 6.7 million, I could get anywhere on foot, by boat, or by tube.

I explored the city every day, hit the tourist traps, saw the Crown Jewels up close, got my first Hard Rock Cafe T-shirt, and toured inside Saint Paul's Cathedral, where Prince Charles and Lady Diana were married, but I never got to see Chelsea play a football game. I also took a river cruise with Barbara and Harold and their son, Lane, down to Greenwich on the south bank of the Thames, where we got to straddle the Prime Meridian line. I spent a lot of time in Covent Garden, a heavily trafficked tourist area known for its cafes, pubs, shopping, and music. It was artsy, lively, and a place for young musicians to try out new material on a willing crowd. I met English pop singer Samantha Fox in Piccadilly Square and saw George Michael perform live at Earl's Court just a few blocks away from my flat.

After a few weeks, I got bored, bought myself a BritRail pass, and traveled all over the UK to visit major cities in England, Scotland, and Wales. I spent most of the next month and a half in Oxford, Bristol, Cardiff, Birmingham, Manchester, Liverpool, Edinburgh, Glasgow, and Inverness, and traveled back to London once a week to get a home-cooked meal and wash my clothes before leaving on the next trip. My most unusual stop was the four days I spent in the Scottish Highlands camped out on the edge of the giant lake looking for the Loch Ness Monster. I never laid eyes on Nessie and eventually headed back to London to pack up and head home. I thanked my aunt and uncle for a great summer and flew back to Charleston to start my junior year at The Citadel.

I had a few days at home before I reported back to school, so I rounded up a few buddies to meet up at The Windjammer, grab a few beers, and play some beach volleyball. Since I didn't have any pockets in my swimsuit, I threw my fake ID under the driver's seat of my car and completely forgot it was there. The next Saturday, my mom, who'd begged me to clean out my car since I'd gotten back from England, decided she'd do it for me and discovered my priceless gem. She came inside, held the license inches from my face, and said, "Who is David Webb, and why does he look exactly like you?"

Junior year without an ID was a drag, so instead of hanging out in bars, I poured myself into a new, three-pronged business venture called Par-T's. My company made custom T-shirts, booked local bands for parties, and ran a pizza delivery business—all out of the barracks. I already had the basic equipment I needed to make silkscreen shirts when I made a run of twenty-five INXS concert tees to sell outside of Gaillard Auditorium on July 15, 1987. The band was promoting their album *Listen Like Thieves*, so I photocopied a promo group shot, turned it into a single-color screen image, and printed it with silver ink on a black T-shirt. I made all of them by hand, wore one to the show, and stuffed the rest in my backpack. I stood outside the auditorium, sold them all, and pocketed almost $7 a shirt. When they were all gone, I went inside and saw Michael Hutchence and the boys put on one of the greatest concerts ever.

I set up a bank account with a deposit of $100 and used the remaining money to buy sixteen Little Caesars pizzas the following Saturday night. Back in the day, they were two for $8, and I resold them for $10 each to captive, hungry knobs. I didn't devise this get-rich-quick scheme; I had learned it from entrepreneurial upperclassmen who'd done the same thing to my classmates and me two years earlier. I usually ate one pizza myself, gave one to my roommate, Scott, and sold the rest. That's fourteen pies at ten bucks a pop, so after literally eating some of my profits, I pocketed around $70 for a single night's work. Occasionally, I'd lose one to a senior in exchange for his silence, but for the most part, it was a nice "gray area" way to make some cash for the next weekend.

Once I had more money in the bank, I started making T-shirts—not the handmade customs that I did for the INXS show, but larger orders that required a minimum of one hundred units. These shirts were all Citadel inspired and could be sold to that same group of knobs, but occasionally, I made a shirt with value across all four classes.

A three-color screen print on a white 100 percent cotton shirt typically would cost me $3.50 to mass-produce, and I'd sell them for the same $10 price point, regardless of size. If some of my track buddies, Echo guys, or 1990 classmates wanted to make a few extra bucks, I paid them a $1 commission on every shirt they sold. Having sellers in all four battalions reduced my risk and always guaranteed a sellout. If someone else designed a shirt, I'd pay him a flat $100 for the design, so I usually cleared $4.50 to $5.50 per shirt, depending on the quantity ordered. I certainly made a few duds and had to sell them at cost, but with the right shirt, I could make a healthy profit.

The money allowed me to quit my minimum wage job in the computer science lab and focus on the business. I made $25 to $50 per show by booking local bands in bars or for parties, and I made a Little Caesars run every couple of weeks, but my bread-and-butter business was always the T-shirts. And I wasn't the only guy in the battalion with that idea. There might be three or four guys with off-campus privileges who ran around the battalion trying to sell their shirts, whole pies, or even pizza by the slice. All of us looked to make a fast buck off a scared knob.

One of the best things about my mom was that she loved to take my friends to dinner, and I knew a lot of hungry people. They couldn't come to my house for a home-cooked meal, but she loved taking everyone to Bessinger's BBQ for the all-you-can-eat buffet. I think some of the happiest moments of her life were in that restaurant, surrounded by my talkative and thankful friends. And I know Emily, who was still in high school, enjoyed hanging out with all my brothers. We were one big happy family gathered around the dinner table.

Other nights, if I was on restriction and serving confinements, my mom and Emily would pick up twenty roast beef sandwiches for my roommate, Scott, the rest of the guys, and me. In those days, Arby's ran a "5 for $5" deal, which meant those twenty sandwiches cost $20 plus tax, and everybody I knew loved them. My mom and Emily pulled up between the 2nd and 3rd Battalions, yelled up to my window, and I met them by the side gate and got caught up on the news from home. They slipped the four bags of sandwiches through the wrought-iron gate, and I hustled back to my room. Even after all these years, those loving gestures stand out the most about my mom.

The rest of my junior year was uneventful, and London kept calling, so I reached out to my aunt again to see if I could return to the study center. She said they had a room I could use, but this time, it would cost me $5 per night. So, I withdrew $1,000 from my Par-T's checking account and handed it to my dad the next time he came home.

"What is this?" he asked, perplexed.

"It's for me to go back to London," I said.

"Who said you could go back to London?" he asked sternly.

"Aunt Barbara said I could stay for $5 a night, so I'm giving you enough money for two months of rent and hopefully enough left over for a plane ticket."

"What will you do for food? How will you get around?" he asked.

"I've got money," I said modestly.

"But from what? How?" he asked, confused.

I filled him in on Par-T's, the three business units, and handed him a few sample T-shirts. I told him I earned the money myself, wanted to spend more time in London, and then backpack through parts of Western Europe. With the $1,000 down payment, he booked my round-trip flight and got me both a BritRail and Eurail pass. Deep down, I know he liked the hustle and felt comfortable knowing I could navigate my way around the world.

I spent the first week back in London at many of my old stomping grounds, met up with a friend from The Citadel who grew up there, joined him and his mates for a pub crawl and football match, and was able to see R.E.M. live at the Hammersmith Odeon Theatre on their Green World Tour. I met a lot of people from all over the world, enjoyed backpacking, but mostly loved getting to see new cities. Charleston, and especially The Citadel, were small echo chambers focused on history and tradition. I found a much bigger world waiting for me, and I wanted to see as much of it as possible.

As Mark Twain wrote in his book *The Innocents Abroad,* "Travel is fatal to prejudice, bigotry, and narrow-mindedness, and many of our people need it sorely on these accounts. Broad, wholesome, charitable views of men and things cannot be acquired by vegetating in one little corner of the earth all one's lifetime."

After two months of gallivanting overseas, it was time to head home. My cousin, Lane, had moved to South Africa to teach school and play polo, but I still had one more year to complete to get my degree. And I still hadn't decided if I would take my Army commission. There were a couple of girls I wanted to ask out, but to be frank, I was bored being back in South Carolina. There simply wasn't anything to do in Charleston that compared to my adventures in Europe. With very limited options, I began an intense training regimen at Porter-Gaud to get ready for my final track season. There were no concerts, no knobs, and nothing for Par-T's to work on, so I applied for a cashier's job at the Record Bar. Yes, I took a job and worked in the same record store that I'd stolen from for so many years.

I spent those last few weeks of summer thinking about what I really wanted to do. I loved Madrid, so my first thought was to call Paloma to see if I could live with her family while I looked for a job. Then I thought about calling my Aunt Barbara again to see if I could rent my old room in the Daniel House and try to find work in London. I knew that taking my commission with the Army might have made my dad happy, but the more I thought about it, the more I wanted to move to Los Angeles and make films. I had nine months to figure out my next steps, and there were far more important things to do first.

Instead, I turned my focus toward an epiphany I had that involved three of my good friends. Two days before school started, I met up with Ted, Don, and David at our favorite bar, Cumberlands, for some beers. We'd all heard about the lip-synch concert scandal with Milli Vanilli a few weeks earlier, so my proposal wasn't entirely off the wall.

I explained that my sister thought of a cool idea for a band name and said I could use it if I ever formed a group. So, I thought, *If I can be a fake fighter pilot, why can't I front a fake band?* I gave the guys my thirty-second pitch on the band's name, T-shirt design, marketing campaign, and the unlimited potential for instant connections with women everywhere we went. And just like that, Miles to Go was born.

However, on September 22, 1989, Hurricane Hugo said, "Hold my beer," and ravaged the city of Charleston with its Category Four winds that reached 140 mph and devastated large chunks of the coastline. Thousands fled the city in the days leading up to the storm, so when I was granted leave from The Citadel on Thursday, the 21st at 0715 hours, I raced home, boarded up our windows, packed up the station wagon, and fled with my mom and sister to stay with my dad, who had left Texas and moved to Atlanta. What we thought would be a nice seventy-two-hour break turned into a ten-day hiatus away from our school and senior festivities.

Charleston, the islands, businesses, homes, and both colleges were hit hard. The National Guard helped maintain security, prevented looting, and aided in cleanup efforts, but there was still a lot of work to do. Stores were flooded, beachfront property was wiped from the map, my Audi had been washed away, and things would never quite be the same for those of us who experienced all the heartbreak in the wake of that storm. We finally resumed classes and turned our collective attention to celebrating our senior year.

Parents Weekend was the first major event for the senior class. That Friday afternoon, all qualified cadets marched from our barracks across the parade deck and into Summerall Chapel to be presented with our class rings. Every aspect of that ring is symbolic. When I look at it, I'm reminded of the words duty, honor, God, and country. The ring is a testament to the history, sacrifice, and traditions of the Cadet Corps. It represents conflict, freedom, infantry, lives lost in defense of our nation's ideals, and victory blessed by peace. However, more importantly, it signifies the brotherhood forged between total strangers and all walks of life dating back to 1842. That unique bond between previous generations and those yet to come is often called the Long Gray Line.

Things had returned to normal on campus, and we now had our rings. We again focused on our fake band, Miles to Go, and scheduled a photoshoot with my sister as part of her high-school senior project. We took the photos at The Windjammer on the Isle of Palms. The storm had decimated the area, leaving only faint clues about the location of the venue. Emily rattled off a single roll of black-and-white film in ten minutes, and once developed, I knew right away that we had the shot we needed. We made band tees, tour shirts, flyers, and posters—but we never played a single note.

For Christmas Break, I headed to The Marque Hotel in Atlanta and spent time with my mom, dad, and Emily. But before leaving campus, a few of us decided to throw a party in Columbia, South Carolina, at a small venue called The Old Police Hut. The pre-party buzz was enormous, and I'd hired the Uncertain-T's, one of the top cover bands from Charleston, to drive up for the Friday night show. Two of my Echo Company classmates, Gerald and Eddie, along with a friend who was a year behind us, helped me set up and promote the event. Gerald secured our rental agreement with the Columbia Police Department, and flyers went up all over the city but were deliberately concentrated at all the major sorority houses on the University of South Carolina campus.

The Old Police Hut was off Greystone Boulevard heading toward the zoo. Most guests came from the north, so they took the exit, turned left crossing over I-26, and then hung a right turn onto Candi Lane. It was a three-quarter-mile drive down the county frontage road, past a set of railroad tracks, and then a little further to our mostly hidden entrance at the end of the road. I'd set up a rectangular card table at the start of the dirt road with signs that let our partygoers know they were in the right spot. It was BYOB, but we charged $5 a head to cover the costs of the venue and the band. Gerald rented the place for $100 and put down a $50 deposit, which authorized us a twenty-four-hour window to set up, host the party, and tear down the next day. After our guests paid their cover charge, they drove down the dirt road and parked in a large gravel lot. A footpath led to the white, 800-square-foot building, where off-duty policemen often went to relax and unwind.

We didn't know that our little event had gone viral. Our flyers had been photocopied and distributed to a half dozen local high schools. Cars backed up for a half mile down the frontage road, and the end of that line kept getting closer and closer to the top of the hill and Greystone Boulevard. There were cars, station wagons, and vans squished full of kids, sometimes brimming with ten or more teens inside. With the entrance at a standstill, my teammate, Ronnie, walked out of the woods drinking a beer, saw the line, and shook his head.

"Rob, where are we supposed to put these people? The Hut is already overflowing," he said.

"I have no idea, but we've got to get all these cars off the road. Someone's going to see this and want to know what's happening," I replied.

"What do you want me to do?" he asked.

"Just get as much money as you can from each car before you let them in," I said with a smirk on my face.

We didn't recognize a soul. No cadets. No sorority sisters. Just car after car full of teenagers. The word was out, and it felt like every high school student in the city was waiting in our line. We couldn't clear them fast enough, and there was no time to check IDs. A car would pull up full of people and ask how much to get in, and my reply was always the same.

"Just give me whatever cash you have in the car."

They threw bills at us to get into the party, and our pockets couldn't hold them all. We'd envisioned throwing the biggest Christmas bash in Columbia history, blending our closest Citadel brothers with a ton of

USC coeds for the ultimate senior party. But ninety minutes into our shindig, things took a turn that we didn't see coming.

SLED stands for the South Carolina Law Enforcement Division, and its primary mission is to provide manpower and assistance for other state law enforcement agencies. This elite team conducted investigations and executed raids on behalf of the governor and attorney general, and that Friday night in December, they were assigned to our bash. Ronnie and I saw them before we heard a thing. With the right lane completely backed up and idling cars still waiting to pay, we saw a wave of police vehicles crest the hill with lights flashing—headed right at us. A second later, we heard the sirens, and I knew we were cooked.

"I gotta go warn the guys!" I yelled at Ronnie.

"What do you want me to do?" he asked, completely befuddled.

"Just hold them off for a few seconds," I shouted, and then I took off in a full sprint, disappearing into the tree line.

I ran up on the most incredible rager I'd ever seen. The Hut was packed; kids sat on the windowsills. Four hundred people were outside dancing around two massively unsafe bonfires as the Uncertain-T's covered the song "What I Like About You" by The Romantics. The music blasted out of the speakers and into the brisk night air. I frantically searched for the guys to warn them about the cops hot on my tail, but it didn't matter. SLED had arrived.

The police sirens stopped everyone dead in their tracks. A dozen squad cars with flashing lights and high beams screamed down the road and slid into our parking lot as a swarm of officers waving flashlights emerged through the woods and into the clearing. I had a flashback to all those nights in the barracks when the upperclassmen yelled, "The party's over," and my heart sank.

"Meetze! Gerald Meetze!" one of the officers thundered out into the crowd.

"Who's in charge?" another officer bellowed.

A few seconds later, I heard my name loud and clear from another officer, "Hornak! Where are you? Hornak!"

This powerful display of might had instantly overwhelmed the group. Kids ran screaming to their cars, beers were poured out, red solo cups were thrown into the woods, and the band franticly packed up their gear. The one road in was the only road out, and it was completely blocked by the police. No one could escape. We were crammed onto a half-acre of land, so the cops found and surrounded Gerald and me quickly. Our backs were literally and figuratively up against the wall when the lead tactical officer broke through and identified himself.

"I'm Lieutenant Chris Osborne. You boys have really messed up tonight. We've got you on so many charges, including underage possession of alcohol, open container, disorderly conduct, and contributing to the delinquency of minors."

"We didn't provide any alcohol—not a single drink," I said. "It's a twenty-one and over party only."

"So, who was checking IDs? How did all these underage kids get in?" Lieutenant Osborne pressed.

I chimed in again, "The line was so long, there was no time to check every single ID in every car. It would have been impossible."

"Did you check any IDs?" the Lieutenant grilled.

"I spot checked every car." I'm not quite sure how I came up with that explanation.

"Spot checked? What does that mean, son?"

Lieutenant Osborne detested all my answers and said, "At this time, we're going to place both of you under arrest, and we'll sort out the charges at the station."

Gerald asked if he could speak as he pulled a folded piece of paper out of his back pocket. "Lieutenant, we have a legitimate right to be here tonight. I have a copy of our signed contract with the Columbia Police Department," he explained.

"Let me see that," Lieutenant Osborne huffed as he snatched the document from Gerald's hand.

"Sergeant Downs signed off on this Christmas Party, and everyone at police headquarters was made aware that there would be drinking and live music here tonight. It was agreed to in advance and approved a few weeks ago," Gerald continued.

Lieutenant Osborne read the document.

"You have no right to arrest us, sir. We all have copies of this agreement," Gerald summed up.

Lieutenant Osborne splintered off with a few members of his team, huddled up just out of earshot, and discussed the situation. They were clearly agitated, and their body language was animated, but after a few minutes, they came back to us.

"Every guest here will vacate the premises immediately. That includes the band. The four of you guys on the lease and the skinny guy we picked up on the frontage road will stay behind and remove every piece of trash from this property and leave it exactly as you found it. You have until 0700 hours to fully comply with these orders," Lieutenant Osborne commanded. "Do you understand?"

"Yes," we said in almost perfect unison. And just like that, the police returned to their vehicles and left the scene. I paid the band, and the five of us spent the next few hours cleaning the property and picking up all the trash we could find. We were scared to leave even a single cigarette butt behind. Gerald, Eddie, and the other guy took off together while Ronnie and I hit a Waffle House for an early breakfast and then crashed at a nearby hotel for a few hours. The next morning, I headed back to Atlanta, 100 percent aware of how fortunate we all were.

MY DAD AND I HAD AVOIDED THE LOOMING DISCUSSION about my potential employment after graduation. We stayed in the same two-bedroom suite at The Marque, and it felt like a grenade was ready to explode.

"Where's your head at with the whole job search? What's your plan?" he asked.

"Well, you know how much I love to travel, so I'm thinking I could sell popsicles in Madrid or work at Tower Records in Lon..."

He cut me off, "Are you trying to be funny?"

Sensing the seriousness of the conversation, I decided to pivot for my sake.

"Totally," I said. "I have a big job fair coming up in Atlanta, and I already have some interviews lined up, but what I'd really love to do is move to Los Angeles after graduation, go to film school, and then try to get a job with Lucasfilm or Industrial Light & Magic."

His silence was deafening. I don't know how long we sat and stared at each other. His normal reaction time was only a couple of nanoseconds, so I knew something was way off. My dad, the ex-Army Ranger instructor, looked me dead in the eyes and said, "No son of mine is going to Hollywood to make movies."

That was it. The discussion was over. If I had a vote, it had been stripped away, and I felt so sad. Making movies with my buddy Luke in Atlanta had been one of the only joyful memories I had as a kid. I loved my dad, but I respected him much more. I decided now wasn't the time or place, and I closed the book on that dream forever.

After stewing on my dad's decree over Christmas, I decided that two could play that game. My first move was to avoid any meetings with Army brass concerning my 2nd Lieutenant commission for Active Duty or the Army Reserve. That would show him. So, after slamming the door shut on a guaranteed job in the military that I was already good at, I drove six hours to Atlanta for the regional job fair.

I felt great after my second interview for a sales job with a company in Atlanta, but they later informed me that I'd failed the personality test and stopped returning my phone calls. Strike one. But things were going well for me with another national organization. I'd aced multiple interviews, everyone seemed very cool, but I tripped up during what was presumably the final interview. The young, blonde manager was about twenty-five years old, and she was stunning. After knocking my interview out of the park, I asked her if she was down to grab drinks at a local nightclub. Strike two. Back in Charleston, I made an appointment at the Medical University of South Carolina to see if I could get into medical school. Apparently, the dean frowned upon any applicant who had failed Chemistry four times and applied with a 2.5 GPA. My options were drying up quickly.

I called my dad, explained the series of bad interviews, and asked for his advice. He told me he always thought I'd make it through The Citadel and how proud he was of my decision to go there. We joked about some of my close scrapes and how I always wiggled free. He said I was a natural-born salesman and believed I had the potential to be a great leader. He asked me to call two gentlemen he knew, which I did. Those calls turned into a series of conversations, a trip to Rockaway, New Jersey, face-to-face interviews, a group dinner, and finally a job offer in medical sales.

I'd just wrapped up my track and field collegiate career with a personal best in the 400m intermediate hurdles at the Southern Conference championships in Boone, North Carolina. I was excited that I'd pulled a rabbit out of the hat in front of my dad in my final race, but I was also bummed that I didn't help the team score any points in my main event. I'd been running competitively since my first 800m race way back in sixth grade and felt a little melancholy that it was all over.

With no more practices on my daily schedule and no meets the following weekend, it was time to enjoy my final days before graduation. Sure, I had some exams looming, but why would I kill myself studying when the most I could hope to achieve was a negligible increase to my GPA?

I had a few calls with my new boss about my move to Washington, DC, onboarding documents in hand, my start date on the calendar, and upcoming sales training to look forward to. Everything was lining up on the employment side, and I was excited about living in our nation's capital. The only thing left was to enjoy my last two weeks in Charleston.

One evening, I met up with my buddy, Ted, and we drove down to his girlfriend's house near Colonial Lake. The plan was to swing by her place on Rutledge Avenue and convince all her roommates to join us for one last blowout evening. I was in a great mood, and both of us walked into the apartment already gassed up. Ted was always easygoing, but I get loud and animated when I'm drunk and like to take over a room. We walked in, and I cracked open another beer. I was in the middle of hijacking DJ duties when the most beautiful girl I'd ever seen stormed out of one of the bedrooms.

"Can you stop making so much noise?" she exclaimed. "Some of us are trying to study."

My gaze was squarely fixated on the tall, long-legged brunette who was clearly frustrated that I'd taken over her apartment.

"I'm sorry. I'll turn it down," I said.

I'd been out with my fair share of ladies during those four years, but half were good friends, and I considered those to be dates without an agenda. It might have been an Echo Company party, Parents Weekend, Homecoming, or some other Citadel event. On my occasional free weekends, I wanted to be with someone I knew would have a good time in any situation and be great company. As for the rest of my dates, there were a few relationships that might have produced something more substantial, but The Citadel had a funny way of dooming things from the start. But this tall drink of water was different. There was just something about her.

"Hey, I'm Rob."

"You're too loud. I'm trying to study for exams," she said.

"It's my first weekend off in months, and I'm making up for lost time," I said.

She wasn't amused. "Well, you need to turn it down a notch."

"Happy to," I said. "Didn't catch your name."

"It's Bentley."

"Bentley?" I echoed.

"Bentley—like the car," she said.

I'd never met a more stunning girl in my life. I hung out with Bentley and the others for an hour or so, listening to music. I don't remember what we talked about, but reality was closing in fast. The class of 1990 would graduate next weekend, and I was moving to DC the following Monday. She and I didn't exchange numbers, but I wished her luck on her exams. Nine days later, I moved to Alexandria, Virginia, bummed out that I'd never see Bentley again.

On Saturday, May 12, 1990, I sat in the McAlister Field House with my mom, dad, sister, and cousin, DeWitt, along with the rest of my senior class. Dick Cheney, President Regan's Secretary of Defense, gave our commencement address. But rather than listening, I reflected on a quote I'd read the week before I checked into this place. Winston Churchill said, "Never give up on something that you can't go a day without thinking about."

"I lift up my eyes to the mountains-
where does my help come from?
My help comes from the LORD,
the Maker of heaven and earth.
He will not let your foot slip-
He who watches over you will not slumber."

—Psalms 121:1-3 NIV

8

VIRGINIA IS FOR LOVERS

"There's not a word yet for old friends who've just met."

—*Jim Henson*

I graduated on a Saturday and made the eight-hour drive to Northern Virginia with my dad the next day. We left at the crack of dawn, and shortly after lunch, we looked at apartments in the Old Town area of Alexandria. My buddy, Ted, and I planned to live together, but he was delayed a couple of weeks and trusted us to find a decent place. Our first stop was at Potowmack Crossing, and I quickly decided to rent a two-bedroom, first-floor unit from a sweet girl named Lee. The location was perfect, and my dad didn't like messing around, so I signed the paperwork within an hour. The property was three miles from Washington National Airport, seven miles from Capitol Hill, and just two miles from a plethora of bars, restaurants, and shops on King Street. My new residence had been the oldest district of Washington, DC, until 1846, when it was ceded back to Virginia.

I needed a new car, so my dad tagged along and helped me select my biggest purchase yet. I loved the candy apple Saab, but he thought the cappuccino brown Honda was more practical, so we settled on the

Accord. We went suit shopping in Seven Corners and capped off the thirteen-hour day with dinner at Hard Times, a local chili restaurant about a mile from my new digs.

The next morning, we picked up the key from Lee, and I moved into my first apartment. My dad wrote me a check for one month's rent, another one for my first car payment, and wished me luck. I dropped him off at National Airport for his flight home, and I set off on the 250-mile drive to Rockaway, New Jersey, to begin training for my first real job.

The first few weeks were a blur. I spent time between Alexandria, Baltimore, and Rockway and studied medical terminology, product knowledge, and surgical protocols. I was responsible for more than fifteen medical device product lines. Work was a rude awakening, and learning everything was like drinking out of a firehose. I never would have made it in medical sales without my first mentor's help, kindness, and patience. Chuck taught me so much about the business and how to navigate a hospital, but the greatest thing he instilled in me was the power of handwritten communication. In those first two months, he wouldn't let me leave a building or hospital without stopping in the lobby to write personalized thank-you notes.

My roommate, Ted, arrived in Alexandria by early June, and within a few weeks, we'd fully settled into the next chapter of our lives. I sold medical devices to eight area hospitals, he had taken a job in finance, and we had established new friendships with Lee, some of her co-workers and friends, and many of our neighbors in the complex. The pool was the best social hotspot. It always bustled with young professionals eager to unwind from the busy work week. Occasionally, management would supply all the food and alcohol to host a community mega party, and on some of those nights, the remaining die-hard revelers grabbed the leftover drinks and rolled over into our apartment 50 feet away.

A few weeks into our Virginia residency, Ted called up a few guys he knew from high school, and we made plans to meet for drinks after work at The Union Street Public House, an old colonial warehouse located two blocks off the Potomac River. He introduced me to Benton, Keith, JT, Nelly, Tim, Tom, and Trey at happy hour, and the rest, as they say, is history. We were all the same age, had just graduated from college, liked to play sports, and had all convened in the DC area to commence adulthood. I never made a meaningful connection with any of the guys I went to high school with, but Ted gave me the opportunity to meet a bunch of his friends, a few of whom dated back to elementary school, and we bonded quickly.

The group expanded to include Anne, Belinda, Gretchen, Kate, and Susan in those early days, and our ranks expanded rapidly as more friends moved back to familiar surroundings or to start their careers. Almost everyone could rattle off multiple connect-the-dot stories about being neighbors, attending the same elementary school, playing on the same youth sports team, or lifeguarding at Lake Barcroft during the summer. Any combination of our bunch got together multiple times per week, whether it was pickup basketball, catching a live gig at Bad Habits, grabbing lunch at Chadwicks, having drinks at the Hamilton Grill, golfing at Hains Point, or going to a Bullets, Capitals, Orioles, or Redskins game. We always hung out together.

Why was that so special? This group of people so easily and willingly welcomed me into their inner circle. They let me be part of their lives, which was completely foreign to me. I'd never experienced anything like that while growing up. My mom never allowed me to have a friend over, and it was socially stunting. And even though I'd once had two friends in Atlanta, I never developed a single normal relationship while living in the round tower or bouncing from school to school. I made brothers for life at The Citadel, but the beginning of those relationships was under extreme duress and constant threat. I shared an incredible bond with the guys who'd survived that ordeal, but it was different. My new life and friends in Alexandria and my very existence felt normal for the first time in my life.

As Richard Bach, author of *Jonathan Livingston Seagull,* wrote, "Your friends will know you better in the first minute you meet than your acquaintances will know you in a thousand years."

One afternoon, while I was at my local bank, I was offered the opportunity to lead a soccer team at T.C. Williams High School. I accepted the position without hesitation. Ted agreed to be my assistant, and we kicked off our coaching careers when the new school year began that August.

The first practice was a doozy. We were nervous, but probably not as apprehensive as the kids or their parents. We'd never coached anything in our lives, and the team had canned their last coach because he didn't know anything about, as Pelé would say, "the beautiful game." Both of us had played competitive soccer, and we knew the terminology. But everyone was skeptical, and we were under the microscope after we lost our first three games.

We kept hectic schedules and burned the candle at both ends. I hit the basketball court at least two nights a week, we coached soccer three times a week, we played in a co-ed softball league, we hit bars and clubs regularly, and we lounged by the pool to drink beers every Sunday afternoon. We had a routine. And in early October, Ted got a call that would change my life forever.

"Rob, I just talked to my old girlfriend. She's planning a trip this way with her roommates, and they asked if they could crash with us for a few days," he said.

"Which roommates?" I asked.

"I think all of them," he said.

"What about the tall brunette?" I asked.

"I think she's still a roommate, so yes, the brunette's making the trip," he said.

The girls had a few days off for Fall Break and drove north from The College of Charleston to our place in Alexandria. The six of us packed into that 900-square-foot, two-bedroom apartment. We also had a king-sized pull-out couch in the living room, but for the life of me, I don't know how we divvied up the living space that weekend. And it really didn't matter because there are only three things I remember about that weekend.

The first was our Friday night out in DC. We rode the Metro to Dupont Circle because we wanted to take the girls to one of our favorite hangouts, The Brickskeller, a hotel and tavern famous for offering more than 1,200 bottled and canned beers from all over the world. For a group of first-timers, selecting a beer could be a daunting task, so we made some suggestions. The lower level of the tavern resembled a rustic saloon, and the six of us chatted away. But I was focused only on the lady with the big hoop earrings who sat directly across from me. The conversation flowed with such ease that I thought, *There's no way a girl this beautiful would ever be interested in me.* I couldn't keep my eyes off Bentley. The rest of our table could have stood up, waved a giant flag, and walked out the door, and I wouldn't have noticed.

The second thing I remember was a relaxed conversation with her about my work in medical sales. She asked a bunch of questions about what I did. Most of my friends weren't sure what my job entailed, so I gave her the CliffsNotes version.

"I sell a bunch of disposable, interventional gadgets to radiologists and a wide swath of surgical devices and fabrics to vascular and cardiac surgeons."

"Have you ever seen an open-heart surgery before?" she asked.

"Absolutely. I cover different kinds of procedures and surgeries every week. I've probably seen a dozen heart-related surgeries," I said.

"I've actually been cut open three times," Bentley said.

"Seriously? Do you remember what surgeries they were?" I asked.

"I had some congenital defects and was a blue baby, so I had my first surgery at three, my second at seven, and my third at nine years old," she said.

I pressed for details, but Bentley was foggy about the specifics and told me everything had been fixed with her last surgery about twelve years ago and that she currently didn't have any health issues. I learned that she was born with a hole in her heart and that it had been repaired over fifteen years ago.

Back at the apartment later that night, I pulled out a sample Dacron patch from my sales bag and handed it to her.

"Your surgeon probably used something like this to close the opening between your two ventricles," I said. "When was the last time you saw a cardiologist?"

"When I lived in California," she said.

"How long ago was that?" I asked.

"At least ten years," she replied.

"Bentley, you need to see a cardiologist," I pressed.

"Well, my parents haven't taken me back to the doctor since we moved to Atlanta," she said. "I'm not sure there's anything to do. They told me I was fixed."

I was only twenty-two years old, so I probably knew as much about cardiac surgery as any first-year medical student, but I was 100 percent sure that no follow-up in over a decade was unacceptable. I said that she needed to talk to her mom and dad immediately and that the next time she made it back to Atlanta, they should take her to see a cardiologist. Bentley said she'd do that, and the weekend continued.

The third thing I remember was their last day in our apartment. It was a lazy Sunday morning, and everyone was whipped from our Saturday night escapades. Everybody else was still asleep, but when I came out of my bedroom, I was excited to see Bentley awake on the pull-out sofa, watching *The Princess Bride* on VHS.

"One of my all-time favorite movies," I said as I approached the couch.

"Mine too! Everyone was still sleeping, so I grabbed this from the shelf," she said.

"Can I join you?" I asked.

"Of course, you can!" Bentley exclaimed.

Time was running out on our weekend. I didn't want it to end, and I didn't want her to leave. Like Wesley and his love for Princess

Buttercup, I only needed to be near her. Everyone else eventually woke up, ate breakfast, and started packing, but we were oblivious to it all. They ignored us as we lay on that pull-out sofa in the living room and watched one of the greatest love stories of our time.

As the girls loaded up the car to leave, I knew I couldn't make the same mistake I'd made in Charleston. I had to see her again.

"Bentley, can I call you? My family is having a get-together in Atlanta over Christmas and New Year's, and I'd like to see you if you're free."

"I would like that. Here's my home number. I'll be there after I finish exams," she said.

THINGS IMPROVED FOR US ON THE COACHING FRONT. We moved some kids to new positions, found a center back that bolstered our defense, changed our formation in the middle and up top, and started scoring goals. We rattled off a few wins in a row, word got out at school that the team was improving, and the boys were having fun. In the final game of the season, we knocked off the top-ranked team, and our Jaguars finished with a winning record. The parents were thrilled with the turnaround, and as we all celebrated our big victory, they asked us to coach the team again next year.

"Only if we can change the team's name," I said, and in that moment, the Alexandria Attack was born.

My Virginia friends had become the center of my universe, and we did everything together, from playing Monday night basketball at O'Connell High School to playing softball on The Mall in front of the Smithsonian Institute, where a well-placed hit could scoot between the outfielders and into traffic, guaranteeing an inside-the-park home run. We gathered for Independence Day in the grass by the Washington Monument and watched the fireworks show that captured the dual backdrops of the White House and the Capitol. We went to concerts and played golf, paintball, and video games until the wee hours of the morning. We went to the beach, dressed up for Halloween, and did it again for some amazing 70s parties. The baseball diehards checked off games in Boston, New York, and Philly. But mostly, we loved hanging out together. I finally had a family of friends.

"This is My commandment, that you love one another as I have loved you. Greater love has no one than this, than to lay down one's life for his friends."

—John 15:12-13 NKJV

9

GEORGIA ON MY MIND

"The road leads back to you."

—*Ray Charles*

B entley went back to Charleston with her roommates to study for exams and wrap up the semester. Then came a period of around eight weeks that did a number on me. I didn't have a way to speak with her. We'd had a great weekend together; she'd opened up about her surgeries, and we both loved romantic comedies. When I asked if I could call her over Christmas, she said, "I would like that." While that response was incredible in the moment, the wait was excruciating.

Around the middle of December, I couldn't wait any longer, so I called Bentley's home number, got the answering machine, and left a message. Did she still want me to call? Would her dad listen to the message and then delete it? Was he that kind of guy? He didn't know me from Adam, and what if he confused me with some jerk named Robert he'd met years ago? After five minutes, I decided to call a second time and left an even more detailed message. I didn't go Jon Favreau certifiable in *Swingers* on her machine, but the temptation to call one more time started to gnaw at me.

I called two more times the next day, and the next one, too, and left at least six lengthy messages and maybe more over a four-day span. My mind felt like a speeding locomotive that was headed off the rails. This couldn't be the end of our story, but I was afraid she might never call back after all my voice messages. I was mentally spent and close to giving up hope when the phone rang. It was Bentley's mom.

"Hello, Robert, Margaret Bentley is finishing up exams and will be driving home from Charleston in a couple of days. I will make sure she gets your messages." She had just thrown me a lifeline.

Bentley called me later that week, and as soon as I heard her voice, all my anxieties vanished. She was happy I called and told me to call her at the same number when I got to Atlanta.

I reached out to my dad to see how Christmas was shaping up, and he said that my mom had already rented a two-bedroom suite at The Marque, an upscale hotel right across the street from Perimeter Mall. She normally booked the property from the week before Christmas through New Year's Day. This was my dad's present to her, and she, in turn, gifted it to her family, inviting her brother, sister, and their families. Sometimes we'd go to Callaway Gardens in Pine Mountain, Georgia, but she liked The Marque better because it was closer to everyone in Atlanta, and the suite had an enormous dining and sitting area between the two bedrooms. She supplied the food, music, and the gathering place, and the family could swing by the hotel to visit any time they wanted.

My dad knew I wanted to carve out time with Bentley, but he mentioned going to see the Georgia versus Georgia Tech basketball game at the Omni. Whenever I was in town over the holidays, we usually saw the Atlanta Hawks play, but on this occasion, he said that he'd gotten a few extra tickets, and I could invite Bentley, too.

Bentley said she loved basketball and asked if we could pick her up at her parents' house on our way downtown. While I was sure that my dad's gesture wasn't completely altruistic, it didn't matter much because my wait to see her was almost over.

We headed to Bentley's house in my dad's Jagolet. Never heard of that car? It's an XJ6 Jaguar body fused with the biggest, most powerful Chevrolet engine that could be functionally retrofitted under the hood. Because of all the electrical and transmission problems he'd had with his Jaguar, a forward-thinking mechanic recommended that he install a new wiring harness and do a complete engine transplant. This amalgamation was a beast, and it sounded like one when we pulled into her driveway.

I was already nervous to see Bentley, but that feeling was exacerbated when my dad gave his new creation a little juice. It sounded like a tank idling on the streets of Buckhead, and I almost expected Bentley to run back inside, but instead, she opened the car door and said, "Is this a Jag?"

In my mind, that game was our first official date, but neither of us had made that declaration. I was petrified that she'd be overwhelmed by my dad, who could either charm or command a room in seconds, or by my cousin Lane, who stayed with us for the Christmas break. He had a charming personality but a comedic dryness that could catch someone off guard. But Bentley was a trooper and quickly connected with them both.

She had amazing poise and an infectious presence. I don't think there was another female in our section, but she hung with all the men, drank watered-down light beer, and watched as Kenny Anderson scored a career-high forty points and led the Yellow Jackets to victory in a three-overtime thriller. That's fifty-five minutes of basketball.

As we left the arena, my dad came beside me and said, "Any girl who can sit through that much basketball with all those guys is a keeper."

My dad and Lane caught a ride back with a friend, and I drove Bentley home in the Jagolet. Instead of using the interstate, I decided to take the long way up Peachtree Street so we could have more time together. It was a Wednesday night, and the game had ended late, so the roads were empty. We didn't know much about each other yet and were chit-chatting about the game when I slowed down and stopped for a red light. We both stopped talking and listened to the engine growl.

"How fast can this thing go?" Bentley asked

"Let's find out," I said as I put the pedal to the floor.

I don't know what that mechanic put under the hood, but the Jaguar rocketed off the line. I felt like Steve McQueen in *Bullitt* racing past the Fox Theatre and through Midtown. Bentley motioned for me to hang a right on 14th Street so I could pick up Piedmont Avenue.

"Less cops," she said.

The XJ6 weighed four thousand pounds, so as we turned north and raced toward Lenox Square, I looked over and said, "I feel like I'm driving a missile."

She smiled, and we found we had something else in common. We liked to drive fast. We made it back to her parents' place, and I walked her to the door.

"Can I see you again?" I asked.

"How's tomorrow?" she said.

"That works for me," I said, trying to hide my sheer excitement. "Do you want to do anything in particular?"

"Maybe something where it's just you and me?" she smirked.

We spent most of the next three days together. But all was not well. When Bentley got home after exams, her parents told her they were getting a divorce. It shattered her world, and she didn't want to be stuck at home with her heartbreak. She got to meet a ton of my extended and immediate family as they passed through the doors of The Marque. We hung out for hours around Perimeter Mall, shopped in Buckhead, and caught a couple of movies, coincidentally at the same theater where I waited in line for hours with my dad to see *The Empire Strikes Back*, but it felt way too early in our relationship to reveal that. We watched bowl games, she showed me around her old high school, and we went clubbing at Petrus with a bunch of her friends. Man, I was hooked.

We spent four amazing days together. I dropped her off at her house, and as we were saying goodbye, I got serious and asked her a question.

"Bentley, would you be up for something a little outside the box tomorrow?"

"What are you thinking?" she asked.

"My dad helped me make a connection with a local cardiologist, and he's agreed to see you to do a complete, non-invasive cardiac workup. All you have to do is say yes, and we'll go together," I said.

"I'm OK with that," she answered. I kissed her goodnight and was thrilled that she said yes.

The next morning, we arrived at Dr. James Sutherland's office. He specialized in both pediatric and adult cardiology, which was not a common practice in the nineties. Bentley could have easily said no to this personal intrusion, but I think she was equally curious about her heart's condition. Not one to miss a show, my dad came along, too. She gave a brief overview of her medical history, made it through the question-and-answer session, and had numerous vials of blood drawn. The doctor then hooked her up for an electrocardiogram, which records electrical signals in the heart.

"Your EKG looks good," he said as the feed rolled out of the machine.

He shifted her to the examination table and prepped her for an echocardiogram, which uses sound waves to take moving pictures of the heart. It was another way to look at her valves and vessels and would provide detailed feedback without an invasive procedure like a cardiac catheterization. As he applied the lubricating gel to her skin, the ten-inch-long vertical scar that ran the length of her sternum was clearly visible. He squeezed more gel directly onto the ultrasound probe and slowly moved it across her chest. The images on the screen were all foreign to us, but Dr. Sutherland interpreted them.

"There's a lot going on here," he said. "First, your valve repair still looks very good for having been done so long ago—as does your VSD patch, Bentley. I don't see any leaks between the ventricles and only mild regurgitation from your aortic valve repair."

"What does that mean—mild regurgitation?" she asked.

"This is typical for a patient like you, Bentley," he said. "The aortic valve has three leaflets, and some mild stenosis has built up. As the calcium builds, it makes it difficult for the leaflets to open and close. When they can't close properly, it allows blood that should be pumped out of the heart and into the body to get pulled back into the ventricle, which causes regurgitation."

"Is that bad?" Bentley asked.

"It's typical for someone with your condition, but not something that will cause you major problems in the next few years. You'll want to follow up with a cardiologist to have these same tests run every year," he said.

"How many years before she would have a problem?" I asked.

"It's hard to say," he said. "With her age and overall good health, she could go twenty years without needing another surgery…"

"I have to have another open-heart surgery?" Bentley interrupted.

"Definitely. Your aortic stenosis will only get worse over time. Just keep exercising and taking good care of yourself, and you'll be able to delay this for a while," he said.

There was an ever-so-brief pause as Bentley absorbed that news. The doctor continued with the assessment, moving the transducer to new positions on her chest. While Bentley only remembered that she was a blue baby born with a congenital defect, we learned much more in that clinic over the next ten minutes.

"Don't be scared about what I'm going to tell you next. This isn't affecting your health, but it's certainly not very common," Dr. Sutherland began. "You have dextrocardia situs inversus totalis, which correlates with your overall congenital birth defects. Basically, all your organs are reversed from their normal positions in the body, and your heart sits more on the right side of your sternum instead of the left."

Even though she couldn't recite that long Latin diagnosis, none of this was news to Bentley. But it was hot off the press for my dad and me. He remained silent with his arms folded across his chest, while I kept asking the questions.

"This all sounds pretty bad. What does it mean?" I asked.

"Given that she was born in the sixties with these congenital defects and anomalies—frankly, she's lucky to be alive. We don't see many patients like this because they typically don't live this long. And for her to be this healthy and of childbearing age—it's very unusual."

"Can I have children?" Bentley asked.

"I don't see why not, but I think your OBGYN will need to follow you very closely—someone who specializes in high-risk pregnancies. They'll need to communicate with your cardiologist every step of the way," he said. "This is all good news, Bentley. You are a living, breathing, walking miracle."

Simply stated, Bentley was born a blue baby and had a hole in her heart, which allowed some of the blood to circulate back and forth between her two ventricles instead of getting oxygenated in the lungs and pumped out to the rest of her body. This type of defect can't remain untreated for long, so a surgical intervention is required. And since Bentley's blood was getting mixed back and forth between the two lower chambers of her heart, she struggled to breathe and stayed in a perpetual state of blueness. Now, imagine that you have to walk a mile up a steep hill, and it's hard to catch your breath. Now, imagine feeling that way when you watch TV or lie in bed. That's how Bentley felt every day as a kid.

However, the simple diagnosis she'd heard as a child didn't correlate with the more complex picture we received from Dr. Sutherland. While she was, indeed, healthy, Bentley would need another surgery sometime in the future, and while we learned she could have children under specialized physician care, that thought had not even entered my mind. Shoot, this was only our fifth date. My empathy for her was through the roof, but at the same time, I couldn't help but feel overwhelmed. And if I felt that way, how did she feel? There was less than a 0.01 percent chance of being born with that many anomalies. She had won the congenital heart defect lottery.

We left the office, and my dad asked us if we wanted to get something to eat. One of his favorite places in Atlanta was Houston's. The restaurant had dark brick interior walls with columns and tables that were constructed from a blend of cherry and mahogany wood. The lighting was reminiscent of a bomb-ravaged English diner during World War II. We slid into our oxblood-red leather booth and looked at the menu.

"What's good here?" I asked.

"The chicken fingers and fries special," my dad said.

"I don't see it on the menu," I said.

"That's because it's not ever on the menu. You have to ask the waitress for it," he said.

"It's that good?" I asked.

"It's that good," he confirmed.

Bentley hadn't said much since we left the doctor's office. The waitress came by, and we ordered three of their secret specials. There was a heaviness to our wait. We'd all heard Dr. Sutherland's assessment. While there were plenty of positive things about her heart health and overall condition, she faced at least one more surgery and substantially more follow-ups for the rest of her life.

When the silence became awkward, my dad looked at me and said, "Are you sure you want to sign up for this?"

I don't know who was more stunned, Bentley or me. My dad never held back or minced words, but this time, he was way out of line.

"Sign up for what?" I asked.

He started waving his index finger in a circular motion toward Bentley, but kept his eyes fixed on me. "All of this. All of her problems."

"She's right there. Why would you say that? And what the doctor said didn't sound all that bad to me. Seriously, why would you say that?" I stammered.

He was callous, his timing was terrible, and I don't remember what we said after that, but I know he hurt her deeply. It's hard to let go of that kind of hurt and impossible to forget. Perhaps, in that moment, he was trying to protect me. But from what?

Bentley and I spent the next ten days together. We celebrated Christmas with an eclectic gathering of family and friends. I showed her around my old neighborhood, and she watched me play basketball with my dad and cousins at the Chesnut Elementary School playground. We saw Indiana play Auburn in the 1990 Peach Bowl, and we celebrated New Year's Eve with a big group of her friends. I knew I loved her. And I could never leave this city without asking her about tomorrow, so as I packed up the car on January 2, 1991, to head back to Virginia, I had to make my move.

"I want to keep seeing you, and I don't want to date anyone else. I know it's a long drive back and forth from Virginia, but I'd like to try," I nervously blurted.

"I feel the same way. I don't want to date anyone else either," Bentley replied. "And I don't know if I'll be in Charleston or have to stay here in Atlanta, but we can figure this out."

We both wanted to be together. I thought back to the rude question my dad asked me in the restaurant a few days earlier. My answer was yes.

"Whatever is good and perfect is a gift coming down to us
from God our Father,
who created all the lights in the heavens.
He never changes or casts a shifting shadow."

—James 1:17 NLT

10

ORIOLES AND ANGELS

"I saw the angel in the marble and carved until I set him free."

—*Michelangelo*

Dating long distance was a monthly exercise of devotion. Due to financial constraints, Bentley had to withdraw from the College of Charleston, and she moved back to Atlanta to enroll at Georgia State. She now lived rent-free, bouncing back and forth between her mom's and dad's condos. She qualified for in-state tuition and took a full-time job at The Ritz-Carlton, working in the fitness center to help make ends meet. With her full-time student status and both of us working forty to sixty hours a week, the 630 miles of interstate separation was a logistical nightmare.

We set a goal to see each other at least one weekend a month. My schedule was more malleable, so it was easier for me to drive to Atlanta than it was for her to come see me. I'd head to Richmond or Roanoke late Thursday evening, knock out my sales calls Friday morning, then hit the road by noon with only a seven- or eight-hour drive in front of me. When my work schedule required me to be in Maryland or DC on a Friday, or if there was a big concert or sporting event—or if

Bentley just wanted to get out of Atlanta for a few days—I'd book her a round-trip flight in and out of Washington National Airport. And on that first weekend of October 1991, I invited her up to catch the final Baltimore Orioles game of the season.

It wasn't going to be any ordinary event. It was the final Major League Baseball game to be played in Memorial Stadium, an old Greco-Roman-style structure named in honor of the local citizens who gave their lives in World War II. It was built in two phases over ten years on old city land formally called Venable Park. I'd attended a dozen or so games in this multi-purpose park since I'd moved to Virginia in May of 1990, and I wanted to witness a rare slice of baseball history.

Every time Bentley came to Virginia, I had one goal: to make it a weekend to remember. So, I planned a two-day excursion to the Inner Harbor in downtown Baltimore, Maryland. This former seaport had been developed into a premier waterfront entertainment district, which included the Baltimore Aquarium and its already famous marine mammal pavilion. We hadn't dated long, but I knew Bentley loved every kind of creature and that her all-time favorite was the dolphin.

We left Alexandria on Saturday morning and made the hour-plus drive northeast to the Marriott Inner Harbor, just steps away from the downtown aquarium. I arranged for us to take part in their dolphin awareness and interaction program, which was exactly the hit I hoped it would be. Bentley and I spent hours in the aquarium walking, talking, and holding hands. We also saw an IMAX movie at the Maryland Science Center. Around 7:00 p.m., we took a water taxi over to Fells Point for dinner at The Waterfront Hotel Bar.

Our day had been spectacular. Any time with Bentley was great, but I especially loved exploring a new city together. After a short walk from the taxi stand to the tavern, we got our table, ordered some drinks, and reminisced about the day while looking at the menu. Then she abruptly changed the topic.

"I have something to tell you, and I don't know how you will take it," she began.

My heart stopped, and I sat motionless.

"I flew with angels when I was seven years old," she said

"You mean you saw the Blue Angels when you were seven—when you lived in California," I corrected her.

"No, real angels, not planes. Angels hovering over and all around me in the operating room," she continued.

"During your open-heart surgery?" I asked, completely puzzled.

"Yes, my second surgery was on my seventh birthday. I woke up, and I saw all these angels floating above me," she said.

"OK. I remember reading that they had to rush you back into surgery because you were bleeding, but you never said anything about it when we were with Dr. Sutherland," I said.

"I didn't want to scare you—or the doctor. And I definitely didn't want to say anything in front of your dad. Only a few people know," she said.

"You remember that? You remember the surgery? Can you describe what you saw?" I peppered her with questions.

"My surgery was oddly scheduled on my birthday, so I remember being really bummed out by that. But I remember it all, like it happened last week. It was beautiful and peaceful, and I didn't want to come back," she said.

"Come back from where?" I asked.

Bentley wasn't a classic storyteller, never embellished for the sake of embellishment, and would probably freeze on an improv stage. But what she does so well is recount details in a linear point-by-point fashion, which is not how I like to receive information. I prefer direct answers to direct questions—and in the order I ask them. But this was her story, and I accepted that she would tell it in the manner most comfortable for her. She took me back to the beginning when she had her first surgery at three years old.

"I was lying on my back and looking up at my mom through a clear, plastic tent that completely covered my crib. I had pneumonia, my chest hurt, and I felt so isolated. I was scared, crying out for my mom with my arms outstretched, but she wasn't allowed to pick me up."

"You actually have memories from when you were three years old?" I asked, completely dumbfounded.

"Of course. I remember that my chest hurt really bad—like constant pain. And I remember when my mom told me I had to have surgery. I was nervous and thought I was being put in a cage. But I also felt an inner peace and knew it was going to be OK. Maybe it was Jesus comforting me, but I really had no way to know. I also had a sense that what was happening to me was only temporary."

"You knew this at three?" I asked again. "How did you know that?"

"I believed, or maybe I'd been taught, that Jesus was close to little children. That He would protect me. And even at three years old, I felt this inner peace. I knew that even though my mom couldn't physically comfort me or stop my pain, something else was making me feel better. And going into that surgery, I wouldn't have known for sure that it was Jesus, but I believe it clearly was."

"What happened after that?" I asked.

"The surgery was successful, but they told me that I'd need another one in a couple of years. My recovery seemed fine, and I felt better right away, but nothing about my childhood was normal. I was fragile, or at least that's how I felt. Actually, that's how I was treated. By everyone. My parents, brother, and teachers. Even my friends treated me differently. I couldn't go anywhere alone and couldn't play games with my friends. Everyone was afraid of hurting me, and I felt completely alone. Just like I was back in the crib with the plastic tent over me."

Our waitress took our order, but we still hadn't gotten to the meat and potatoes of this entire conversation, so I leaned in with more questions.

"Do you have any memories leading up to your second surgery?" I asked.

"Going into the surgery? I remembered enough from my first one that I knew it was going to be tough. My mom said it was going to be a bigger surgery, but I was also older, and maybe I was better prepared. My mom was more influential this time around because she would take me to her Bible studies and so many ladies prayed over me. I felt a lot of comfort from that. And her friends made a bunch of goodie bags for me, so I got to open something every day the week before my surgery. At that age, it was exciting. I was in a pretty good headspace overall."

"What about the morning of surgery? Did you dread it?" I asked.

"I remember that morning very well. My parents asked our Episcopal priest, Father John, to come to my hospital room and pray. And his wife, who was a good friend of my mom's, was there, too, and they were both lovely people. I really adored Father John, but I remember thinking how somber he looked. And then it kind of hit me: *Oh, this is probably going to be a big deal,* and I could sense that everyone was scared. But I couldn't conceptualize that I might not make it through the surgery or see any of these people again. So, I said goodbye with some fear that I might die while they were working on me, which was very unpleasant.

"I remember lying on the operating room table and being jerked into position. Nurses stuck needles in both my arms, someone put towels on my chest, another person swung a large drape over me, and then a person standing right over me put a black mask over my nose and mouth, leaned in close to my face, and asked me to count backwards from ten. The last thing I remember was breathing in a foul mix of gas and smelly rubber as I went to sleep."

"So, when did you wake up?" I asked.

"It felt like I'd only been asleep for a few seconds, but I remember waking up to a lot of chaos and commotion. A doctor standing next to my bed was yelling loudly that I had to be rushed back into surgery because I was bleeding on the inside. I remember a wave of dread poured over me. I didn't see my mom and dad anywhere, and I'm not sure I could even speak. I might have still had that big tube in my throat. Then I heard someone yell, 'We have to open her back up!'

140

"I was still groggy when they raced me down the hall and back into the operating room, where they'd slice me open for a second time that day. Everybody sounded nervous. And they strapped that mask back on my face again. That was so unpleasant."

"What happened next?" I asked.

"I opened my eyes, and I saw angels everywhere! My first thought was, *Oh, I shouldn't be awake. I'm having surgery.* But there were so many angels, and they covered the room. They were all over—everywhere."

"What did they look like?" I asked.

"I couldn't see distinct faces. They were sort of a white, almost cloud-like presence. The coolest part was the wings. Just huge and powerful. And I was hit by this incredible thought that I knew they'd always been there. They didn't just come down in that moment. I understood that they were already there and had always been there."

"These angels. They were just standing there?" I pressed.

"I wouldn't say standing. All the angels formed a circle around me and over me. I could see them, not really understanding what was happening, but it was awesome. And those wings. One of the angels reached down and scooped me up with his wing. And that instant, I thought, *I'm going home.* I was held by an angel and floating above my earthly body. I could see myself below on the operating table with my chest spread open. Doctors and nurses were yelling at each other, and there was general chaos in the room, but all the noise started to fade away as I was carried, lifted, flown up higher with these angels."

"Where were they taking you?" I asked.

"I knew I was going home. And I was so thankful. I was so excited. Because I knew I wouldn't have to go back into that broken body. I looked at myself and thought, *Oh yeah, I don't want to do that anymore.* And my second thought was that my parents would be sad and that it would feel like an eternity for them to lose their daughter. I wished they knew that I'd see them again soon because in that moment, there was no earthly time. I was already in the spirit realm and going to Heaven.

"I have so many questions. You were thinking about your parents as you were being lifted?" I asked.

"Yes, I was very aware of my mom and dad. And then my last thought was that my animals would wonder where I went, and I was concerned because we had two cats and a dog I loved very much. I had a deep connection with them. And then I stopped thinking about my parents and pets and just enjoyed the ride, being cradled in that massive wing while being lifted higher."

"Where did they take you? Did you make it outside the hospital? Did you see anything else?" I asked.

"As I was lifted away in the spirit realm, I closed my eyes. Then I felt a strong vacuum pull on my body. It was a very strong suction, and in a flash, I was back on the operating room table, back in my old body. I could hear all the chaos again, and I heard someone yell, 'She's coming back. She's waking up.' Instantly, I was hit with that putrid rubber smell before I went back to sleep."

"Obviously, you woke up again, but do you remember where?" I asked.

"I woke up in the ICU, and a nurse told me that the bleeding had stopped. But my recollection is that they never found the source of it. It just stopped. And that was the day I flew with angels."

Our food had arrived, and I asked her follow-up questions in between bites. She didn't remember how long the whole encounter had lasted, but Bentley was very clear on other very specific details.

"How far did the angels lift you up before you came back to the table? How high did you get? Did you morph through a wall or the ceiling?" I asked.

"Everything was in the spirit realm. I was lifted to the ceiling, and to me, that was significant because that's when I surrendered to being taken to Heaven. That's when I felt like I was going home, so I just closed my eyes. But I don't know if I closed my eyes or if they were spiritually closed at that point because it felt so good. I didn't have a vision of being outside the hospital or anything like that. It was as if the room kept growing taller."

"So, you first woke up a few feet above the table?" I continued, looking for more details.

"At first, I was just above the table. I could see my broken body. I could see everyone running around. I could see Dr. Myers, but there were so many people in the room. He had a lot of help."

"But you said you kept being lifted—and that the yelling and chaos started to fade away. So where did you go?" I asked, trying to visualize her experience.

"I was lifted toward the ceiling. But I kept going higher in the room until I was very far away. The table and people in the room looked small, but I was still in the same room. I never left the room," she said.

"And then you were sucked back into your body? Did you tell anyone in recovery? Did you tell your folks?" I asked.

"I didn't tell anyone. I wasn't sure how to process everything that had happened. And they kept me in the hospital for a while—almost four weeks, I think, so I missed the last month of third grade. But my mom's friends brought over a ton of gifts, so every morning after I woke up, I got to open a new present. Usually, I got a Barbie and sometimes a stuffed animal, but after I ate some breakfast, a nurse would wheel me to the playroom to visit Lumpy. He was the hospital guinea pig who lived on my floor, and he was there to play with all the heart surgery kids who wanted to visit him. It was tremendously comforting to sit in my wheelchair and hold Lumpy in my lap."

"Besides the angels, and I guess the guinea pig, is there anything else you remember about your time at the children's hospital?" I asked.

"Well, one day we heard that Lee Majors was going to stop by and see all the heart patients on our floor," she started.

Interrupting her, I blurted, "Whoa, you mean Steve Austin from *The Six Million Dollar Man*? I loved that show," I said.

"Yes! The whole hospital was so excited, and it was big, big news. And on that day, I got wheeled around to look for Lee. I'm not sure who pushed me—maybe a nurse or maybe my mom. I don't know. But I was so excited and a little nervous to meet him because he was such a superstar. We raced around the unit until we found him at a nurse's station with an entourage of people. I wheeled right up to him, but I got completely tongue-tied. I think I just said hi, and he asked me my name. I vividly remember that he had such compassionate eyes and a calm demeanor. And that was it. But it was a huge boost meeting the Six Million Dollar Man."

"Any other cool celebrities stop by? You were just a few miles from Hollywood," I said.

"No, just Lee and Lumpy," Bentley said.

"So, after four weeks, they finally let you go home? What was the hardest part?" I asked.

"I was so ready to leave the hospital. That was the easy part. The hardest thing was trying to go back to my old life. I was very restricted by the doctors and my parents. I could play in my bedroom or sit outside. When I went back to school in the fall, I wasn't allowed to play with my friends or classmates. Everyone was afraid of hurting me. I was very lonely.

"When I came home, I started sleeping in my bed right away and would pray to see the angels again, but nothing ever happened. I prayed every night because I thought it could actually be a thing. I prayed for months, cried, and grieved in silence when I couldn't see any angels around me. It was so frustrating, and sometimes I cried myself to sleep."

"What did your parents say when you told them?" I asked.

"I hadn't told them yet. I always sensed there was so much more to God than just going to church and brunch on Sunday mornings. My mom would say prayers with me before bedtime, but there wasn't a lot of fostering or learning about the Bible and Jesus. One night, as I tried to fall asleep, I asked God to see my angels, but once again, nothing. So, I got out of bed and decided that tonight was the night and that I'd tell my parents I got to fly with angels.

"So, I walked into the living room. My dad was strict and looked disgruntled when he saw me. He was in his leather recliner, drinking a martini, and my mom was in the chair next to him. My dad accused me of interrupting their evening and sternly told me to go back to bed."

"What did you do?" I asked.

"I looked at them both and said I flew with angels during my surgery, and I don't know why I can't see them again. My dad dropped his martini glass, and my mom began sobbing and ran out of the room. I could tell it clearly upset her, but I didn't know why. Once they calmed down, I shared my experience, and they both said they believed me."

"Why do you think they believed you so quickly? You were only seven," I continued.

"At some point after they rushed me from the ICU back into surgery, my parents were taken to a padded room in the hospital and were told that I had internal bleeding, that I'd been rushed back into surgery, and the doctors didn't think I'd survive. So, while my experience was so beautiful, theirs was completely gut-wrenching. They were overwhelmed with fear and heartache, thinking that their daughter was dying. So, sadly, we never talked about it again, and I never said anything else because I didn't want to upset my mom. My dad's reaction wasn't comforting either, so I held onto this gift from God in silence and wondered why I couldn't fly with angels anymore. It was such a significant experience. It was more real than anything I'd ever felt before."

"You never talked to your parents about it again?" I asked.

"Not once," Bentley said.

"You had a third surgery in Los Angeles, right? Do you remember anything from that one?"

"I was nine then, and I was excited, thinking I'd finally get another angel experience. I thought it only happened during surgery. And while I was bummed that I needed another heart operation, it would be worth it to see my angels again. But when I came out, I felt a deep

145

despair because it didn't happen. But the comfort I felt two years earlier, knowing that my angels were right there, was a gift that I've treasured ever since. Even though I can't see them, I know they're always there."

"Did you ever tell anyone else?" I asked.

"No," she said. "But there were so many times I tried to cross that threshold as a teenager by doing dangerous activities. I loved to drive fast and put myself at risk physically. I tried to do things that might let me cross into that spirit realm again, and looking back, I realize how many times God saved me from myself."

That's when so many of our dates started to make sense. Bentley always picked me up from the airport in her brother's old BMW 530i and drove like she was Burt Reynolds in *The Cannonball Run*. On one of our early dates, we went gliding in a sailplane over Stone Mountain. And for my birthday, she bought me a skydiving ticket, and we had raced through the streets of Atlanta in my dad's Jagolet on our first date. But that night at dinner, she said that she didn't want to be that kind of risk-taker anymore and thought it was the right time to tell me about the day she flew with angels on her seventh birthday.

The next morning, Bentley and I went to Memorial Stadium for the Orioles' final home game of the season. It had been another dismal campaign for Baltimore, but the team had a chance to end the year on a high note. But Detroit scored four runs in the top of the first inning and effectively ended the game before the crowd had even taken their seats. And like all O's fans that day, I thought about the next season, our new stadium, and whether next year would finally be our year.

I also saw the parallels in dating Bentley. She took a huge leap of faith by sharing her story that weekend, and I saw a future with this woman in my life and its endless possibilities.

"He has put his angels in charge of you.
They will watch over you wherever you go."

—Psalms 91:11 ICB

11

BACKGROUND TALENT

"This is the kid, calls me fifty-nine days in a row; wants to be a player. There ought to be a picture of you in the dictionary under persistence, kid."

—*Michael Douglas as Gordon Gekko in* Wall Street

Bentley and I tied the knot at the end of May in a beautiful ceremony at The Cathedral of Saint Philip, an Episcopal church in Atlanta, Georgia. We drove to Panama City, Florida, the next day for a short honeymoon that was given to us as a wedding present. On our way back, we picked up Bentley's belongings and headed north toward Alexandria to begin our life together.

A few months earlier, I'd purchased a two-bedroom condo on the third floor at Potowmack Crossing. The management company was experiencing financial difficulties, so they offered a significant discount to current or former renters who purchased one of their vacant units. It was too good to pass up, and the timing was perfect, so I bought our first place in the 1710 building.

As a medical device representative, I was required to provide on-site service and support for all the hospitals and physicians I worked with in my territory. One day, after covering a procedure at the University of

Maryland Medical Center in Baltimore, I headed back to our condo in Alexandria. I turned on the radio, and the local disc jockey announced that Central Casting, a local background talent agency, was looking for thousands of baseball fans to be in a new major motion picture. My mind ran wild with questions while the DJ provided the details.

They were looking for fifteen thousand people to fill the stands at Camden Yards, home of the Baltimore Orioles, to film large crowd scenes and stadium aerial shots for *Major League II*, the sequel to the 1989 Cleveland Indians comedy *Major League*—one of my favorite movies of all time. All the relevant information was spelled out, including the shooting dates, start times, and what clothes to wear, which was important since we'd be filming a summer sports movie in the middle of October. I was beside myself with excitement, so I raced home, ran up the three flights of stairs, and burst through the door to share the news with Bentley.

"You're never going to believe this! I just heard they are making a sequel to *Major League!* They're going to film it in Baltimore. There's an open casting call, and all I have to do is show up on the day they're filming crowd shots, and I'll get to be in the movie!" I exclaimed.

"That's great. And you can do that and your job?" she asked.

"Yes. Well, I think so. I'm not entirely sure if I'll be on call, but hopefully, no surgeries will come up for me to attend. But I think it will be good," I said.

However, there was nothing good about it. In the days leading up to the shoot, my schedule changed, and there was no way for me to film in Baltimore and cover surgeries with Dr. Crossland and Dr. Garcia at Northern Virginia Doctors Hospital the same day. This quashed opportunity frustrated me, but it reminded me of another one of my all-time favorite movies, *Field of Dreams*. In the movie, Ray Kinsella, played by Kevin Costner, spoke with Dr. "Moonlight" Graham, played by Burt Lancaster. He asked the doctor what it was like to be called up to the majors, only to play one half-inning in right field and never make a play or get an at-bat.

"It was like coming *this* close to your dreams and then watching them brush past you like a stranger in a crowd," he answered.

I couldn't have described my disappointment any better. My dad had said no to my dream of working in the movie industry, and now the universe had, too.

For two weeks, I stewed over what might have been until I decided to act. I grabbed the yellow pages, called the radio station, and talked to their advertising director, who gave me the name and number of their liaison at Central Casting. I gave them a call.

"Hello, Central Casting," said the receptionist. "How may I direct your call?

"Hey, this is Robert. Could you please connect me with Renee? She's in charge of casting for *Major League II*," I said.

"Of course. Let me connect you," she said.

"Hi, this is Renee. How can I help you?"

"Hi, Renee. I'm Robert. I wanted to follow up with you about the open casting call for extras to appear in *Major League II*," I said.

"We wrapped up those shots a couple of weeks ago, so there's nothing available in terms of open casting. Who are you? How did you get my number?" she asked, her tone quickly changing.

"Well, like I said, I'm Robert. I'm in medical sales, but I love movies. *Major League* is one of my all-time favorites. So, I thought it would be really cool to be in the sequel. And Lloyd at the radio station gave me your number. He said you could help," I explained.

Renee said that neither she nor the agency took unsolicited calls. She thanked me for reaching out and politely ended the call. The conversation didn't go as expected, but that didn't matter to me. I was in sales and got told no or was hung up on every day, so I buzzed her back the next afternoon and tried to explain how real fans of the movie should be in the sequel. She spouted off my long list of disqualifiers, said she couldn't help, and abruptly ended the call.

So, I tried her a third time and then a fourth. She became agitated quickly and hung up on me both times. By Friday, my conversation with Renee was moderately hostile. She told me that not only would I never work on *Major League II*, but I also would never work on *any* movie that she or their agency was casting. I took my beating and apologized for all the calls, but at least I managed to share the story of my dad's repudiation of my Hollywood dream, which appeared to garner some sympathy.

I gave Renee the weekend off but called again Monday afternoon. We had a normal "tell me about your weekend" conversation, but instead of dismissing me as usual, she gave me a small piece of insider knowledge.

"Since they're currently filming nights at Camden Yards, I must finalize my list of extras by 4:00 p.m. every day and get it over to the set. I have everybody I need for tonight, but you can call me tomorrow afternoon if you want and check on the list," she said.

"If I want?" I joked. "You're funny. I'll talk to you tomorrow."

I called Renee at 3:30 p.m. every day for the next eleven days. She began to expect my call. As the days progressed, we began to chat like old friends, and I could tell she wanted to help. And on that eighteenth day, she said the most magical twenty words I'd waited my whole life to hear.

"Robert, can you be on set at Camden Yards by 9:30 p.m. tonight and work until at least 8:00 a.m. tomorrow morning?"

"One hundred percent! I'll be there on time and stay as long as you or they need me. Do you have any advice about what to do or what I should wear?" I asked.

"It's cold right now in Baltimore, especially at night, but they're filming scenes that happen early in the season. If you want to get on camera, you can't be in a sweatshirt or heavy jacket. Wear a white T-shirt when you check in with the second assistant director (2nd AD) and keep your jacket in your backpack," she said.

I'd had no on-set experience, but Renee had crafted a well-designed play for me to execute. I wore jeans and a white Citadel T-shirt, checked in with the 2nd AD, and waited with the rest of the extras in the left field seats. Boy, it was cold. I don't think the temperature got over 56 degrees the entire time I was there, but right on cue, one of the producers got on the bullhorn and said, "I'm looking for the tall guy with black hair and a white tee. I stood up, raised my hand, and made my way down to the second row and into the only empty seat in the entire section. My seat was right behind Randy Quaid, the actor who played Cousin Eddie in *National Lampoon's Christmas Vacation*.

Quaid was a late addition to the cast, and he played the part of an off-kilter fan, so the director needed to go back and do some re-shoots. The other actors had to be the same from the original takes, but the extras could be different. They just needed to dress the same for continuity. So, either Renee already knew they'd slot me in that seat behind Randy, or it was just an incredible coincidence.

We shot all night, and at the crack of dawn, one of the producers verified that we'd all be back that evening.

"Same start time, exact same clothes and look. If anyone can't make it, come see me before you leave."

Did that mean I was in? Was I coming back? Was I an actor? I ran to a pay phone outside the stadium and called Renee to see what was happening.

"You're in, Robert. They want you back tonight at the same time. I assume you'll be there?" she asked.

"Of course. Thank you for this," I said.

"Well, go home and try to get some sleep," she said.

Sleep? I had to go to work. I had sales calls to make and cases to go cover. I raced home, showered, and called Bentley at work as I got dressed.

"How was it?" she asked.

"I had the best time ever. I sat right in front of the camera. I got to meet Randy Quaid, and they asked me to work again tonight!" I exclaimed.

"Another night? Won't you be exhausted?" she asked.

"Probably, but when will I ever get to do this again?" I asked.

I went back that night in the same jeans and white T-shirt and froze again in the stands. When we weren't shooting, I tried to get to know everyone on the set. Renee didn't know it at the time, but she had let the rooster into the henhouse. Not only did I get to do multiple scenes with Randy, but I also got to shoot a scene with Charlie Sheen and Alison Doody, who was in *Indiana Jones and the Last Crusade*. I had different colored T-shirts and light jackets in my backpack, and after we finished shooting a scene, I swapped clothes to change my appearance just enough to throw the producers off my scent, and then I got to work worming myself as close as possible to the camera before the next shot.

Two days turned into three and then four. I was completely exhausted from pulling double duty every day. I caught a few minutes of sleep whenever and wherever I could, sometimes in the stadium concourse or in between rows, and even once on top of the visitor's dugout. Around midnight, with the temperature dipping just below freezing, I called Bentley from inside Camden Yards.

"Hey. I'm just checking in," I said.

"I'm fine. How are you?" she asked.

"I'm OK. It was a lot of fun at first, but it's been long days and not a ton of action. Frankly, the food sucks, and it's freezing up here. I'm literally so cold that I'm shaking," I said.

"I think it's time to come home," she said.

It had been a once-in-a-lifetime experience. I was never worried about getting fired from the set, so I was perfectly myself during filming. I got pictures with Randy Quaid, talked at length with Alison Doody in between takes, and fumbled a golden opportunity to have a line with Charlie Sheen after he saved the game for the Indians. And for four glorious December nights in 1993, I got to pretend I worked in Hollywood.

Major League II premiered on March 30, 1994. I bought a bunch of tickets for Bentley, me, and the rest of our Northern Virginia crew to see the movie on opening night. I kept saying to myself, *Please don't let me wind up on the cutting room floor.* And at the twenty-five-minute mark, I made my big-screen debut. I high-fived a bunch of friends in the theater and couldn't wait to get home and call my dad.

"For he satisfies the longing soul,
and the hungry soul, he fills with good things."

—Psalm 107:9 ESV

12

GUNPOINT!

"Everyone has their day in jail."
—Drivin' n' Cryin'

The evening started innocently enough at a friend's house in Bell Haven, Virginia. It was a Thursday night, and a bunch of the NOVA (Northern Virginia) gang had come out to celebrate the pending nuptials of our good friends, Keith and Kate, but Bentley couldn't join the fun. She was a full-time nanny for twins during the day, and she was finishing her undergraduate degree at George Mason University at night. Her days were much longer than mine, so while she was in class or studying at home, I went out to bars with our friends.

Realizing she'd be home soon, it was time for me to announce my departure to my friends at the bar and head home. Without batting an eye, I downed three shots of tequila, walked outside, and jumped in the driver's seat of my wife's 1983 Honda Accord hatchback with my buddy, Billy—one of Bentley's oldest friends from Atlanta who'd also been welcomed into our group with open arms. We only had an eight-and a half-mile drive to Alexandria, but I thought we could make it back in record time.

Earlier that evening, I'd called Bentley and let her know about my plans for the night in case she might be able to join us. I expected to get the answering machine, but she picked up right away, which caught me a little off guard.

"You're home early. How was school?" I asked.

"Long day. I've got a paper to write. What's that noise? Where are you?" she demanded.

"I'm at Chris and Mary's. We're getting ready to leave their place and head to the Tequila Grill," I said.

"Is that a good idea? You already sound drunk," she shot back.

"I'm totally fine. I've only had a few beers," I said, which was always my answer.

"I don't think you should go," Bentley warned.

"Don't worry. I'll be fine," I said as I hung up the phone.

The bar was a twenty-minute drive, and I thought nothing of it, although I could have easily grabbed the Metro in Alexandria and ridden it to one of two stops that were within walking distance of the bar. I was probably over the legal limit when I left our friends' apartment, but I hadn't even started the real drinking yet. I had two clear choices in that moment: play it smart and safe, get back to the condo, and help Bentley write her paper, or go out with all the friends and family who'd gathered to celebrate the happy couple before their wedding. The pull to join in on all the revelry was too strong to resist.

I grew up drinking beer, never cared for mixed drinks, but could be persuaded to hammer down a few shots given the right circumstances, and this was one of those nights. The bar was jumping, and spirits were flowing, but my Spidey sense told me it was time to go. Whenever I got that tingly feeling, I stopped drinking. But for some unknown reason, I didn't listen that night. I wandered around the bar, one bottle of beer in each hand and one in my back pocket, looking for Billy. In my search to find him, I ran into another friend, and she'd lined up a row of tequila shots that looked like they might go to waste.

I downed all three, said, "I'll see you guys at the rehearsal," and walked out the door with Billy.

We left the Tequila Grill, got into Bentley's Honda—affectionately known as Lady—and started her up. Every car her family had ever owned had been given a human name, a quirky trait I liked so much that I've named all my rides ever since we started dating. Automobiles had personalities, and Lady was no different. She was like a dependable bobsled, tiny and compact with a five-speed gear shift, and she ran like a champ. I loved driving small, low-to-the-ground, manual transmission vehicles because I felt like I was in the cockpit of an aircraft, and tonight I wanted to fly.

We pulled out of the parking lot and onto K Street, headed east past Farragut Square and just north of Lafayette Square and the White House. We took a right on 14th Street just before Franklin Park and turned on the afterburners for the straight shot through the city and into Virginia. We made great time, caught mostly green lights, and I kissed my hand and then popped it on the interior lining of the car every time I blew through a yellow or red light. You know, for luck.

I could see the Washington Monument off to the right as I crossed over Constitution Avenue and started up the slightly sloped hill toward Independence Avenue. I glanced in my rear-view mirror and noticed a bunch of police cars behind me. I had no clue how long they'd been there or exactly where they'd clocked us, but an instant wave of nausea engulfed me. I knew in my gut that this wouldn't end well unless I came up with an escape plan and fast.

I instantly felt like I'd hit five stars in *Grand Theft Auto*, which produced an immediate sobering effect. My senses heightened, my heart rate elevated, and my brain synapses fired way faster than two hundred spikes per second.

"Are they after me? This isn't good. Can I lose them? How fast am I even going?" I muttered under my breath, or so I thought.

"I think you can make it to the Parkway," Billy said.

"Can DC cops follow us into Virginia?" I asked.

"I don't know, Rob, but if you get to the bridge, they might have to stop," he said.

I'd never been in an aerial combat fight before, but I knew this was exactly what it would feel like. We were more than thirty miles an hour over the speed limit in a densely populated city in a car that wasn't designed for high-speed pursuit. I cussed incessantly, barked out questions to Billy, and tried to calculate time, speed, and distance in my head to figure out if we could make it to the Virginia state line. I was wasted but still confident that I could outmaneuver the highly trained officers who were chasing me. Lady flew through the intersection as I crossed over Independence Avenue, and with the Thomas Jefferson Memorial already in sight, I felt nudged to stop. I looked at Billy, came to a screeching halt, and knew I'd just given my wife the biggest "I told you so" moment of our young marriage.

Those cops—a group of charged-up police officers—had been chasing us for the past mile, and they all wanted a piece of me. I don't know how many surrounded my car, but it was a lot. And the guns— so many guns were pointed at me. Were all those weapons necessary? Two officers ripped me out of the driver's seat and slammed me onto Lady's hood.

"Hands behind your back, hands behind your back!" one officer shouted.

"Stop resisting," another yelled as they pressed my face further into the hood.

"I'm not!" I shouted back, getting more pissed by the second.

I've always wondered what my arrest would have looked like on an episode of *Cops*. Would it have been good enough for a greatest hits compilation? Was I snarky, charming, or a bit of a douche? Would I have embarrassed or even disgraced myself and my family? Probably the latter.

Everyone started to calm down, and all the officers started asking questions:

"Do you know how fast you were going?"

"Why didn't you stop?"

"How much have you had to drink?"

"Do you know how many red lights you ran?"

"Didn't you see us behind you?"

"You could have killed someone!"

The barrage felt endless. And I didn't have any answers. I was pretty messed up, and deep down, I knew I was wrong and completely at fault. But I wasn't going down without a fight.

"You could have shot me!" I yelled.

"I got your name," I said. (I didn't.)

"I know people," I shouted. (I didn't.)

"You just physically assaulted me." (I deserved it.)

"I've only had two beers." (Not true.)

"Hope you enjoyed being a cop because it's over for you." (It wasn't.)

The only person whose life was about to change was mine. I took the field sobriety test and was confident that I'd aced it. They stuffed me in the back of the patrol car, while two officers in the front seat berated me.

I wonder if there's a way to get out of this cruiser, I thought, *because then I can jump off the 14th Street Bridge, plunge into the dark waters of the Potomac River, and swim to freedom.*

But then it hit me. How cold was the water, and how far could I swim in handcuffs? Had I given them my name or address? If I had, wouldn't they just head to the condo and arrest me again? As we looped in and out of Virginia on the George Washington Parkway and headed back into the city, the feeling of defeat engulfed my body. My last thought was, *Bentley is going to kill me.*

I'm not sure where I was processed or if they took a mugshot. They said I had to take a breathalyzer test, but I refused and asked for my attorney. I didn't have one, but they didn't know that. I wanted to hold them off as long as I could, hoping my blood alcohol content would fall far enough, fast enough to get me out of this nightmare.

An officer finally came into the holding area and said I could make one phone call. "You should probably call that attorney of yours," he joked.

It was after 2:00 a.m. I didn't know where Billy was being held, and I sure didn't know a single attorney to call. Bentley would be livid. I stared into space for a long minute, picked up the desk phone, and called my wife.

"Hey," I sheepishly said.

"What number is this? Where are you calling me from?" she asked groggily.

"I think I'm in Southeast DC—like a district police station," I said.

"I KNEW IT!" she shot back.

"Hang on. It wasn't my fault. I got popped for speeding, but it's not a big deal. I just need you to come down and bail me out," I said

"You were drunk hours ago, and you're drunk now. I told you not to go, and I'm not coming to get you," she said and hung up the phone.

That sucked. I didn't know it then, but that had been my only chance. No more calls. No redial. No begging for help. The processing officer smirked and escorted me to my cell.

I SAT ON OUR GREEN-AND-WHITE STRIPED COUCH and thumbed through the yellow pages. I had to figure out how to get out of this mess. I couldn't call my boss or anyone at work for obvious reasons, and I sure couldn't call my dad because he'd say, "You got yourself into this, and you'll have to get yourself out." The only thing he would want to know was whether I'd taken care of my business and kept my job, but it was way too early to answer either of those questions.

I sifted through page after page of attorneys with no discernible way to distinguish any of them from another, when my buddy, Mike, who was always down to grab a drink or bug out to an O's game, provided a vital connection. His dad was a judge and had a shortlist of contacts who took on cases in the district that involved extenuating circumstances. I couldn't stomach that I'd been lumped into that category. I faced multiple charges, hefty fines and fees, and my Virginia driver's license would likely be suspended, not to mention that I faced an alcohol evaluation. I needed an experienced lawyer who could help me navigate the system.

Mike's dad introduced me to an ex-federal prosecutor, who'd already reviewed my case. First, he wanted to hear my side of the story to determine if there were any mitigating factors that would help him defend me. My attorney didn't mince words. He said that I faced some serious charges, and then he proceeded to list them.

"For starters, they got you for speeding. That's ticket number one, but they clocked you doing more than thirty miles an hour over the speed limit, so you were also charged with aggravated reckless driving. They hit you with a third ticket for failure to stop after being signaled by police, and then you got the big one—the DUI charge, too. And it looks like they tagged you for an open container as well," my attorney, a former Marine, said.

"That one's not mine. The open container," I said.

"Well, the police charged you with it. The report says there was an open beer can on the floor."

"Again, not mine. That was Billy's beer. My passenger," I said.

He seemed a little put out in that moment. I faced four very serious charges with possible jail time attached to two or possibly three of the citations, and I was upset about the one misdemeanor. It turned out that Billy, who had a front row seat to that night's show, told the cops that it was my beer, not his.

"Sorry, Rob," Billy later confessed. "They were cuffing you, and I thought, *What's one more ticket in the whole scheme of things?* You were already in so much trouble."

"I'll take your case as a favor to Mike's dad," my attorney said. "You can leave a check with my secretary on your way out."

"I have to keep my license," I said, "or I'm screwed."

"I can help," he said.

We stood up, I shook his hand and thanked him profusely, and he said, "I'll see you in court." I desperately needed someone who could help solve my problems, and I'd found the man. Imagine Harvey Keitel's character, The Wolf, in *Pulp Fiction,* and you get the picture.

Court day had arrived. My attorney and I met about fifteen minutes before my appearance in front of the judge. My ability to work and perhaps my very freedom were on the line. My attorney said that there had been changes to the district's DUI limits. The old blood alcohol level limit was .10 percent, but a new law dropped it down to .08 percent, which cracked open a door that gave judges increased sentencing flexibility for a few months. Because of this change, my attorney had negotiated a deal with the prosecution that would allow my judge to significantly reduce my sentence when he rendered his opinion.

What I took away from that conversation was that I would be enrolled in a district-sponsored diversion program. I could keep my license, but I'd have to attend a group educational seminar, typically held on a Saturday, which would cost me roughly $300. It could last up to ten hours. I thought, *That's a number I can live with.*

We entered the courtroom and stood near the back to wait for our case to be called. I scanned the packed room, hoping to see at least one or two people called in front of the judge first who would make me look better. I'd identified a few potential candidates that might agitate the judge, when the bailiff bellowed, "Next case. The District of Columbia versus Robert Hornak."

My attorney and I approached the defendant's table, while the DA remained at the plaintiff's table and rummaged through his towering stack of cases.

"It's my understanding that both sides have come to a pre-trial agreement on this case. Is that correct?" the judge asked.

"Yes, Your Honor," said my attorney.

"Yes," agreed the DA.

"Good. I will defer sentencing until Mr. Hornak completes the diversion program. He will be allowed to keep his driver's license in the interim if he continues to progress through the program. Upon successful completion, he will return to my court and make a formal request to dismiss this case. Mr. Hornak, do you agree to these terms as I have presented them?"

"Yes, sir," I replied.

"Excellent. My bailiff will take you back for processing and program selection," he said.

The judge slammed down the gavel, and in a matter of three minutes, all my worries about losing my license and, thus, my job were erased. I wanted to high-five my attorney in the courtroom. This was a victory no matter how you sliced it. I got to keep my license and go to a one-day class—easy peasy. I thanked him repeatedly as we exited the courtroom.

"You really saved my bacon," I said.

"You're welcome, but this is as far as I can go," he stated.

"I don't know what to say. Thank you again."

"You've been assigned to a case worker tied to the diversion program. She'll handle everything from here," he said.

"Will I see you again?"

"Yes, at the final hearing, once you complete the program," he answered.

"Great, see you in a few weeks," I said as I opened the door to enter the next waiting room.

I felt like I was at a DMV for adult delinquents. Once sentenced, those who weren't going straight to jail were escorted into a cramped waiting area. They told us to take a seat. While still basking in my victory, they called my name.

"Hornak," a middle-aged woman with greying hair called.

"Here," I replied, giving her a half wave as I stood up from my chair.

"Do you understand my role in this process?" she asked as she led me to her cubicle. "I'll determine the specific program details that you'll be required to complete."

"Actually, my attorney already put a deal together with the DA," I stated.

"Your attorney has no jurisdiction when it comes to program details. His arrangement with the DA was to get you into this program—nothing more," she huffed back.

"He told me I could take a class on a Saturday," I said.

"Honey, did you get that in writing?" she quipped.

"He said I could do a Saturday," I stated again as we both sat down at her desk.

"We've reviewed your case, Mr. Hornak, and you are not eligible for the Saturday diversion class," she said. "In fact, I'm not even sure how he got you into this program at all. You've been assigned to a twenty-six-week diversion program during which time you will abstain from all drugs and alcohol. You'll submit to a weekly urine test, which will be observed by an employee of the program. Should you miss a class or test positive for any banned substances, you'll be sent back before the judge, will lose your license, and be re-sentenced."

I was numb. This couldn't be right. They had the wrong guy. The wrong paperwork. After a lengthy pause, I said, "Are you sure that's for me? What happened to my Saturday class?"

"You're not eligible for that program, Mr. Hornak. The arresting officer's report said that they pulled you out of the car at gunpoint following a high-speed pursuit and that you were verbally abusive to everyone at the scene," she stated.

"Yes, ma'am," I said. "That's true, and I'm terribly sorry about that. My wife and I had a fight earlier that night, and I was racing home to mend some fences."

"Well, it does look like you were racing," she said sarcastically. "It was also reported that you passed the majority of their roadside tests."

"The reverse alphabet tripped me up," I said jokingly. "That's a good thing though, right?"

"For most people, but not for you. You see, your breathalyzer wasn't administered until an hour after your arrest, and you blew almost twice the legal limit," she said.

"OK," I replied, waiting for the blade to drop.

"You see, Mr. Hornak, we believe you're a chronic drinker and have developed a high degree of alcohol tolerance. We think you're a threat to the road," she said.

I still thought I could wiggle free. "But I work in all the area hospitals and coach a youth soccer team. I don't have time to go to all those classes."

"Then you won't like this part either, Mr. Hornak. You must also attend 104 Alcoholics Anonymous (AA) classes over the next six months to coincide with your coursework. You must turn in your AA paperwork each week to your program manager. Should you fail to complete any portion of this process, you will lose your license and go back in front of the judge."

"You've got to be kidding me," I blurted out.

"Do you accept the requirements as I have presented them to you? Failure of any one of these stipulations will end your participation in the program."

The meeting ended, and what seemed like a slam-dunk victory twenty minutes earlier had turned into an absolute nightmare. I felt betrayed. Could I appeal this? Was there anything in between Saturday school and all these drunk classes, piss tests, and AA meetings?

I went to my first diversion class, signed in, and an intimidating man followed me to the bathroom. He stood inches away and watched me fill a plastic urine cup. He didn't know this wasn't the first time I'd had someone in my face while I was taking a leak. Sure, this level of testing should be required in prison, or I would have understood it a little better if I'd been busted for drugs, but they sentenced me to this personal intrusion because I was a deft driver and could handle my alcohol. I was sure they'd hit me harder than usual because I'd told the two cops who drove the squad car that I'd memorized their names and would report them for assault. I gutted my way through that class and went home dejected.

One day later, the thing I dreaded most was upon me. I pulled up to a building that looked a lot like an abandoned Pizza Hut for my first AA meeting. I listened, didn't say a word, asked some dude to sign my paperwork, and left as quickly as I could. That place wasn't for me, and I sat in the parking lot wondering how I could get through three more of those that week, much less the 103 meetings that remained in my sentence.

I thought I'd try a new plan. What if I could pay someone to go in my place? Everyone was supposed to be anonymous, so I felt confident I could get a friend or neighbor to go into a meeting as "Rob" and get my sheet signed. The first week, I offered $80 to anyone who would attend my four mandatory AA meetings. It was a great deal for everyone. I got out of the one thing they couldn't trace back to me, and a friend could put a little extra money in their pocket. I thought it was ingenious and didn't see the harm. But apparently others did, so I copied the signature from my first meeting and forged the rest of the attendance forms. After all, it was anonymous, so how could anyone verify who was there or who had signed the paperwork? This second iteration of my plan didn't cost me a dime and spared me from any judgmental blowback.

However, I couldn't get out of my educational classes, those urine tests, or the guy looking over my shoulder each week. And some of the videos and testimonies started to hit me hard and got me thinking about my recklessness that night. I started to wonder how I would explain my actions to Bentley if it came out that I'd lied on my paperwork four times a week. It was painfully obvious that I couldn't get out of these meetings.

Hoping for a fresh start, I found a new meeting location and prayed that no one would recognize me. For the first couple of weeks, I shared my name and told everyone I was there only to serve my sentence. My desire to rebel was bubbling under the surface, and I still felt like the court had gotten my punishment wrong. After all, I wasn't like anyone in those meetings. I just liked to drink with my friends and was always on time for work. I knew my limits and never hurt anyone. The people who shared told horrible stories about their drinking, drug abuse, and their failed relationships. I couldn't relate.

Then one day, a gentleman who had spoken a handful of times shared more of his story. He talked about his DUI and how he'd lost his driver's license and then his job. He talked about the struggles of finding new work and making enough money to support his family. He described his worsening relationship with his wife and how he drank even more to cope with all the stress that got stacked on top of him. He talked about his divorce and how he rarely got to see his little girl. His story hit me like a ton of bricks, and I felt so sorry for him. I reflected on the sheer stupidity of my actions and how I had risked my entire future with Bentley every time I got drunk and got behind the wheel. I had to change.

Alcoholics Anonymous took on a whole new meaning for me after that. I listened intently to everyone's stories. I started sharing with the group and would speak with people after the meeting ended. I realized how stupid I'd been on countless nights before my arrest, too, and how badly I could have wrecked my life or someone else's in the blink of an eye. It was the wake-up call of my lifetime.

"They disciplined us for a little while as they thought best;
but God disciplines us for our good, in order that we may share in his holiness.
No discipline seems pleasant at the time, but painful.
Later on, however, it produces a harvest of righteousness and peace
for those who have been trained by it."

—Hebrews 12:10-11 NIV

13

DA BOYS

"I get knocked down
But I get up again
You're never gonna keep me down"

—*Chumbawamba*

Bentley was born in 1969, near the infancy of successful cardiac surgery for complex congenital abnormalities. Only about 1 percent of children in the US are born with some type of congenital heart defect, and life expectancy five decades ago for those infants was tenuous at best. However, increased procedural knowledge, decreased surgical mortality, improvements in patient management, and long-term follow-up greatly improved survival rates for this subset of the population. Even with these improved outcomes, there weren't many pediatric patients who had aged into adulthood who were available to study, especially women of childbearing age. In fact, there were only a handful of cardiologists who had advanced fellowship training in both pediatric and adult cardiology.

Dr. Sutherland was one of those physicians, but his practice was in Atlanta, and we were ten hours away in Alexandria. A year earlier, I'd taken a job with a company that specialized in aortic and pulmonary valve transplants. They harvested donor saphenous veins and repurposed them as cardiac bypass grafts. After a few phone calls to some key physicians I worked with, we found our new cardiologist.

When we had our consultation with Dr. Morton Kalus, we were entertaining the idea of starting a family, so he advised that while a pregnancy was possible, it would need to be closely monitored. Furthermore, he suggested that we make an appointment at Johns Hopkins University in Baltimore to undergo genetic testing. He wanted to rule out the possibility that Bentley's cardiac anomalies were anything more insidious since congenital heart defects appeared to run in families.

Bentley and I struggled with the notion that any amount of pre-determined knowledge or risk analysis would sway us from trying to have children. And to be honest, we only looked at it from a cardiac perspective. Certainly, there was a higher possibility that we could have a child born with a congenital defect, but with all the improvements in patient care, especially those related to survival, we decided it was a risk worth taking. And within a few months, Bentley took a home pregnancy test. It was positive.

Her OBGYN confirmed the pregnancy. I detailed her medical and surgical history, and we all agreed that Bentley would be monitored closely. However, as her belly quickly grew, and based on family history, she felt confident she was having twins. We had an appointment for her next follow-up, but I called to schedule an earlier visit due to Bentley's suspicion. The nurse said Bentley couldn't possibly know she was having twins and that they'd see her in a few weeks for her regularly scheduled checkup and sonogram. I wasn't pleased and immediately reached out to my friend Stanley Crossland, who organized our Monday night basketball games at O'Connell High School. I asked if he could help me out and get Bentley a sonogram.

Stan was my friend and teammate most nights, but he was also a vascular surgeon at Northern Virginia Doctors Hospital. He had all the necessary imaging equipment and confirmed Bentley was, indeed, having twins, but more specifically, twin boys. Her intuition was correct, and we were elated with the news, but I was seething mad with the OB's office for dismissing this possibility out of hand. I wanted to call and blast them immediately but decided to call my dad first. We got stuck in a traffic jam on Route 7 on our way to the condo. So we pulled over, and Bentley and I called him from a pay phone on the side of the road.

"Hey, Gramps!" I exclaimed.

"What did you say?" he asked.

"I called you Gramps. Bentley's having twins! Twin boys!" I said excitedly.

My dad was beside himself with joy and couldn't contain it on the phone. His exuberance would be completely justified as a first-time grandparent under normal conditions, but what I'd told him would bring a combination of elation and relief for the entire Hornak family. I was the last male descendant of our Slovak line, and while I never felt pressured or carried any emotional baggage to preserve our family's lineage, the significance of having not one, but two, male heirs to carry on our name was not lost on me.

My next, less pleasant call was to the OB's office. While I'm sure they received calls daily from expectant mothers seeking early ultrasound scans, Bentley wasn't your run-of-the-mill patient.

"Hey, this is Robert Hornak, Bentley's husband. I tried calling two days ago to schedule an appointment because she believes she's having twins."

"Yes, sir. I remember, but your next sonogram is still a few weeks away. You can talk to the doctor then," she said.

"Well, what if I knew with 100 percent certainty that Bentley was having twins? Would you bring her in for an appointment then?" I said in the snarkiest tone I could muster.

"Now, sir, how could you possibly know that?" she said, talking down to me like I was a child.

"I'm actually looking at a picture of my twin boys right now," I arrogantly stated.

It was the greatest poker hand I'd ever played in my life and, boy, did it ruffle some feathers. I was on the phone with the nurse and then the doctor within seconds, and they both wanted the answer to the same question. And I wanted to have a little fun at their expense.

"Who did this for you?" they both asked.

"Just a basketball buddy," I said.

I ultimately told them that I played basketball with Dr. Crossland at least once a week and that he'd done this as a favor for Bentley and me. I gave them all the details from her sonogram and used the situation to emphasize that I'd go to any length to ensure my wife's health and that of our boys.

In the subsequent weeks, we coordinated care between her OB, cardiologist, and an excellent cardiac surgeon who agreed to be on standby should anything catastrophic happen during delivery. As the boys grew, Bentley's heart was under greater stress, and there were some discussions about protecting her health, yet she marched on. On one visit in the third trimester, both boys weighed in at over six pounds each, and they told us Bentley wouldn't make it full term because she'd be at risk for a stroke or worse. But she soldiered on. With her due date a month away and both boys still growing, the doctors put her on bed rest.

Our Virginia friends came to the rescue in the weeks leading up to the births. They visited with Bentley, brought her lunch or a chocolate milkshake, and helped her pass the time. I made Philly Cheesesteak runs to Jerry's Subs and Pizza at all hours of the day and night and probably put on more baby weight than she did.

At thirty-eight weeks, the doctors said it was time to induce. Bentley's mom picked up our sister-in-law and nephew, and they all made the four-state drive to northern Virginia. On the day of delivery, my dad hustled to the airport and boarded a flight. When Bentley went into labor on that Tuesday afternoon, the waiting room was full of our friends and family.

The boys were born at Alexandria Hospital and arrived a little after 9:00 p.m. Cade was first and weighed in at 8.7 pounds, and one minute later, Davis was born and weighed 7.9 pounds. That's 16.6 pounds of baby that Bentley carried to full term without a single complication. I came out of the operating room, saw all those faces, and a wave of pure joy rushed over me. Bentley was fine, and both boys were healthy. That was all that mattered.

After a bit of a wait, everyone got to meet Cade and Davis, including my dad, who got to hold his grandsons for the first time. That was perhaps the happiest I'd ever seen him, when he shouted out "Da Boys!"

"It will be like a woman suffering the pains of labor.
When her child is born,
her anguish gives way to joy
because she has brought a new baby into the world."

—John 16:21 NLT

14

SUICIDE SEASON

"Everyone you meet is fighting a battle you know nothing about.
Be kind. Always."

—*Robin Williams*

I t was the most ominous and eerie feeling I'd ever felt.

"Paging Robert Hornak. Please pick up the nearest airport courtesy telephone for a very important message."

My heart sank. I'd just gotten off my flight from South Carolina and stepped into the Charlotte Douglas Airport when I heard that message broadcast over the loudspeakers. Had something happened to my wife or the twins? Bentley and the boys had dropped me off two hours earlier at the Myrtle Beach International Airport. They were going to spend the week with her brother, sister-in-law, and their one-year-old son, while I was in Phoenix attending my National Sales Meeting for Boston Scientific. Expecting to hear terrible news, I sprinted through the airport and looked for a white phone.

"Hello! Hello! Anyone there?" I shouted as I picked up the first courtesy phone I found.

"Yes, sir. How can I help you?" the operator asked.

"I just heard my name over the airport paging system. I'm Robert Hornak. Is everything OK?" I asked.

"You need to call your sister. She's been trying to reach you and left a number."

As the panic I felt over what might have happened to Bentley, Cade, or Davis waned, I still felt mild trepidation. The operator had given me the number for my aunt and uncle in Birmingham, Alabama. I found a bank of pay phones, pulled out my calling card, and dialed the number. My sister picked up.

"Everything OK?" I asked.

"I need to tell you that Pops has died." My mind went blank.

Completely stunned, I said, "What?"

"I just spoke to the police department in Atlanta, and they said he's dead."

"When? How?" I retorted.

"The officer said they found him last night on a security sweep. He was in his car, and there was a fire. They identified his body at the morgue this morning. Someone needs to go there to officially identify the body and pick up his belongings," she said.

"Last night? Why are they just calling now? Fire? How does the coroner know they even have the right person?" I asked, peppering her with questions.

Emily said, "The officer gave me the number for the county morgue and said for you to call with any questions."

"OK. I'll call right now and figure out how to get to Atlanta," I stammered, then hung up the phone.

My dad was an intimidating man who owned every room he walked into. He was the son of a Slovakian immigrant, stood 6 feet, 5 inches, played sports throughout his childhood, and later excelled at both varsity basketball and golf at Marquette University. After college, he enlisted in the military, went through OCS, Jump, and Ranger schools, got shot while on a reconnaissance patrol in Vietnam, was evacuated to Japan to recover from his wounds, and was awarded a

Purple Heart and Bronze Star with the "V" device for heroism in combat—all before he turned twenty-six years old.

I picked up the pay phone again and called the number Emily had given me. I spoke to an officer with the Cobb County Police Department who, for the most part, echoed what I'd already learned. He said a tip had come into 911 about a burning car in a hotel parking deck somewhere in Smyrna, Georgia. He said the fire happened the night before in the bottom level of an empty garage and that both police and fire trucks had been dispatched to the scene. When they arrived, the car was already engulfed in flames. He confirmed that my dad was the only one in the vehicle.

None of this made any sense. A burning car? Sunday night? At a hotel one exit from his apartment? Nothing added up. My dad and I had spoken on the phone just three days ago, and our conversation seemed normal and upbeat. He always wanted to know how Da Boys were doing and loved hearing every update and all the funny stories. We talked about Bentley, how she was holding up, and if she was getting any sleep. We briefly discussed the Hawks' overtime win against the 76ers and Marquette's victory over Southern Mississippi. As we said goodbye, I told him I'd call again on Sunday when we all got to Myrtle Beach. There wasn't anything unusual about our call.

The conversation with the officer continued. "How quickly can you get to Atlanta?" he asked.

"I'll try to get on the next flight or rent a car," I said.

"You'll need to go straight to the medical examiner's office and identify your dad's remains," he said. "It has to be you, not your mom or sister."

"What are you saying?" I was completely befuddled by his comments and frankly still trying to understand what I'd learned over the last five minutes.

"The burns your dad sustained cover his entire body. We could only identify him through dental records and a few items that were still intact in his wallet. It's important that you take care of this and not your family," he said emphatically. He gave me the name, number, and address for the coroner's office in Marietta and said he was sorry.

It was still very early Monday morning. Flights were full, and my only way to get to Atlanta quickly was in a rental car. I set off on the four-hour drive from the Charlotte airport to the Cobb County Medical Examiner's Office. I had a portable cell phone and called Bentley to let her know what had happened.

The drive was filled with equal parts shock and denial. I'd heard what they told me, but the sequence of events didn't make sense to me. In fact, I couldn't comprehend that my dad's entire body had been burned in a hotel parking deck and was now completely unrecognizable. As I replayed those thoughts, it dawned on me that I hadn't called his brother or sister. What would I say to them, and what would I discover when I got to the morgue or his apartment?

The thing that connected my dad and me the most was our mutual love of basketball. Some of my favorite memories as a kid involved going to NBA games with him and his friend, Marvin, who had season tickets right behind the Atlanta Hawks' bench. I got to meet players like Dominique Wilkins, Tree Rollins, Dan Roundfield, Spud Webb, and my dad's friend from Marquette, Doc Rivers, but frankly, I simply enjoyed spending time with my dad. Out of all my trips to the Omni, I vividly remember two games because of what happened off the court.

Pizza at the Omni was my absolute favorite meal as a kid, so getting a slice or two at the game was often the high point of the night. Once, when I was ten or eleven, my dad gave me a $20 bill and told me to grab a whole pie. I took the cash and sprinted into the concourse to find the nearest stand. I paid for the large pizza and was headed back to our seats when I fumbled the monstrous box and watched helplessly as the pizza slid out of the cardboard container and landed face down on the floor.

I picked up the crust as fast as I could, tossed it back into the box, and then used the side of my hand to slide along the concourse floor to scoop up as much cheese as I could. I set the box on top of the nearest trash can and tried my best to evenly spread that massive gob of cheese back across the eighteen-inch pizza. It looked disgusting, but what was I supposed to do? When I finally made it back to our seats, I sheepishly handed my dad the box as if nothing had happened. He popped the lid open, looked down, grabbed a slice, and dug in. I expected the worst, but we sat together and ate our mutilated, germ-infested pizza and watched the rest of the game.

My other favorite Omni memory occurred a couple of months before we packed up and moved to Charleston. My dad and I were sitting in Marvin's good seats near the bench, watching a loud, unruly fan two rows behind us berate the players and referees. He was a wobbly drunk and made everyone around him uncomfortable because of his foul language. My dad got madder by the minute, and I knew this drunk had lit the fuse to a stick of dynamite.

My dad knew a lot of regular-season ticket holders in our section who were just like his friend, and the group's collective effort to politely ask the unruly fan to sit down and be quiet had failed. In fact, that guy got more boisterous as the game went on. Everyone wanted a solution. There was no security in sight, so my dad stood up, turned to his right to face this pugnacious man, pointed a finger at him, and in his most forceful tone said, "Stop ruining the game for everyone, or I'm coming up there."

It felt like the earth had stopped rotating. It was so quiet. I've often wondered if the players on the court slowed down and turned to investigate what was going on. I don't remember this guy's response, but like a cheetah launching itself at a gazelle, my dad came out of his seat in a slow-motion blur, grabbed the man's neck with his right hand, and put him in a Darth Vader-like chokehold. He pinned him forcefully against the back of the plastic seat and used his left hand to motion for security. The fans erupted in cheers, not for one of Dominique's high-flying slams but for my dad, who was strangling a man with impunity in the stands. Everyone stood up, causing a ripple effect that spread into the neighboring sections. It looked like a tsunami of spectators had risen from the epicenter and then fanned outward from this one-sided clash. The man struggled like a fish out of water, and he gasped for air as his beer rhythmically splashed all over him each time my dad pressed him deeper into his seat.

Two security guards rushed down the stairs to intervene, and I thought for a moment they would tackle my dad, but as they approached, a group of spectators pointed at the man being choked and shouted, "You want him!"

The first time I saw the film *Gladiator,* I had an immediate flashback to that game when I heard the line, "Win the crowd and you'll win your freedom."

That night, my dad won the crowd, and it was like sitting with a celebrity for the rest of the game. Folks patted him on the back, thanked him for shutting that guy up, and even random strangers gave him high-fives on their way to the bathroom. What a game!

I PULLED INTO THE PARKING LOT at the Cobb County Medical Examiner's Office and went in. I gave the person at the desk my name and asked for the coroner.

"I'm Robert. I'm here about my dad."

"Thank you for coming," the examiner replied. "We have some items to show you."

He pulled my dad's burnt wallet from a plastic bag. Inside were three personal items, two of which were slightly charred photos of his twin grandsons taken at the hospital after they were born. Each photo had an inscription of their full name and date of birth.

None of this seemed real. "Can I see my dad?" I asked.

"I'm going to advise against it," he said.

"What do you mean? Why can't I see him?" I asked.

"Robert, your dad was completely burned over his entire body. The fire was so hot that it melted parts of the car. I've seen a lot of terrible things, and trust me, you don't want to see your dad like this. If you go in there, the image will haunt you the rest of your life."

I struggled with the decision for about five minutes, asked additional questions, but eventually relented to his better judgment. The office had identified my dad through his dental records, but they weren't 100 percent sure about the cause of death. They thought it was a clear-cut case of suicide by vehicular carbon monoxide poisoning, but the fire made things a little fuzzier.

The examiner said that the first responders didn't find a suicide note, but they also didn't suspect foul play. They surmised that due to his location on the bottom floor of the parking garage, which had zero ventilation, coupled with how long the car had been spewing out carbon monoxide, an ignition fire had been created, which burned for an extended period because it wasn't immediately discovered by security.

I didn't call anyone after I left the coroner's office. I drove around aimlessly, not sure what to do. My dad's car had been impounded, and I didn't have a key to his apartment. He'd moved from Texas back to Atlanta a few years earlier, but I didn't visit often and never got a key. We'd never discussed his daily life. I knew a little bit about his work but nothing about his neighbors. Our relationship was relatively superficial. The most serious subjects were off limits, except for my DUI arrest, my job, and Bentley's and the boys' health.

I pulled into his apartment complex, parked in front of the leasing office, and gathered my thoughts. I introduced myself to the property manager, explained the situation, and handed him my driver's license and a copy of the preliminary police report. I begged him to let me into the apartment before my mom and sister arrived and saw who knows what.

I'd been to my dad's apartment a handful of times over the years. I'd crash with him if I came in town to see Bentley when we were dating, catch a Braves game, or when Atlanta hosted the 1996 Olympics. In fact, one of the best nights of my life was in this very complex. I knew I wanted to marry Bentley for a while and had already bought an engagement ring. I worked out a cover story to go to Atlanta two weeks later, made reservations for dinner at an upscale restaurant, and reserved a quiet table at our favorite dessert bar, the original Café Intermezzo on Peachtree Street. That's where I would propose. Great plans, right?

But my flight was delayed, she couldn't get her car to start after work, and we had no way to communicate. I walked out of baggage claim an hour late, and she was nowhere to be found. She worked in the fitness center at the Ritz Carlton in Buckhead, so I called there first, but her co-workers said she'd already left. The restaurant would close soon, and my proposal plans were going up in smoke.

Another hour passed, and I was still sitting on the curb at the airport when she pulled up. We had missed our dinner reservations, and the cafe would close soon, so we headed to my dad's apartment, where I'd stay for the weekend. While random flight delays and car troubles had successfully derailed my plans, that ring was still burning a hole in my pocket, and there was no way I was going to board my flight on Sunday with it still in my possession.

We pulled up to the building. I asked if she wanted to go for a walk, which was highly out of character for me, and I'm sure she knew something was up. We crested the top of a hill and walked toward the community pool patio. We sat in a couple of lounge chairs and chatted for a bit, but I was desperate to know the answer to my question, so I proposed right then and there. It was perfect.

Now that was a distant, but happy, memory. I inserted the key in the apartment door, but I physically couldn't get myself to turn the knob. The medical examiner said he was confident beyond a shadow of a doubt that my dad took his own life, so I had no idea what I'd find when I opened the door. Turning the doorknob, I took a few steps in and felt my legs go weak.

Before that, I'd only cried two other times in my life. The first time was during the emotional ending to the father-son movie *Field of Dreams*, but not for the reason you think. I didn't cry because I remembered playing catch with my dad; I cried because we'd never done that. The other time was at the end of the movie *Major League*, the baseball comedy I mentioned before. In this film, the overmatched Indians were up against the perennially powerful Yankees in the bottom of the ninth in a 2-2 game. With two outs and a runner on second, actor Tom Berenger stepped to the plate for Cleveland. His character, Jake Taylor, was a washed-up, injury-riddled catcher who hung on to life by a thread. He was desperate for a second chance to right some wrongs.

In the final play of the film, Jake laid a bunt down the third-base line and began his hero's run to the first-base bag. Willie Mays Hayes, played by Wesley Snipes, was the runner on second, and he took off on contact. As Jake lumbered down the line as fast as he could, twenty years of pain, lost opportunities, failed relationships, and two banged-up knees covered every inch of his face and body. Jake stepped on the bag just ahead of the throw, was called safe, and then fell to his knees in agony.

That's exactly what I did that night. I fell to my knees. There was no happy ending, and in fact, the nightmare had just begun. I stopped crying, picked myself up off the floor, and scoured the apartment, looking for clues that could exonerate my dad from the suicide thesis.

It was a weird feeling to search and hope for signs of foul play. That was followed by chest-crushing guilt. My dad and I were supposed to talk the night he killed himself, but Bentley and I were still driving from Alexandria to Myrtle Beach with the boys, and I never called him. The thought that I could have saved him or convinced him to get help gnawed at me for years. I believed my failure to call led directly to his death and everyone's pain.

My dad missed a lot of my life, but he often showed up out of the blue and at some of my more notable events. I'd qualified to run in the 400m intermediate hurdles for The Citadel at the Southern Conference Track & Field Championships in Boone, North Carolina. Unbeknownst to me, my dad drove from Atlanta to watch me run that day, and it ended up being the last race of my career. We grabbed a quick bite to eat at Wendy's and joked about the twelve hours he'd ultimately spend in the car just to watch me run one lap. I'll never forget how good it was to see him there that day.

My dad never talked about the war, so I won't speculate about what might have happened to him during his time in Vietnam or if he came back with PTSD. I think most reasonable people understand that combat can affect the brain in ways that experts don't fully comprehend. Perhaps there'd been some signs of unusual behavior leading up to his death, but I realize I'm reaching for an answer I'll never get. Less than four months after Cade and Davis were born, he took his own life.

The visitation was on Thursday, and on Friday, his funeral service was at Saint Philip's Cathedral in Atlanta. I gave the eulogy, but I didn't want to share stories that everyone already knew. Yes, he was a great basketball player, a war hero, and an amazing friend to many, but everyone already knew that. I wanted to share two stories that had been private until then. So, I shared the courthouse drama surrounding my arrest at seventeen and how he may have saved my life with his tough love. Then I talked about his twelve-hour round-trip drive to see me run a single race and how I knew how much he loved me.

On that cold, dreary day at Arlington National Cemetery, almost three full weeks after he'd died, friends and family gathered around the tent and witnessed a moving military memorial, but they were also still in shock about why he'd take his own life. Anger, grief, and sadness filled the beautiful but somber ceremony that day. He was only fifty-six years old, the exact same age I am at the time of this writing. We all buried something that day—a husband, a father, a brother, a son, an uncle, and a friend. My dad decided that the entire world would be better off without him, but he couldn't have been more mistaken.

"The righteous perish, and no one takes it to heart;
the devout are taken away, and no one understands that the
righteous are taken away to be spared from evil."

—Isaiah 57:1 NIV

15

SWEET HOME ALABAMA

"They say the only constant is change."

—*Ty Burrell as Phil Dunphy in* Modern Family

I stepped off the plane in Birmingham, rented a car, and drove to meet our realtor. I'd submitted a relocation request a few weeks earlier, and it had been approved. I told our realtor that it was imperative that I find the perfect house for Bentley and the boys because Bentley did not want to move—not at all. In fact, I was struggling with the decision I'd made to pack up our lives and leave everything we'd built together in Virginia for a new, uncertain life in Alabama.

I was hoping the realtor would show me an assortment of plantation-style houses like the Southfork Ranch on the 1970s prime-time TV series *Dallas*. To soften the blow, Bentley and I agreed we wanted a large house, a bunch of dogs, and a fenced area so we could buy a few horses and let them run free on the long drive up to the property. I don't think we knew how big an acre was, but we had to find something that could accommodate all those new animals.

"Make sure it has a barn so our horses will have a place for shelter in bad weather," Bentley said as I left for the airport.

However, we couldn't afford to buy a plantation house for a whole host of reasons. And after looking at homes in six different pockets of Birmingham, I struggled to narrow it down. I was worried that what I thought would be the right community would be wrong for her and the boys. Our home in the historic section of Old Town Alexandria was priced similarly to a three- or four-bedroom home in a few of the over-the-mountain communities just outside Birmingham's city limits. And even though we were a few years away from worrying about schools, homes in those areas always sold in a day or two. My frustrations mounted, and I decided we should rent an apartment, sell our home in Alexandria, move the family south, and start a new search for a home when Bentley was here. But how would I explain this barrier to her? The biggest draw for us to make this move—that plantation house—wasn't a possibility now.

I've read that following a significant life-altering event, you should avoid making major changes since it could hinder your ability to properly adjust to the initial change. Many clinicians think it's best to focus on your physical and mental health and to reduce stress by leaning on a solid network of friends to get through those difficult moments. However, we didn't go that route. Our burgeoning happy life, wrecked by my dad's suicide and compounded further by my decision to move us closer to my mom and sister, saw us walk away from our home, our closest friends, and our entire support network—all because I felt the need to be the dutiful son. In ten months, we'd celebrated the birth of Cade and Davis, mourned the death of my dad, and uprooted everything.

We rented a three-bedroom apartment across the street from The Summit, a large outdoor mall at the crossroads of Highway 280 and Interstate 459, and only a few miles from both I-65 and I-20. For me, the location was perfect. I had access to four of the biggest roadways in the state and could easily get around for work. Bentley had a decent amount of space and a pool on the property for the boys. It was a short walk or quick drive to grocery stores, multiple restaurants, and even a movie theater. But the apartment felt sterile. It wasn't what we'd envisioned, but it gave us a lot of what we needed. Our home in Alexandria sold quickly, and my company covered the real estate commissions and all our relocation expenses, so we had a lot of flexibility when we decided where to go next.

The move south put us closer to family, but we viewed it as temporary. It felt like the right thing to do at the time and given the circumstances. My sister had graduated from high school in Charleston four years after me and went to Samford University, a private Christian university in Homewood, Alabama. By Emily's junior year, my dad had bought a townhouse for my mom in a neighboring community just a few miles away, and he'd often drive over to spend time with them on the weekends. My aunt and uncle, who'd hosted me in England all those summers ago, worked at Samford and lived in the area, as did their daughter and her family. And Bentley's parents, who lived in separate apartments just north of downtown Atlanta, were only a short two-hour drive away.

So, after eight years in Virginia, we said goodbye to all our friends to relocate to a state where neither of us had ever lived. I was going to be the rescuer who could quickly wrap up my dad's affairs and get my mom's life back on track. But here's the thing: no one had asked me to swoop in and be the hero, and I didn't foresee my mom's unwillingness to accept that my dad's suicide would change everything about the way she lived. He had always been the sole provider, and his income vanished overnight. Someone had to make sense of the disarray he left behind, but my mom was neither capable nor prepared to take on such challenges. So right or wrong, I appointed myself to fill the void.

However, a funny thing happened during that first year in Birmingham. I dove into my work and had some quick success. I cleaned up most of my dad's estate issues, and Bentley and I began to make new friends. We enjoyed the more relaxed lifestyle, with plenty of places to take the boys on outings, making it incredibly easy to make friends and feel safe. Bentley needed a community like that because I was still on the road so much for work. With all that family around, Bentley and I could get away for an occasional date night, and in those early days of parenthood, dinner and a movie once a week or so was exactly what we needed.

Halloween was approaching, and my aunt and uncle recommended that we take the boys to see all the trick-or-treaters in a small suburb of Birmingham that had everything we wanted in a community. It was roughly a fifteen-minute drive to all the major hospitals in the area, had multiple fields and playgrounds for the boys, a village with a grocery store, two gas stations, plenty of shopping, pharmacies, and restaurants. And all these places were within walking distance of an outstanding elementary school. So, on that brisk October evening, we drove to Crestline Village in Mountain Brook. It felt like something out of a Charles Dickens novel. The houses had been decorated with lights and pumpkins, families were everywhere, and kids ran from door to door in their search for candy. We knew we were home.

We never got our *Dallas* plantation, but we found the perfect place for us, a three-bedroom ranch house in the heart of the Crestline area. We needed that extra bedroom because we'd just learned that Bentley was expecting again, and this time, we were having a baby girl. Elizabeth (EB) arrived in the fall of 1999, and she changed our lives in two major ways. First, we had the obvious challenges of juggling three children under three years old, and second, Bentley's cardiologist said that this pregnancy had put such a significant strain on her heart that we had to be sure that she never got pregnant again.

The next ten years went by in a blur. We went from Barney, red wagon rides, lemonade stands, jumping on the trampoline in the back yard, slushie runs to the Chevron, and playing H.O.R.S.E. in the driveway to an overflow of homework, practices, road trips, and way too many sporting events. All three of the kids played basketball and soccer, and the boys' baseball schedule added an obscene number of games to the calendar. I juggled my work schedule and coached as many of their teams as I could. That required Bentley and me to divide and conquer, which we did well, to attend all of Cade's, Davis's, and EB's other activities. But we were also blessed with a multitude of memories from those elementary and middle-school years in Birmingham, and we built an incredible network of friends through church, school, and sports. While I didn't pay much attention to it at the time, I soon became thankful that Bentley had amassed an army of spiritual women who prayed for and looked out for each other and their children.

But it wasn't all Mai Tais and Yahtzee.

One afternoon, when I was out of town, Bentley temporarily lost vision in her left eye. She described it like an eclipse. The light faded to black from the top of the cornea to the bottom, as if someone had slowly pulled down a window shade. She said it was brief and that she soon recovered her sight. She drove herself home, didn't have any other symptoms, could see clearly again, and wasn't in any pain. Nothing like that had happened before, but we both agreed it could be serious, so she made an appointment with a local ophthalmologist for the end of that week.

Before I got home the next day, it happened again. This time, she was driving the boys home from baseball practice and had the exact same symptoms over the same short period of time. So, she pulled over and waited it out. She called the doctor's office and explained what happened, and they told us to come in first thing the next morning.

After multiple tests, a thorough eye examination, and a review of her medical history, Bentley was directed to immediately make an appointment with her cardiologist. We learned that Bentley probably had a transient ischemic attack (TIA), which is basically a mini stroke. It happens when blood flow to the brain is temporarily blocked. Six or seven major symptoms can present when a patient has a TIA, but Bentley had only one—the sudden loss of vision. The sense of urgency was palpable.

A TIA greatly increases a patient's risk for having a full-fledged stroke within the next ninety days. It's an early warning sign that the brain isn't getting enough oxygen. Symptoms of a TIA don't last long, sometimes presenting for just a few minutes and up to twenty-four hours. I called Bentley's cardiologist, explained the situation to the nurse, and got her added to the schedule the following Monday morning.

Bentley hadn't been operated on or had any kind of event since she was nine years old. And when my dad and I took her to see Dr. Sutherland, she'd gotten a relatively clean bill of health during that full cardiac workup in Atlanta. She was closely monitored during her pregnancy with the twins and again when she was carrying EB. Bentley exercised regularly, was always active with the kids, and ate well. She'd defied the odds, and most people were shocked to learn what she'd been through compared to how healthy she looked.

But her two TIAs threw us for a loop, and we needed answers. During that painfully slow week, while Bentley waited for her cardiology appointment, she had two more events, one at home and one when she was with some of her family. Her brother, who was also in the medical field, observed her fourth episode in real time and said, "Don't stroke out on me."

I took Bentley to see her cardiologist that Monday morning, and after another detailed workup, he explained that, on occasion, a single blood vessel that leads directly to the eye could become blocked and cause temporary vision loss. He went on to speculate that Bentley had an episode called *amaurosis fugax,* or more simply put, transient monocular blindness. With four such events in rapid succession and Bentley's history of heart disease, he performed a far more invasive test.

A transesophageal echocardiogram (TEE) is a study that uses sound waves to create a picture of the heart. But instead of putting a transducer on Bentley's chest, her cardiologist inserted a probe with a transducer down her esophagus, which gives a much clearer image of the heart because the sound waves don't have to pass through skin, muscle, or bone.

The prognosis wasn't terrible. Her cardiologist started her on 75 mg of Plavix, an antiplatelet therapy that stopped Bentley's blood cells from sticking together to form a clot. He gave her medication that helped lower blood pressure, taking some of the workload off her heart and arteries. He then prescribed a prophylactic antibiotic, normally used to prevent infections during routine dental work. Generally speaking, he thought her cardiac function looked good and that the new medications would quickly eliminate her TIAs. But he also said that she'd need another open-heart surgery in the not-too-distant future.

Suddenly, Bentley's health deficiencies became real again. We'd heard all the warnings through her pregnancies, yet nothing had ever happened, but these four mini-strokes, a new diagnosis, and new prescriptions set off the alarm bells. Both doctors had said that any one of those attacks could have led to catastrophic damage or a full-on stroke. She'd literally and figuratively dodged four bullets in the last seven days.

That night after the kids went to bed, Bentley and I talked about her new reality and how this crisis could have changed our entire existence. We didn't think morbid thoughts; we discussed how each day was a gift and what we really wanted to do in life before it was too late.

"If you had a bucket list, what would be number one?" I asked.

"I want to drive a Porsche on the Autobahn," she rattled off instantaneously, like it had been on the tip of her tongue her entire life.

"Jesus Christ *is* the same yesterday, today, and forever."

—Hebrews 13:8 NKJV

16

THE AUTOBAHN

"No matter how fast you're driving in Germany,
someone is driving faster."

—Tom Hanks

We had good friends who lived in London. Bentley had always wanted to visit Paris, and now that she had just revealed her big bucket-list wish, I went into full travel-agent mode and started researching Porsche facilities that were directly connected or very close to the Autobahn. The only city that made sense to target was Stuttgart, the capital of southwest Germany's Baden-Württemberg state. Porsche's headquarters, museum, and dealership were in the heart of the city. The Bundesautobahn 8 connects major German cities like Munich and Karlsruhe, is a significant east-west route, and runs directly through Stuttgart. So, I focused my attention on finding a friendly staff member at the Porsche Zentrum Stuttgart to ask if they'd let Bentley test drive one of their newest models. To me, the pitch seemed straightforward. American Porsche aficionado facing fourth open-heart surgery, looking to test drive the newest 911 on the A8 during the Christmas holiday—how could they turn us down?

I targeted a handful of individuals in the sales and marketing departments, used Google Translate to bridge the language barrier, sent my first wave of emails, and learned that almost everything in the Porsche world would be shut down during the holidays. In fact, the only place that would be open had limited hours—the new car selection shop. After a few days, a sales manager sent me a lifeline. I tried to explain what I hoped to accomplish for my wife and threw out words like Porsche lover, bucket list, top speed, and pending surgery, but I had no idea how the computer would translate any of those words or phrases.

We zeroed in on a date and time, and I made sure he understood that there was zero chance that his efforts would lead to a sale. I absolutely wanted to make this happen for Bentley but didn't want his act of kindness to come back and bite him if his manager became part of the discussion and determined I had strung him along. With everything lined up in Stuttgart, I could organize the rest of our trip.

We started in London, and it was magical. We stayed with Tom and Julie, old friends from Virginia who lived in an apartment at Kensington Palace Green, part of the Kensington Palace grounds that had been home to Princess Diana. We rode all over London in double-decker buses to see the holiday lights, shopped on Oxford and Regent streets, checked out Big Ben, and saw the Christmas tree in Trafalgar Square. The boys and I rode the London Eye, and they got to experience the bungee trampoline on the River Thames.

Tom and Julie even babysat the kids so Bentley and I could ring in the New Year at a West London nightclub, Cherry Jam, owned by Ben Watt, half of the musical duo Everything but the Girl. I had emailed Ben two weeks earlier and asked if he was playing anywhere in the city over the holidays. He informed me there weren't any tour dates scheduled but was kind enough to invite us to his private New Year's celebration.

We left London on New Year's Day and took the Eurostar high-speed train bound for Paris. I never made it to France during my three summers in Europe and had no idea where to stay, but I was a Marriott guy and wanted to impress Bentley with an exquisite hotel, so I booked us at The Renaissance Paris La Défense, about four miles northwest of the city center. We exited the station located just below the Grande Arche monument, a 360-foot-high cube that was designed by a Danish duo and constructed in the heart of Europe's largest purpose-built business district, and arrived at our hotel much later than planned.

On the train ride, we told the kids that the first thing we would do upon arrival would be to visit the Eiffel Tower, so after checking in at the hotel, we dropped our bags off in the room and got right back on the Metro headed to the Trocadéro station.

"OK, gang. I've never been to Paris before, and I don't know a single word of French," I said.

"You know cinq," Davis said. "That means five."

"And you know how to say bonjour and baguette," Cade added.

"Yes, correct," I replied. "I do know a few words, but I don't know anyone in this city, and the healthcare system here is not the same as back home. I don't want to have to take anyone to the ER while we are here, so stick close to your mom and me and keep your head on a swivel. Got it?"

"Got it," they all said.

The Palais de Chaillot was a building at the top of the Trocadéro overlooking the Seine and just opposite the Eiffel Tower, and the view from the esplanade was simply stunning. Cade, Davis, and EB had seemingly forgotten our entire pep talk on the Metro ride into Paris and were running and chasing each other all over the square. It was late in the evening. There was only a smattering of people around us, and the kids were having a blast. But in one split second, our cheerful mood was flipped on its head.

EB was chasing her brothers and snagged her unzipped jacket on one of the black metal bars surrounding a large air vent, knocking her off her feet and twisting her body toward the pigeon spikes on top.

It was a direct hit, and the sharp spear tip missed her eye socket by a couple of centimeters and split her temple open with a one-inch gash right next to her left brow. The bleeding was instantaneous and poured down her face. There was so much blood that I honestly couldn't tell where she'd been punctured. I scooped her up and ran to the last open street vendor a few hundred feet away. They gave me paper towels and wrote the name of a nearby hospital on a piece of paper, which I then handed to our cab driver.

He took us to the Necker–Enfants Malades Hospital, which I later learned was the world's first children's hospital, founded in 1802. It was 10:00 p.m. on New Year's Day, and the hospital looked deserted. We ran in through the emergency entrance and saw one woman sitting at the front desk and a ghost town in the waiting room. The paper towels and my shirt were soaked in blood, so without saying a word or explaining the situation, she quickly paged the emergency team overhead and rushed us down to a vacant procedure room. A few seconds later, a young doctor and nurse ran into the room.

I frantically tried to explain what happened in English, and he tried to respond in French, but neither of us knew what the other was saying. The doctor grabbed a bottle of saline solution and cleaned her forehead thoroughly, but it was still bleeding. He opened a syringe pack with local anesthetic and began numbing the area while the nurse kept rinsing the blood off with saline and holding pressure with a towel.

The doctor opened a drawer, pulled out a suture kit, and was clearly going to try to close her wound with a needle and synthetic thread. I immediately stopped him and tried to ask if they had a liquid adhesive, which is a non-invasive alternative to skin sutures or staples. He had no idea what I was saying, and I couldn't remember the name of the J&J product. There was no easy way to mime "skin closure adhesive," so I pointed to myself with two fingers and said, "doctor."

I knew the hospital had to have the surgical adhesive somewhere in the ER, so I rummaged through drawers as quickly as I could. The nurse kept pressure on EB's temple while the doctor watched me rapid-fire every drawer in the room until I found it. As soon as he saw the box, we were on the same page. The Dermabond only took a minute to apply and dry but had the same effect as stitches. The glue was transparent so we could still see the wound. It was a miracle she didn't lose her eye. The young doctor placed two butterfly bandages across the cut horizontally, and that was that. We shook hands, did a lot of smiling and nodding, and I carried EB back out into the waiting room to see her mom and brothers.

The next day, we visited The Louvre and got to stand in front of the *Venus de Milo*, a marble sculpture that was carved by Alexandros 150 years before Christ. And of course, we saw the *Mona Lisa*, a portrait by Italian artist Leonardo da Vinci considered by many to be one of the best-known masterpieces of the Italian Renaissance. We took pictures in front of the Arc de Triomphe, walked up and down the Champs-Élysées, and visited the Palace of Versailles, the former royal residence commissioned by King Louis XIV about ten miles west of Paris.

On our last night in the city, we went ice skating on the Eiffel Tower, and the next morning, we piled into a BMW hatchback that I rented from Hertz. I thought driving through Paris and seeing the French and German countryside would be an extraordinary opportunity, but I couldn't have been more wrong. It was raining when we left the hotel and snowing by the time we left the rental car facility. I knew I'd made a terrible decision when I missed my first turn and dropped onto one of the busiest roads in the city. I couldn't read a single road sign, and at that time, there wasn't a Google Maps or Waze app to bail me out. So we kept moving forward toward Stuttgart and Bentley's date with destiny.

We walked into the Porsche dealership the next morning, a few minutes before our 11:00 a.m. appointment, and were greeted at the door by a brand ambassador. I introduced myself, and she said the salesman would be with us soon. It was the most beautiful showroom I'd ever seen. Millions and millions of dollars' worth of luxury cars were parked in front of us. As she walked around the shop with the kids, Bentley grinned from ear to ear.

"*Guten Morgen, Herr Hornak. Ich bin Sebastian,*" the salesman said.

"Hi, I'm Robert. I'm very sorry, but I don't speak German."

"We all wondered about that. Your emails were well written for an American, and we thought you knew the language," he joked.

"Thank you for setting this up for my wife. She's so excited to drive today," I said.

"Oh, we have a slight problem. Our lawyers have informed us that since your wife is so sick, we cannot let her drive one of our vehicles today," he said.

"I don't understand. She only has heart issues but gets around just fine. She drives every day at home," I said.

"I'm sorry, Mr. Hornak, but she will not be able to drive a car today," he firmly stated.

I was devastated. I was only mere seconds away from pulling off the biggest, most amazing surprise of our entire marriage, and the rug had been pulled out from underneath me. This was my bucket list gift to Bentley. Clearly, something I'd said about her health in my emails had been lost in translation.

But Sebastian continued, "We all felt so bad about your wife's condition and the fact that you came all the way from the United States, so we arranged for one of our performance test drivers to take her out on the Autobahn today. We hope you will find this satisfactory."

So we walked over to Bentley and introduced her to Jörg, her assigned driver for the day.

"What do you mean, my driver?" she asked.

"You told me this was the number one item on your bucket list, so today's the day," I said.

Jörg had arranged to take her out in a Porsche 997, a sixth-generation 911 Carrera S coupé that had only been available for a few months. He said there was room in the back for "*zwei kinder,*" so Cade, Davis, and EB drew straws for the two open seats. Davis and I stayed behind for that great adventure, and while I knew I couldn't buy Bentley a Porsche that day, I was completely at peace knowing that she was having the time of her life racing up and down the Autobahn.

"Teach us to realize the brevity of life,
so that we may grow in wisdom."

—Psalms 90:12 NLT

17

CHASE FIELD

"I've circled him a couple of times—
but never had the opportunity to touch him."

—*Jason Bateman on* Smartless

With twin boys, it's natural that they share a lot of the same interests, and ours were no different. They shared the same classroom until the fifth grade, had the same friend group, and played the same sports on the same teams. It was a built-in buddy system, but Bentley and I also wanted Cade and Davis to have their individual collections of memories, so we purposely planned trips that would take them, and EB, in different directions.

Bentley always enjoyed taking the kids on a relaxing weekend trip to the Southern Cross Ranch in Madison, Georgia. It offered bed and breakfast accommodations, home-cooked meals with family-style seating, and a herd of horses to ride, and it was considered one of the largest ranches in the southeast. She considered it her home away from home. I, on the other hand, preferred sightseeing and catching a baseball or basketball game in a new city, no matter which child was traveling with me.

One time, Davis and I traveled to Dallas to see the Mavericks take on the Memphis Grizzlies. He was able to meet Dirk Nowitzki, Jason Kidd, Rick Carlisle, and Mark Cuban before the game. We ate lunch at Maple & Motor, where we very randomly met and had lunch with Eric Stonestreet, who played Cameron Tucker on *Modern Family*, and we followed that up with a tour of the Book Depository building, where President John F. Kennedy was assassinated.

EB asked for an entirely different trip. She wanted to visit New York City, see a Broadway play, do some shopping, and ice skate at the Rockefeller Center. We targeted Harold Pinter's *No Man's Land* on Broadway, starring both Sir Ian McKellen and Sir Patrick Stewart, but we missed the play entirely. After we skated, we stumbled into the standby tickets and the waitlist line for *Saturday Night Live*. EB's age prevented us from seeing *SNL* that night, but as luck would have it, she got to meet and get a picture with the *Lord of the Rings* actor as Sir Ian exited the theater that cold, snowy night. We wrapped up the long weekend with a Knicks game at Madison Square Garden, and EB successfully spent her entire trip allowance shopping in Times Square.

Yet another memorable weekend was when Cade and I traveled out west. His favorite NBA team, the Phoenix Suns, was scheduled to take on Steph Curry and the Golden State Warriors. I'd spoken to a very sweet lady with the team the week before, who agreed to escort us to the Suns' tunnel before the game. This allowed Cade to meet Suns' great Tom Chambers, newcomer Robin Lopez, and former Duke legend Grant Hill. Sadly, he missed meeting his basketball hero, two-time MVP Steve Nash, by mere seconds.

That same weekend, just down the street, the Los Angeles Dodgers were in town to play the Arizona Diamondbacks. Cade's all-time favorite baseball player, Luis Gonzalez, played left field for the D-Backs, and my favorite player, Greg Maddux, was scheduled to start for the visiting "Boys in Blue" in the Friday night matchup. The game lasted over five hours and ended when Orlando Hudson hit a two-run homer in the bottom of the fifteenth inning to give the Diamondbacks the 9-7 walk-off victory.

Cade didn't get to speak with Luis Gonzalez that weekend, but I have three of the most incredible and generous stories about "Gonzo" and my son that would absolutely amaze you. Luis repeatedly proved to be one of the most kind-hearted athletes I've ever met.

Saturday morning, while on a tour of Chase Field, Cade dropped off a letter for Greg Maddux at the security desk and asked the officer if he would deliver it to his locker before the game. When the gates to the stadium opened that evening, we went straight to our seats on the first base side, in between home plate and the Dodgers' dugout. Ten minutes later, during batting practice, Greg came out to speak with Cade.

"Are you Cade?" Maddux asked. "I got your note."

Cade was still young, a budding pitcher, and they had a genuine baseball conversation about changing speeds, pitch location, and how to keep a hitter off balance. It was surreal. "Mad Dog" signed a ball for Cade, a second one for Davis, and then I got to meet and chat with my baseball hero. *Sports Illustrated* stated it best on the cover of their August 14, 1995, issue when they referred to Greg as "The Greatest Pitcher You Will Ever See."

I thought to myself, *How could this day possibly get any better?*

We'd settled into our seats when the ceremonial first pitch announcement was made over the public address system in the stadium. Actor Jason Bateman walked to the front of the pitcher's mound. "Cade, do you know who that is? That's the main dude from *Arrested Development*. It's a show your mom and I used to watch." Cade was eight years old, had no clue who I was talking about, and kept looking at the signed ball that Maddux had just given him.

Jason himself did an interview on *Jimmy Kimmel Live!* where he recounted the very details of throwing out the first pitch in Phoenix, so I won't go into any great detail here. What you need to know is that Bateman is a diehard Dodgers fan who wanted to goof around with the Arizona faithful that night. He made a solid throw to the catcher at home plate and was rightfully booed as he walked to his seat.

You can hear his side of this story by searching for the video on YouTube, but as the great radio broadcaster Paul Harvey always said, "And now, the rest of the story."

Bateman took his seat between home plate and the third base dug-out, while Cade and I, for the most part, sat in seats that mirrored his on the first base side. Jason sat with a buddy, and all that kept us from meeting him were the thirteen seats across the first row of Section J, located directly behind home plate. I forgot about the game because all I wanted to do was meet Jason Bateman. The reason? It's easy. If you've ever watched an episode of *Arrested Development*, you'll remember Bateman's character, Michael Bluth, and his constant motivation to try to keep his family together. It was smart and funny and sometimes hit close to home. I completely related to his character.

I assumed I'd have to wait patiently for my big moment, but no long line of autograph seekers materialized. I recall a couple of folks who shook his hand or waved as they walked by, but it was all extremely subdued and polite. The Diamondbacks recorded the final out in the top of the second inning, and it felt like the perfect time to strike. So I grabbed Cade, and we set out to meet his first Hollywood star.

"Hey, Jason, big fan. Mind if I introduce you to my son Cade?" I asked.

"Yeah, of course," he responded. "Where are you guys from?"

"Alabama." Then I summarized everything we'd done since our arrival in Phoenix.

Bateman and I are about the same age. We had baseball in common. I loved watching movies, and he starred in them. For one brief second, I thought our conversation might be going so well that I could invite him and his buddy to grab a burger and drink at the Hard Rock Café down the street after the game. But I lost all my nerve, confident I'd look like a loon. He very politely said it sounded like an awesome trip; we shook hands again, and Cade and I headed back to our seats before the bottom of the inning started.

I'd never had a problem introducing myself to celebrities or inserting myself into an awkward situation before, if meeting a star was on the line, but I kept replaying my ridiculous one-sided conversation with Jason in my head. For starters, why didn't I ask him more questions?

Everyone knows the first rule of sales is to get the other person to talk about themselves, and I'd clearly dropped the ball. *Why didn't I ask about his favorite Dodger—or if he had any nerves when he threw the first pitch? I could have asked him to sign Cade's ticket or even a baseball.* I'd blown it, stewed in my seat over the entire incident, and hatched a new plan designed to reset the discussion.

The home half of the fifth inning ended. I grabbed Cade and the Diamondbacks logo ball we'd bought in the team store and hustled back over to Bateman's section. My anxiety percolated on the walk over, and when I get uneasy, I talk fast.

"Hey, Jason. It's us again," I said. "Really sorry to bother you, but we've been talking and realized that Cade's mom—you know, my wife—is a super big fan of yours, too, and would be upset if we came home without some kind of memento from meeting you tonight. Would you mind signing this ball for her? Her name's Bentley, like the car," I rattled off.

"Sure," he replied, giving a quick glance to his buddy.

"Yep. It's going to mean a lot to her," I said. "She'll be so excited when we get home. You know, back in Alabama…"

"Here you go. We're just going to keep watching the game." He politely cut me off before I could launch into my next monologue. The Dodgers were coming up to bat, and I quickly thought that I may have crossed a line returning for round two. I felt a tinge of tension, apologized for the intrusion, told him he made a great first pitch, and walked with Cade back to our seats.

As soon as my butt hit the seat, I kicked myself for not getting a picture. I'm a photo guy. It's what I do in these types of situations. And having a photo just adds another layer to the story. *I should have gone with the picture the first time we went over,* I said under my breath, so I devised a new late-inning strategy to get my photo.

Bateman's a true baseball fan and loves his Dodgers, and I assumed he'd stay the whole game, so I laid out the latest plan to Cade.

"When the last out of the game is recorded and everyone gets up to leave, we'll make our way back over to his section, make it look like we accidentally bumped into him, and casually ask for the photo. It'll be easy," I said.

Unexpectedly, a Diamondbacks executive approached Jason and his friend with a large envelope, spoke with them for a few seconds, and then they all stood up and walked toward a tunnel next to the Arizona dugout.

"Cade, we've gotta move!" I shouted as I grabbed his arm and our gear.

I rattled off a different plan on the fly as we beelined it for the same tunnel. I had my backpack over my left shoulder, my Nikon DSLR over my right, and pulled Cade every step of the way. Fifteen seconds later, I saw the three men walk down the ramp, headed into the bowels of the stadium. Out of nowhere, an usher stepped in between me and our destiny.

"I'm sorry. You can't go down there. It's for players and personnel only," he stated.

I glanced over the top of the usher's right shoulder and saw Jason make a left turn as he walked out of my line of sight. He was about 20 feet away, and the picture was about to slip through my fingers. *When will I ever get this chance again?* I looked at the usher, then looked back over at Cade and nodded.

Right on cue, Cade said, "I have to poop, sir—poop, really bad."

"I can't let you guys go down this tunnel," he restated.

"Listen, man, my boy's gonna poop his pants right here!" I shouted.

"OK, go! Bottom of the ramp and take a right," he instructed.

Slowed down by mere seconds, we ran down the ramp, made the same left turn, and ran right into Bateman, his friend, and the executive. One more step and I would have plowed into all three of them.

"Whoa! Hey, Jason. Glad I caught you. Cade told me he was so bummed out that he didn't get a picture with you—and then I saw you slip into this tunnel. Can I get a quick shot of you guys together?"

Bateman was looking at an enlarged photo of his ceremonial first pitch and was right in the middle of a conversation with the executive. He just stood there and stared at me. Never said a word. Nothing. I have no idea what was running through his head, but I'll never forget that look. I did get a great picture of him and Cade, but I didn't dare ask if I could get one with him, too. That might have been too much.

"Knock and keep on knocking and the door will be opened to you."

—Matthew 7:7 AMP

18

CLEVELAND (PART I)

"It is not the strength of the body, but the strength of the spirit."

—*J.R.R. Tolkien*

For eighteen years, we'd known this day was coming, but it always seemed so far off. Even after Bentley's series of mini-strokes two and a half years earlier, we thought we'd bought more time, yet here we were. We had a decision to make. Although we were in a great mecca for cardiac medicine, the physician I'd hoped would operate on Bentley had retired in 2006. He'd spent his entire career at the University of Alabama at Birmingham and had performed over 25,000 surgeries. His retirement created a vacuum for patients like Bentley, who had extensive genetic abnormalities that required multiple complex reconstructions.

By December, Bentley's breathing was labored, even if she was lying down. Her feet and ankles were swollen, and she was easily fatigued. We took her back for another TEE procedure, and the physician confirmed that her aortic valve had thickened, and she'd developed moderate to severe regurgitation. The blood flowed backward into her heart instead of pumping out and moving through her body. The doctor recommended that she undergo an aortic valve replacement and stated she would receive a mechanical heart valve, which would require a lifetime of anticoagulation therapy to keep it functioning properly.

A mechanical valve is durable, easy to implant, and may be the right choice for an older patient who only needs one surgery, but younger patients—or those with other risk factors like Bentley—should have multiple options. But in her case, the only choice she was given came with a litany of complications due to the anticoagulation medication: bleeding events, strokes, infections, and a negative impact on her quality of life. She'd have to have blood drawn every week, and since she was only thirty-nine, she was facing a lifetime of crippling complications. Someone needed to think outside the box. And if all that wasn't enough, I knew we needed to get another provider when I heard the doctor say, "I've only read about one of her."

I was desperate to find another solution, so I reached out to my cardiology and cardiac surgery friends from around the country and asked them one simple question: "If this were your wife or child, where would you take them and who would you see?"

I was given names from all over, but I heard about one specific place again and again. I reached out to the Cleveland Clinic and scheduled an appointment with Dr. Richard Krasuski, the director of the Adult Congenital Heart Disease Service. They had an entire team dedicated to treating adult patients with congenital heart disease, so I felt comfortable that we were on the right track to find the best solution. I gathered all her old medical records from the Children's Hospital of Los Angeles, scanned everything, burned it onto a CD, and shipped it off to the Clinic ahead of Bentley's appointment.

Bentley had always been apprehensive about going to a new hospital for fear of being treated like a sideshow carnival act. Her condition and medical history were unusual, and during her many past appointments, the doctors frequently brought in medical students to examine her or listen to her heart. They always said, "You may never see anything like this again." Bentley did not like that.

So, our first meeting with Dr. Krasuski would say a lot about whether Bentley was willing to be treated in Cleveland. To our surprise, only the doctor and a nurse came in to discuss her treatment options. When Bentley asked about her special circumstances and if a cavalcade of students would be involved, he simply replied, "You are not special here. I've seen three like you this week." I knew we were in the right place.

Dr. Krasuski did a transthoracic echocardiogram. He was pleased with what he saw but also verified that she had moderate to severe aortic regurgitation. She also had moderate ascending aortic dilatation, a well-known complication of patients with Tetralogy of Fallot. He said it wasn't an emergency but that she'd need a re-operation in the next three to six months. He referred us to Dr. Gosta Pettersson, a surgeon born, raised, and trained in Gothenburg, Sweden, who'd come to the United States and specialized in adult congenital and acquired heart and aortic diseases—including re-operations and aortic valve repair. Dr. Pettersson had spent his lifetime training and doing the exact repair that Bentley needed.

While Dr. Pettersson's credentials were impeccable, Bentley still needed to meet him. She'd always spoken highly of her previous surgeon in Los Angeles and wanted to have that same kind of intimate connection in Cleveland. She told Dr. Pettersson that she was a young mother, didn't want to have her activities limited, and still wanted to be able to ride horses. It turned out that Dr. Pettersson was a passionate outdoorsman and enjoyed riding horses himself. He told Bentley that he'd do everything he could to repair her aortic valve first and would only implant an allograft (human) or a porcine (pig) bioprosthetic valve if necessary. The very last option would be to implant a mechanical valve. We left that meeting knowing that Bentley's wishes had been heard and that we'd found the best man for the job. He didn't want to delay, so she was scheduled to be back in Cleveland four weeks later.

That month was tough on everyone. Cade, Davis, and EB were young, but old enough to know their mom wasn't in great shape as she headed into her fourth surgery. There was a lot of planning and scheduling to do, especially considering the cities, flights, kids, and school. Bentley needed to go early for a series of procedures and tests before the surgery, so we shared our needs and timing with a few close friends and some family.

About a week before the big day, Bentley and I flew the kids to Richmond, Virginia, and made the thirty-minute drive to her brother's house. We knew it was important to keep the kids occupied, especially on the day of surgery, so what could be better than spending time with their Uncle Dave, Aunt Janet, and four cousins?

Bentley and I left the next afternoon to go to Cleveland. We stayed downtown in an old bank building that had been converted into a hotel and traveled back and forth to the hospital. Over the next couple of days, Bentley had blood tests, a chest x-ray, an electrocardiogram (EKG), and an echocardiogram (echo). Last on that list was a cardiac catheterization (cath), a minimally invasive procedure to evaluate her heart and blood vessels. With all the pre-testing complete and everything lined up for surgery, we had one free night to spend in Cleveland. To keep her mind off surgery, we went to Quicken Loans Arena and watched the Cavaliers take down the Knicks.

The night before surgery, Bentley checked into the hospital, relaxed, and read cards and letters from friends, family, and the children. Our mood was somber due to the seriousness of the surgery, but it allowed us to have a frank conversation about her mortality. She told me it was a win-win situation—that she'd either go to Heaven or keep being a wife and mother. Of course, she wanted the surgery to be successful and see Cade, Davis, and EB in a couple of days, but she was also fine with whatever God had planned for her.

"It's like choosing between chocolate and vanilla ice cream," she said. "I like them both, but I prefer chocolate."

Then she told me she would love to see the angels again, but not if it was permanent, only if it was without going to Heaven. I just wanted her surgery to go well and for all of us to be back in Birmingham the next week.

The next morning, everything moved at a lightning pace. Bentley's complex re-operation was the first surgery of the day and had been scheduled for a minimum of six hours. That didn't include the time to get her into the room, get prepped, or begin the actual procedure. In actuality, the elapsed time was closer to eight hours. One of the nurses gave me a hospital pager and told me not to leave campus. Meanwhile, back in Virginia, my sister-in-law was doing her best to keep everyone occupied. Janet took all seven kids to make pottery, play in the park, and eat at Chick 'Fil 'A. Bentley had given me a list of people to message, so each time I got an update on my pager, I passed the information to the list of friends, family, and the women who had prayed over her for the last month.

And just like that, it was over. The last pager update told me to head to a private room and wait for Dr. Pettersson. My anxiety was sky high, but in a very calm and matter-of-fact way, Dr. Pettersson explained that he'd repaired her aortic valve and reconstructed her aorta with a 26 mm Hemashield graft, which coincidentally was one of the first products I ever sold after college. He was pleased that he didn't need to implant a mechanical valve and felt confident that his repair would buy her at least ten years with a good quality of life.

"We'll keep an eye on her, but Bentley will eventually need another surgery," he said.

I let out a huge sigh of relief, feeling I'd managed to get her to the best cardiac surgeon at the top heart hospital in the country. It was clear that she was in great hands, and the stress of the past three months melted away. I called or texted everyone on the list, gave them the great news, and then touched base with Bentley's brother to arrange for him to bring our kids to Cleveland to see their mom. They were a little nervous about seeing her the first time, but they knew her heart had been fixed, she was on the mend, and that we wouldn't have to worry about her health for a while. Our friend, Susan, flew up from Birmingham to spend a couple of days with Bentley and then took the kids home.

After three more days, Bentley and I left Cleveland and arrived late for our connection in Atlanta, so it was a race to get on our plane to Birmingham. I'd arranged to have transport meet us at the bottom of the ramp on the jet bridge, but they showed up with an "aisle wheelchair," which wasn't built for comfort or speed. The agent slung her around on the bumpiest ride imaginable while we raced through the concourses to make our connection. We made it onto the flight, and Bentley said, "That was one of the worst experiences of my life. I don't want to ever do that again."

"I can do all this through him who gives me strength."

—Philippians 4:13 NIV

19

BOOT CAMP

"You have to grab moments when they happen."

—*Denzel Washington*

Bentley's recovery from her fourth open-heart surgery had been nothing short of stellar, the kids were thriving in school, the boys were playing baseball, and I was coaching EB's soccer team. This "thing" that had been hanging over her for the past thirty-nine years had been relegated to the back burner. The new lens with which we viewed life—that each day was a gift—was about to present me with a unique opportunity.

One evening while enjoying dinner at our favorite Mexican restaurant, Sol Azteca, Bentley asked, "So what's on your bucket list?"

Now that was a loaded question since I had a bucket list about a mile long. I'd always wanted to finish the Appalachian Trail or run along the Great Wall of China. I never got to jump out of a perfectly good airplane or see the great pyramids in Giza, Egypt, or the rock-cut architecture in Petra, Jordan. I'd always wanted to touch the Berlin Wall or hike the Inca Trail into Machu Picchu, but perhaps the one thing I wanted more than anything else was to go to an Atlanta Braves

Fantasy Camp and play baseball. I'd never played hardball growing up and had just turned forty-three, so that seemed like a missed opportunity. But a random dinner conversation with a co-worker one night led to something I never imagined.

My entire acting career consisted of one uncredited role as an extra in *Major League II*, but that had allowed me to check off "Be in a movie" from my bucket list. I loved my on-set experience, walked away with perhaps a little less than thirty seconds of total screen time, and felt oddly satisfied that I'd done something that few people get the chance to do. I also understood that I was married with three kids, had the weight of all the responsibilities that go along with those two jobs, and still enjoyed coaching. That's why I stopped playing golf and never thought about doing any more movies. Other things were a higher priority.

A few guys I worked with gathered for a meeting in New York, and we casually talked about life and things we'd done, were doing, or wanted to do. We were a close-knit group and had worked together for a few years, so we already knew a fair amount about each other. I don't remember if I'd told any of them about my one film role, but it came up that night, and one of the guys made a surprising revelation. My buddy, Dave, mentioned he had a friend from college who worked in the film industry and offered to make a connection.

"That would be really cool," I said.

Anthony gave me a call a week later, and we got to know each other a little bit as we shared a couple of stories about our mutual friend. After quickly feeling each other out, he cut straight to the chase.

"I hear you want to work on a movie," Anthony said. "What do you want to do?"

"I'm not 100 percent sure. I've only been on one movie set almost twenty years ago, and that was as an extra," I said.

"Yeah, you definitely don't want to do more extra work. Trust me," he said.

"Well, I don't want to sit in an office or trailer all day and manage a budget either," I said. "I'd prefer to do more movie-related things on an actual set. Other than that, I'm kind of game for whatever. So what would you recommend?"

"Here's what I'll do," he said. "I'll connect you with two people in my production office. I'll say you're an intern doing special projects for me on set, but I'll also make sure you get to spend time across a few departments. This will be your film boot camp, and that way, you can figure out what you like and don't like. Sound good?" Anthony asked.

"Absolutely! So where am I going, when do you need me, and what's the movie?" I asked.

"Meet me in New Orleans in April and text me when you get to the city. I can't put you up in a hotel, so you're on your own there," he said. "We're turning a book called *Cogan's Trade* into a movie."

I had to pitch that phone exchange to Bentley. I knew she'd ask a lot more questions than I had answers. I had a name, number, and city, but no address and no hard date for arrival. She'd want to know why I wanted to do this now, how long I'd be gone, if I'd be paid, when I was coming back, what the movie was about, who was in it, and on and on. But I trusted Dave, he trusted Anthony, and she trusted me, so we both agreed I should go to New Orleans and check it out. And that left only one last thing to do—call my boss.

I'd met Rick when the company he worked for acquired the company where I worked. That merger had been tenuous at best because there was considerable overlap in the two sales departments. It was clear there wouldn't be enough slots for everyone to keep their current positions. His company had focused on delivering radiofrequency energy to kill cancerous tumors, and ours specialized in manufacturing vascular access ports that could be used for repeated access to a patient's bloodstream to deliver chemotherapy agents. They didn't know any of us, and we were easy targets for elimination. Somehow, I survived the cut, and we'd now worked together for almost seven years.

"So you want to take a vacation to work on a movie?" Rick asked, confused.

"Yes," I said.

"When do you leave?" he asked.

"Not sure," I said.

"How long will you be gone?" he asked.

"Not sure," I said.

"What's the movie?" he asked.

"Not sure," I answered again.

"And Bentley's good with all this?" he asked.

"Not sure," I chuckled.

Rick signed off on my vacation request and told me he wanted to hear all about it when I got back. He was very laid back in that regard, and I think deep down he enjoyed the fact that I was willing to do something so unorthodox. I'd be going to New Orleans the first week or so of April to work as an unpaid forty-three-year-old intern for two people whose names I didn't know on a movie about a book I'd never read.

I made the five-hour drive to New Orleans and texted Anthony the Sunday night I arrived. He instructed me to report to the production office the next morning and ask for John or Ashley, and then he texted me the address. Ashley was the production coordinator for the film. She helped me with paperwork, made my ID badge, gave me a crew call sheet for the day, and told me to head down to base camp.

I finally arrived on set, got to meet Anthony, and he introduced me to Andrew, the director and screenwriter for *Cogan's Trade*. And just like that, I was on set and under the same tent with two of the most important people for the movie. Almost immediately, Anthony's phone rang, and he asked me to go meet their accountant, Melissa. She needed help getting payments delivered to multiple departments and handed me a lot of cash. That was my entire first day. I spent five minutes sitting within earshot of the director, but before I could learn anything, I spent the rest of my time running around town, tracking people down, and handing out wads of money. There was no time for a drink and idle chit chat, which is what I expected. They were on a tight budget and had a schedule to keep, and I was there to work.

Anthony was true to his word. I got to know John, the film's production supervisor, and of course, I spent more time helping Ashley and Melissa. I spent an entire afternoon with a stunt double who filmed an exploding car sequence. I spent the next two days with the department heads and team members of craft services, hair and makeup, sound and video, and even the set decorator. Each day was its own little mini-bootcamp, and everyone treated me very well. Surprisingly, many of the staffers wanted to know about my job. I told them I was in medical sales, a little bit about what my day-to-day life entailed, and learned that most people liked to talk about things other than their current project.

Around the fourth or fifth day, Anthony brought me an assignment that really got my juices going. It was a working draft of a storyboard sequence that needed to be reordered and trimmed for time. He also wanted me to verify that all the needed props were accounted for and available on-set so Andrew could film the sequence later that evening. It reminded me of the storyboards Steven Spielberg or George Lucas used when filming *Jaws, Raiders of the Lost Ark,* or *Star Wars.* My project was surely edited further after I turned it in, and it may have only been on screen for a minute or so, but it was exciting to have tangible proof that I'd made a real contribution to the film. With twenty years of sales and management experience under my belt, I realized that my strengths in filmmaking might lie in producing. Now I had another item on my bucket list.

The film had a star-studded cast. I had the opportunity to work and spend time with Ray Liotta, James Gandolfini, Sam Shepard, and Scoot McNairy, and the longer I was on set with those guys, the more I wanted to be in it myself. So, I asked Anthony to throw me a bone, and he made me an extra in the bus terminal takedown scene with Ben Mendelsohn, but unfortunately, I hit the cutting room floor. And maybe the most painful revelation of my time on set was that Anthony could have used me as a background actor in a scene with Brad Pitt. That novel, *Cogan's Trade,* was renamed *Killing Them Softly* by the time the movie premiered at the 2012 Cannes Film Festival.

> "Be wise in the way you act toward outsiders;
> make the most of every opportunity."
>
> —Colossians 4:5 NIV

20

TALLADEGA

"God takes care of babies and fools."
—*Mrs. Annie Blossom Green Brown*

With Bentley in the passenger seat and our three kids strapped in the back row of Wolfgang, my titanium silver 2006 BMW 750Li, we shot out of turn two and the 33-degree banked section of the Talladega Superspeedway doing slightly more than 150 mph. With a three-quarter-mile straightaway in front of me, I pressed the accelerator down further and touched 158 mph before I eased off the pedal heading into turn three. This was instantly and absolutely the greatest Mother's Day gift I'd ever given Bentley.

I first fell in love with the BMW brand when I was fifteen years old. My dad had come home to Charleston for a long weekend and asked me if I wanted to tag along to pick up his new car. It was a brand new, black-on-black automatic BMW 528e, circa 1984. He said the car was a perk from his company, and he planned to leave it in Charleston as a second car since I'd be taking my driver's test soon. He thought that parallel parking would be much easier in the 528e than my mom's station wagon. He was right. I nailed that portion of the test and passed the rest with flying colors.

My mom was happy with her station wagon and had no interest in driving my dad's new car. I don't think she liked the orange hue on the electronic instrument panel, so I was the lone operator of this beautiful piece of German engineering. I was ecstatic because I had my license and complete freedom to drive anywhere in Charleston. My life was changing before my eyes, and this BMW would elevate my social status to new heights. A week before I turned sixteen, my dad called to say he had something big planned for my birthday and that we'd be road tripping in the BMW over spring break.

"So where are we headed?" I asked.

"Texas," he replied, very tight-lipped.

"Texas? What are we going to do in Texas?" I asked.

"We're going to Freeport to drop off the car," he said.

"I thought I was going to get to drive this car. Why are we getting rid of it?" I asked.

"Because no sixteen-year-old son of mine will ever drive a brand-new BMW."

That was it. End of the discussion. We made the trip in relative silence for more than 1,100 miles over three days from Charleston to Freeport. When we pulled up at his apartment, there was a burgundy 1979 Oldsmobile Cutlass with a T-top in his driveway. It was personally devastating. He'd already sold the BMW to one of his co-workers and purchased the used Olds for me. I vowed that day that I wouldn't rest until I pulled up at his house in my own BMW.

I'd been trying to think of something cool to do for Bentley for Mother's Day, and a buddy of mine mentioned a fundraiser hosted by the Talladega Superspeedway to benefit the American Red Cross and tornado relief efforts. A week earlier, Alabama had been hit by a violent, high-end EF4 tornado that passed over large swaths of Tuscaloosa and Birmingham, as well as countless other communities and rural areas in between. The damage that day was heartbreaking—cars thrown into the air, homes destroyed, and trains blown off their tracks. The people hit hardest needed help, and the relief came quickly.

Churches, charities, animal shelters, hospitals, banks, police and fire stations, the American Legion, and the Salvation Army all chipped in. Music superstar Rihanna added Birmingham as a stop on her Loud Tour to raise money for tornado victims and efforts to rebuild in Birmingham and Tuscaloosa. And the American Red Cross's fundraising event at Talladega Superspeedway the week before Mother's Day was too good to pass up.

For a $50 donation, Talladega allowed race fans to drive their personal vehicles around the high banks of the tri-oval asphalt track. When I first heard about this Donate and Drive event, I stopped at the ATM to withdraw $300, just in case Bentley and I wanted to take the BMW out for a few laps.

We drove forty-five minutes to Lincoln, Alabama, and followed the signs to the infield and pit road area. As we pulled in, we saw a pace truck with a flashing light that led a group of five cars down the backstretch. Another seven or eight cars were lined up in the pit row, waiting for their turns.

We met a sweet volunteer, Kristie, and she outlined the rules we had to obey. Everyone in the car had to be in a seatbelt, no passing was allowed under any condition, and the group had to stay lined up behind the pace truck, which would keep speeds between 70 and 80 mph. We also had to stay in the lower, less banked lanes. She told us that our $50 donation allowed us to complete three full laps, and then a volunteer would wave us back into pit row.

I gave Kristie the $50, entered pit road, and waited for the next wave of cars and trucks to go out. Our group included a Corvette, a Kia, a Tahoe, a Porsche, and a Cadillac—and, of course, my BMW.

I wasn't a NASCAR fan, and neither was Bentley, but we both liked to drive fast. As our family sat in that beast of a BMW and waited to start our run, I couldn't help but think back on my love for this brand and the handful of cars I'd bought before Wolfgang. My first was a

Sahara 1976 BMW 2002 with a modified, five-speed manual transmission that I got for $2,000 from my buddy Ike, which made me an official badge owner. But as much as I loved that car, it was always a little bittersweet because it was too late to show it off to my dad.

That BMW served me well in Virginia and made the trip to Birmingham with us, but it had a terrible rust problem that I chose to ignore. And one day, part of my floorboard gave way under the clutch, and I could see the road whizzing by under my left foot. I donated that car to charity and replaced it with a black-on-black, six-speed stick shift 1995 BMW 540i, which was unceremoniously trashed when a semi-truck blew a tire in front of me and destroyed the front of the car, the engine, and its undercarriage. With an insurance check from the trucking company and a clean slate to pick my next car, I bought a 1988 BMW 635CSI. This black and tan, two-door coupe was the sexiest car I'd ever owned, and it turned heads. It even had a built-in cooler nestled between the two rear seats.

But now, we were in pit row waiting for our turn on the track in my 750Li, the biggest, heaviest, fastest—and as the kids would say, baddest—vehicle I'd ever owned. It featured a new-generation V8 engine with direct fuel injection and twin turbocharging. The 4.4-liter V8 generated 400 horsepower and 450 lb-ft of torque, incredible numbers for an engine of its size. It had dynamic stability control and dynamic traction control, and it came with a built-in sport suspension and was equipped with nineteen-inch rear alloy wheels and Pirelli performance tires. My 4,500 pound behemoth weighed almost a half-ton more than a NASCAR Cup Series car and could go from zero to sixty in under six seconds and zero to one hundred in under twelve. While the speedometer goes up to 160 mph, the electronic readout stops at 150 mph. This car was built for the Autobahn and was about to be tested at Talladega.

A couple of friends had made the trip, too, and we'd discussed the best strategy to maximize speed on our laps around the speedway. With the pace truck leading the group, three other drivers went out next, and then the three of us came out of the pits very slowly. Our plan had been for the pace truck and three cars to get way ahead of our group, so we'd have ample room in front of us to drive much faster. There was no way we would comply with all the rules, especially the one that said we had to drive 70 mph on the bottom part of the track.

Talladega Superspeedway was designed to be the nation's largest and fastest oval racetrack. It's the longest NASCAR oval with a length of 2.66 miles. It has four turns with 33-degree banks, and it's 48 feet wide without the apron at the bottom of the track. The tri-oval bank is 16.5 degrees, and while average speeds are now in the 190-mph range, cars routinely traveled at well over 200 mph before NASCAR required restrictor plates. The 33-degree banked turns are as tall as a five-story building, so a driver must go fast on this track to stay up in the turns.

The pace truck pulled out, followed by the Cadillac, Tahoe, and Kia. As planned, our group of muscle cars slow-rolled it out of the pits. The Corvette was in front, followed by me in the BMW and my other buddy in his Porsche. We were ready to roll.

We were a little bunched up on the first two laps and never got faster than 110 mph, but we figured out spacing and timing quickly and hit the backstretch doing 135 mph on the third lap. It was such an incredibly smooth ride, and we had no cabin vibration at all. And when you know there aren't any idiot drivers in front of you, it makes for an incredibly relaxing ride. We came off turn four and were waved back into the pits. Most people would have been thrilled with that speed-induced adrenaline adventure and gone home, but not us. Our day was just beginning.

Bentley drove two sessions back-to-back and tallied six laps, while I filmed her and the kids from the front passenger seat. She's technically sound and was certainly aggressive that day, but with all three kids in the car, she didn't take a lot of risks behind the wheel. And I would argue that she wasn't quite as aggressive as she might normally have been because the 750Li wasn't her daily driver, so her top speeds on the straightaways ranged from 110 mph to 120 mph. As she made her way back into pit row, we noticed a new driver, a young man with a family history of driving on Talladega.

Jeffrey Earnhardt was a stock car race driver, the grandson of Dale Earnhardt and nephew of Dale Earnhardt Jr. His family was NASCAR royalty and was beloved by millions of fans. He'd made the trip to Talladega to help support the Red Cross by taking fans out for three lap runs in the Aaron's pace car.

The pit area had been buzzing with excitement since Jeffrey pulled up in his Camaro, but I wanted to get in one more run before he took over the track. I pulled another $50 bill from my wallet, handed it over, and said, "Three more laps, please."

Bentley and I had completed nine laps and traveled just under twenty-four miles at speeds ranging from 100 mph up to 135 mph, so I was pumped up for my last laps. I came out of pit road looking for faster splits than I had thirty minutes earlier. And here's the critical blind spot for Bentley and me. Neither of us thought about checking each other, and that's not a good thing. We know we're both good drivers, and the kids were having a blast looping the speedway, but no one in that vehicle acted rationally, least of all us parents. It wasn't our finest hour.

I drove so confidently coming out of pit road that I was going over 100 mph into turn one, 120 mph out of turn two, and I hit 140 mph on the back stretch before backing off as I headed into turn three. A photographer stationed high above the track in the spotter's stand snapped shots of all the cars as they passed the "This is Talladega" sign in between turns three and four. I felt good, and the car was handling like a champ.

Bentley hadn't said a word about that lap, so I felt like I had room to pick up the pace. I flew down the front stretch for my second lap, entering turn one at almost 130 mph and exiting turn two at over 140 mph, before easing my foot off the pedal at 150 mph. My heart rate was elevated. I felt a little nervous because I'd never driven that fast in my life, but I knew I had the right car for the job and a supportive wife.

And to offer some perspective, Talladega has a 4,000-foot backstretch, making it the longest in NASCAR, and it's 1,000 feet longer than Daytona's track. It mathematically translates into three-quarters of a mile and can be covered in slightly over seventeen seconds at 155 mph.

I prepared for my final lap, knowing I might never get this opportunity again. I clocked my fastest time down the front stretch, attacked turn one, and came out of turn two just north of 150 mph. But I wanted a little bit more, so I pushed down the pedal another couple of centimeters and took a very quick glance at the speedometer halfway down the backstretch. It was floating just under 160 mph. Turn three came up lightning fast, so I took my foot off the pedal because I approached the turn hotter than I had during my previous five laps. Even without acceleration, Wolfgang crept into the top lane, which was a big no-no according to our briefing earlier in the day. The last thing to do was decelerate enough to enter pit road safely. Bentley and I had broken a lot of rules that day, but those last 7.98 adrenaline-fueled miles were the most exhilarating of my life.

The day wasn't over yet. Bentley approached Jeffrey Earnhardt and asked if he could take her and the boys out, so I donated again to the American Red Cross. EB and I watched their three laps from an infield tower, and it was obvious that he wasn't driving a stock Camaro. The entire drive lasted about four minutes, and he drove at a completely different level. They pulled back into pit row, and I introduced myself and asked if he'd take some pictures with Bentley and the kids. While he was still talking with Davis, Bentley leaned over and said, "You have to ride with him."

So, I handed over my last $50, and Bentley, EB, and I got into that Camaro and exploded out of pit row. Earnhardt gripped the steering wheel with his left hand in a supinated position at seven o'clock, while his right hand rested gently on the gearshift knob. He casually carried on a conversation as we entered turn one, doing more than 150 mph. He was as cool as a cucumber, and I didn't feel the least bit uncomfortable with him behind the wheel. Jeffrey and Bentley talked like they were out on a Sunday drive through a school zone, while I tried my best to hold my DSLR camera steady and film that incredible run on the Talladega track. He broke 160 mph while we were in turn two of the first lap, and we went faster from there.

After that extremely invigorating day, my BMW was riding horribly, so Bentley and I took it back to the dealer and told the mechanic that something seemed off. We waited while they drove it on the interstate and did an inspection.

When our service rep approached us in the lounge, he said, "The mechanic told me there was no doubt that the car was riding rough on his drive, so he put it up on the lift and noticed very strange tire wear," he said. "Have you noticed anything unusual when driving it over the last week or so?"

"Nothing unusual at all," I said. "Actually, it's been driving great, and I haven't had any issues. It's a used car, but I just bought it from the dealership about a month ago. I'm pretty sure the sales guy said it had a new set of tires. Maybe those guys weren't being completely honest," I said in an accusing tone.

"My guy says the tire wear isn't at all normal. I even had a couple of other BMW mechanics come over and look at them. Nobody's seen wear like that on a passenger vehicle. Are you sure you haven't done anything unusual in the car?" he asked.

Bentley and I looked at each other and simultaneously said, "Talladega!"

"What do you mean, Talladega?" he asked.

"We drove it on Talladega for a Red Cross tornado fundraiser," I said.

"Seriously? You drove this car on Talladega?" he asked. "How fast were you going?"

"We got over 150 mph on a couple of laps," I told him with a confident smirk on my face. What I heard next was not the compliment I expected.

"Do you realize you were only a few miles away from blowing out one or more of your tires? Had that happened on the track at that speed, you would've surely smashed into a wall, or worse," he said.

Bentley and I looked at each other in silence.

"I'll be honest. That never crossed our minds," I said, a bit stunned.

I could have killed my whole family that day. Not because I had some kind of death wish but because I was a fool. In hindsight, I know Bentley felt the same way. Driving fast and racing cars was our mutual blind spot, and we didn't think through all the possibilities or potential consequences when we entered the track that day. I'd donated $200 to drive twelve laps in Wolfgang, but I had to pay almost $3,000 for a new set of tires—and it could have cost me a lot more than that.

"Our God is a God who saves!
The Sovereign LORD rescues us from death."

—Psalms 68:20 NLT

21

LOST AND FOUND

"I wear the ring."

—*Pat Conroy,* The Lords of Discipline

I started my sales career in the medical field two days after graduating from The Citadel, but I'd been "selling" a lot longer than that. And like most who choose sales as a career path, I wanted to be rewarded for outstanding performance. Early on, a letter from my boss or being mentioned in the company's monthly newsletter did the trick. But soon I wanted to be recognized in front of my peers with a large trophy or plaque to put in my home office. Then, after a while, those trinkets stopped having any meaning, and all I wanted was a reward trip—an all-expenses-paid vacation for an exceptional year, the kind of trip that would let Bentley and me get away to live the high life for a few days.

For a sales manager, victory as the top region in the country was even sweeter because it meant my entire team had performed at an incredibly high level. One of my salespeople would be representative of the year, I'd be sales manager of the year, and our entire team would win the region of the year. It meant that our combined efforts came together to pull off the trifecta. It meant awards, bonuses, and a fabulous trip for our team, and everyone in the company wanted a shot at the title. When they called my name as the winner that year, it meant that Bentley and I were going someplace special and, most likely, somewhere we'd never been before.

The award was a trip to Maui, Hawaii. And I got permission to bring Cade, Davis, and EB along. The Four Seasons hotel was more than we ever imagined, and while the kids had the best time at the pool, we also got to eat a traditional sunset luau dinner with live music and see hula and Samoan knife dancing. We drove along the road to Hana, chartered a helicopter, and soared above the vast moon-like crater of Mt. Haleakala. We even took surf lessons at Lahaina.

Bentley had grown up in Newport Beach, attended surf school, and ridden Morey boogie boards while living in California, but she didn't plan to get in the water that day. Since only one of us could surf at a time, she wanted to keep an eye on each of the kids and me. So, with Bentley sitting on the beach watching us like a hawk, the kids and I checked in for surfing lessons, were assigned an instructor and photographer for the session, and changed into our wetsuits. We had a quick lesson about how to stand up on the board and were deemed seaworthy within minutes.

It was quickly evident that Cade and EB were not enjoying themselves. The instructor took Cade out beyond the breakers, spun him back toward the shore, and timed his launch to coincide with a moderately sized wave. Cade made no attempt to stand up on any of his four runs and asked if he could go to shore. EB tried to stand once, got rocked off the board, and called it a day only minutes after entering the water. Davis, on the other hand, wobbled to get up and stood on his first run to shore. He seemed destined to become proficient in his new sport.

With Cade and EB safely back on the beach with Bentley, I relaxed and learned how to surf with Davis. Neither of us was great out of the gate, but we leveled up quickly and had a blast trying something outside our collective wheelhouse. We surfed for about an hour, made several runs, and caught a few decent waves. I won't make any excuses for myself here; Davis was a much faster learner, and he crushed it. It was like he'd secretly taken lessons for the past month, and I was amazed that he picked it up so easily.

After our lesson was over, I bought the package of digital photos from the cameraman, and we drove back to the hotel. We spent the rest of the day relaxing, sipping tropical drinks, and watching the kids wear out the slide in the gigantic pool. After a couple of hours, we packed up our gear and went back to the room to get ready for dinner. While I was shaving, I noticed my Citadel ring was not on my finger.

I looked frantically but couldn't find it anywhere in the room. I retraced my steps down the hall and to the lobby. I searched through the Lost and Found box, scoured the pool area, and made one more run up and down the hallways. Nothing. I was upset and became a little more frantic when Bentley asked if I'd worn it surfing. I grabbed my laptop and the flash drive and sifted through all the photos, zooming in on my right hand to see if I still had my ring. About fifty pictures in, my heart sank. The ring was gone.

In a world where everyone was on island time, I was in full panic mode as I headed back to the beach. The sun was almost down, so time was limited. I searched the main lot and walked in a slow, straight line from where we'd parked to the surf shop and then to the part of the beach where Bentley and the kids had camped out. I knew I'd lost it at the beach, so I marked off a search grid from where they'd sat all the way to the ocean. I crawled back and forth across the sand in a deliberate fashion until I was soaking wet from the tide. It was like looking for a needle in a stack of needles, and with darkness looming, I stood up and stared out into the Pacific, wondering how I could have been so dumb.

I didn't have to tell Bentley. She could see the look on my face. It was my deeply personal, symbolic, gold reminder of my time in hell. Typically, I would have spent the evening cursing the situation or blaming Bentley or one of the kids, but I knew it was my fault for wearing the ring out there. I don't know if I had an epiphany or not, but I felt a sense of peace. It had been such a wonderful day with my family, and I enjoyed that incredible bonding experience with Davis. I didn't want to forever taint that memory.

Bentley asked if I could order a replacement ring, but a new one wouldn't have the same significance. I assured her I'd call The Citadel when we got back home. As we left Hawaii, I reflected on our incredible family trip and was reminded of Mage's desire to make Hawaii his permanent home, our helicopter ride over the world's largest dormant volcano, and the time spent surfing with my son. As a bonus, we took some of the best family photos ever, so I forgot about my ring, chalked it up to karma and the cost of having that experience, and never called the school to order a replacement.

About five years later, a woman from The Citadel's Alumni Office reached out to me. She said that a man named Dave had called their office and was looking for me specifically. He claimed to have found my class ring in the Pacific Ocean.

"Could this be true?" she asked.

"It's absolutely true!" I exclaimed.

"Wow. Everyone in the office thought this man might be trying to scam you," she said.

"How do I connect with this guy?" I asked.

It seemed too good to be true. I peppered her with questions, but she didn't have many answers. She said to call Dave with Dave's Metal Detecting in Honolulu, Hawaii. I hung up and dialed his number.

"Dave's Metal Detecting, how can I help you?" he answered.

"Dave, this is Robert Hornak. I just got a call from The Citadel, and they told me you might have found my ring."

"I sure did, just off the coast of Lanai," he said. "I was able to make out part of your name inside the ring. It was pretty worn, but I'm so glad to track you down. How long has it been in the ocean?" Dave asked.

"About five years now," I told him. "How did you find it?"

"I run a metal detecting and diving service here on the islands and was hired to find an expensive engagement ring for a woman who lost it while swimming off the coast. While I was looking for her ring, I found yours buried smack dab in the middle of my dive zone.

"That's absolutely unbelievable," I said.

"That's what I hear most often, especially when I make a discovery like this," Dave said. "I can get it shipped today, and you'll have it next week. I just need your full name and address, and I'll get it out to you," he said.

"But what can I do for you?" I asked. "I still can't believe you found it after all these years."

"You know, Robert, it would be cool if you could cover the dive because I never found her ring and she refused to pay me."

"That's the biggest no-brainer ever," I said. "Just let me know how much. Is there anything else that would help you out?"

"It would be great if you'd write a testimonial about this that I can put on my website," he said.

Dave sent the ring back as promised, and I was, again, absolutely shocked when I opened the box with Bentley. While it looked a little more weathered and beaten from five years on the ocean floor, it was in surprisingly good shape. But having it back didn't instantly change my life. Since I hadn't worn it in so long, I stuck it in the top drawer of my dresser until one day Bentley walked into my office with the ring in her hand.

"You should wear this," she said.

"That's OK. I don't really like wearing jewelry anymore, except my wedding band," I said.

"No, you should wear it. You were blessed to get this back, and you're being given a chance to share this story with the people you meet," Bentley said.

And she was right. My ring is unique, and I'm asked about it more often than I realized. I've been on sales calls, at dinner with friends who'd never seen me wear it, with co-workers, or just talking with a stranger on a plane, and someone will inevitably ask, "Can I see your ring?"

My old response was cocky and arrogant. It was all about me and the hell I'd been through to earn it. I'd talk about the brutish cadre and how so many people washed out. I'd recite that brash Pat Conroy line, "I wear the ring." But I'd lost it in the surf that day and, with it, a piece of my identity.

I don't know why I got my ring back. I used to think I was being rewarded for not losing my cool or blaming my family for something they played no part in that day. Or maybe it was because I'd never tried to replace the ring. But my most prevailing thought is that I now have a new story to tell—a story about losing my ring in the Pacific and the miracle of its return. When I first got it back, I didn't really know what constituted a miracle. I simply chalked it up to karma, good juju, or the fact that I was generally a good guy. But then I came across a quote from one of the unlikeliest of sources, Jon Bon Jovi. Here's what he said:

"Miracles happen every day. Change your perception of what a miracle is, and you'll see them all around you."

Both Bentley and Bon Jovi were right. I had a new story to tell, one that opened doors to discuss a real-life miracle. It was a cool surfing story that didn't turn people off or cause them to put up a wall. I'd been given free rein to share this story with anyone who had the gumption to ask. It was a gift on multiple levels.

"And when she has found *it*, she calls *her* friends and neighbors together, saying, 'Rejoice with me, for I have found the piece which I lost!' Likewise, I say to you, there is joy in the presence of the angels of God over one sinner who repents."

—Luke 15:9-10 NKJV

22

PANZER

"I couldn't find the sports car of my dreams, so I built it myself."

—*Ferdinand Porsche*

When Bentley returned from her Autobahn drive in Germany, the urge to buy her a Porsche was always in the back of my mind. It wasn't a topic that I could openly discuss with her because if she got the slightest inkling that I was thinking about it, we would've raced to the dealership that very second. I knew the exact car she'd always dreamed of owning, so I kept my search process quiet.

I went to our local Porsche dealer and met two salesmen. I gave them a little background on Bentley, her love of the brand, and her once-in-a-lifetime high-speed drive through Germany, and I told them the exact specifications of her dream car. It had to be a black-on-black Carrera-based older model with a manual transmission. Anything short of that, and they didn't need to call me.

The search went on for months. Occasionally, I'd swing by to check in with the guys to see if they'd found anything. Each time they said, "Not yet. We'll call you when we get something interesting."

Deep down, I knew they were actively looking, and it seemed like they were on as much of a mission as I was. Then one day, I got the call.

"Robert, we just got a black-on-black Carrera S trade-in," the salesman said. "Do you want it?"

"I have a couple more conference calls this morning. Can I swing by after lunch?" I asked.

"We can give you until 11:00 a.m., and that's all we can do," he said. "We have a list of people who will immediately buy this car sight unseen."

I quickly cancelled my morning calls, walked out of my office, and found Bentley.

"Hey, sweetie, I just hung up with BMW service. I left them a message a couple of days ago about my car driving funny. They just called back and said they have an open slot if I can bring it in right now. Can you follow me over in case I need to leave it overnight?" I asked.

My story was plausible enough and didn't raise any red flags, so we hustled over to the dealership. Bentley followed behind me and waited in the parking lot while I pulled into one of the service bays. I explained the situation to the service manager, got permission to leave my car in there for the next hour, and walked back outside to meet Bentley.

"They're going to look at the car and let me know in the next thirty minutes if it's going to be a quick fix or a much bigger deal. Do you want to peek in the Porsche dealership until they call?"

"I'm never going to say no to that offer!" she said.

We drove 100 feet across the street, and before we could even park, she caught a glimpse of the car I'd brought her to see.

"That's my car!" Bentley screamed.

The two salesmen walked out of the showroom and saw her examining the 911.

Bentley looked at me and said, "This is the one I've always dreamed of."

By that time, the guys had gotten close enough, and I boisterously said, "We'll take it!"

She looked at me in disbelief and said, "Are you serious? We can't afford this."

I suggested the car could be a gift for her birthday, our anniversary, and both our Christmas presents for at least the next three years. Before I could say anything else, she jumped in the car and started crying. She had fallen in love with this brand, this exact car, when she was five years old, living in Newport Beach, California. It seemed like the emotional weight she'd carried her entire life—and through all those surgeries—had suddenly been lifted.

I'd been a saver my whole life and would have never contemplated a purchase like this prior to her strokes or surgery. But what was I saving for? What if Bentley was gone tomorrow? What if I was gone tomorrow? And if I had the resources, why would I deny her something she'd wanted her entire life? I'd never spent frivolously, and I knew deep down this was the right thing to do. And just like that, I was at peace with the purchase.

Bentley's story had spread like wildfire throughout the dealership, and it seemed like everyone had come out to congratulate her. You could see the genuine joy on her face, and one of my favorite pictures is of her standing in front of that Porsche 911 Carrera S after it was washed and parked in the delivery bay. It was the biggest impulse purchase I'd ever made, but was it really an impulse? It took me eight months to locate the car Bentley had waited a lifetime to receive, and it was worth every penny. And, true to her form, she named it Panzer.

Soon after, Bentley was invited to attend the North American Porsche Driving School as their guest. Out of the thirty people there, she was the only woman in the group. All the men had paid a hefty sum for the experience, but someone in the Porsche family had given it to her as a gift. She spent the day at Barber Motorsports Park, a multi-purpose racing facility just outside Birmingham. She got to drive the seventeen-turn, 2.38-mile road course on the track that was referred to as "The Augusta National of Motorsports." She even got to show off her skills driving on the wet-dry skid pad and was the only person that day to complete a driver-induced 720 maneuver, which means Bentley completed two full rotations in her Porsche before coming to a stop. And if that experience wasn't enough, Porsche invited her back the next year to do it all over again, and she didn't pay for that one either.

Bentley drove Panzer everywhere, even though there was barely enough room to hold all three kids. It was the road car that took EB and one or two of her teammates to soccer tournaments, or it was used for carpool to pick up a few kids at school. Once, Bentley did a burnout in front of her friend Paula, her daughter, and a host of kids as she left the elementary school pickup line. I occasionally drove it to get groceries, but there wasn't enough space in the front storage compartment to stash a large pack of paper towels. Panzer was impractical on so many levels, but he looked fabulous, and she got great joy from driving him.

But I got a weird call one day. Bentley said that Panzer had hit a concrete pole at the Texaco gas station near our house.

"What happened?" I asked.

"I don't know," she said.

"What do you mean you don't know?" I asked again.

"I don't know. I just ran into it," she said.

As a highly skilled driver, Bentley's lack of an explanation made no sense to me. It would be a couple of years later until we found out what really happened.

"Delight yourself also in the LORD,
And He shall give you the desires of your heart."

—Psalms 37:4 NKJV

23

FANTASY CAMP

"Twenty-one greatest days of my life."
—Kevin Costner as Crash Davis in Bull Durham

I had never felt more nervous in my life. I approached the batter's box with a blend of anxiety and self-doubt, yet enormous reverence for the man on the mound. I stepped in with my left foot first, then my right, which I slowly inched closer to the front edge of the chalk line, the left-handed pitcher now toeing the rubber. I placed my wooden Bones bat on my left shoulder and slightly bent my knees. I thought both legs would buckle as my quadriceps started to tremble, as I watched the future Hall of Famer go into his motion.

Tom Glavine had a career spanning twenty-two major league seasons between the Atlanta Braves and the New York Mets. He was a two-time Cy Young winner, a ten-time All-Star, and was named the 1995 World Series MVP when he pitched eight scoreless innings to help bring Atlanta its first MLB championship. Tom was only one of twenty-four players and just one of six left-handers to earn three hundred or more wins in major league history. In his illustrious career, Glavine faced 13,239 professional batters. This was my fourteenth career at bat.

"Strike one!" the umpire called out.

I never played baseball as a kid. Basketball was always number one with my dad, and most of my free time was spent in a gym or on a court. However, during a school track meet when I was twelve, I ran at a blistering pace and recorded an excellent 800m time for my age. An observant coach pulled me aside and said that running was now going to be my thing. And because track and baseball seasons overlapped, I never took up the sport.

Growing up, my dad took me to Atlanta-Fulton County Stadium to see the Braves play, or I could watch them six days a week on TBS. After I moved to Virginia, I became a fan of the Orioles and could catch a game whenever work took me to Baltimore. Neither team had much success in those days, but I enjoyed getting out to a ballpark whenever I could.

But the Braves went on a run during the 1991 season and won the National League (NL) pennant and a trip to the World Series. They had another outstanding regular season in 1992, but found themselves in a pickle against the Pittsburgh Pirates in the National League Championship Series (NLCS). The Braves were down to their final out in a must-win Game 7.

A trip to the 1992 World Series was on the line. The Pirates led the Braves 2-1 with two on and two outs in the bottom of the ninth. Sid Bream was on second base and David Justice stood at third when pinch-hitter Francisco Cabrera, who had batted only ten times in the 1992 regular season, stepped to the plate for Atlanta. CBS Sports announcer Sean McDonough had the call that night.

"Line-drive and a base-hit! Justice has scored the tying run, Bream to the plate—and he is safe! Safe at the plate! The Braves go to the World Series!" McDonough exclaimed.

That play, simply known as "The Slide," was the most exciting sports moment I had ever witnessed. And average baseball fans who watched Bream slide just underneath the tag to score the winning run will tell you it was one of the most exciting and unbelievable plays they had ever seen. Still don't believe me? The MLB Network ranked that game the fourth best of all time. I always liked the Braves; they were my hometown team, but Sid's heroics that night catapulted my fandom to stratospheric levels.

I played on a couple of men's softball teams and in one co-ed league with Bentley when we lived in Virginia, while the rest of my free time was spent playing basketball or golfing with my buddies. But all that changed after we moved to Alabama and Cade and Davis were old enough to play team sports.

I spent much of my free time coaching all three kids. I'd been around basketball my entire life, so that was a logical fit, but I'd also played soccer growing up and previously coached a team for five years in Virginia, so that was a natural fit, too. However, baseball wasn't my strong suit, and there were many willing dads ready to step up to the challenge.

Cade, Davis, and I played catch on the street. I hit them grounders on the field, threw soft toss in the cages, and occasionally, took a few cuts myself. I loved watching them compete; we often went to Birmingham Barons games, and we made it a point to take one or two trips a year to see different MLB stadiums all around the country. Then one day the boys said, "You should try to play."

I visited the Atlanta Braves website and discovered they hosted a one-week Fantasy Camp at the ESPN Wide World of Sports Complex in Kissimmee, Florida. I completed the inquiry form, and a couple of days later, I got a call from Greg McMichael, a former Braves pitcher who ran the program for the big-league club.

"I see that you want to join the Braves down in Orlando," Greg stated.

"Yes. I've never played organized baseball before, but I love the game, and I love the Braves. Will I be the only guy who's never played before?" I asked.

"That's a real possibility, but we have a wide range of people spanning all ages and abilities who will spend the week with us. You must be twenty-five or older and willing to have a good time with other like-minded fans of the team and the game," Greg explained.

"What about gear? Uniforms? Coaches?" I asked.

"We'll have two uniforms with your name and number hanging in your locker when you arrive. You'll have to bring your own gear. I'll send you a letter with everything you will need. And we've got some great instructors, too. Each team will be assigned a pitching and hitting coach, and those guys will observe you during the skills evaluation," Greg concluded.

"I don't know, man. I've never played, and you're telling me I need to try out in front of a bunch of ex-major league players? I'm going to suck," I emphatically stated.

"Don't do that to yourself. The former players we've pulled together are awesome, and they'll coach you up. Besides, the best part of the week is just hanging out with all the guys and the camaraderie that goes with it," Greg replied.

"Who would be my coach?" I asked.

"I can't tell you that today, since we won't know the teams until the draft," Greg outlined.

"Hold it. There's a skills evaluation and a draft? You're not selling me on this like you think you are," I quipped.

"You'll be fine. I see you've played a lot of sports and you're only forty-three, so I think you'll be in good company. Besides, the coaches are all guys you grew up watching in the 1990s," he said.

"Who are we talking about?" I asked.

"Guys like Bream, Clontz, Freeman, Grissom, Lopez, and Perez. We're still adding to the list every day," he said.

"Well, I know who all those guys are," I replied. "Can I bring my wife?"

"You can. There's an opening night get-together in Orlando on January 24. Can I add you to the roster?" Greg asked.

"Sure, count me in," I replied.

I spent that entire winter getting into shape. I was on the treadmill three days a week and running hills and doing sprints the other four. I lifted weights two days a week and was in the cages with the boys as often as we could get there. They had just turned fourteen, but they were now coaching me. They helped fine-tune my swing, taught me how to play a few different positions, and explained the most important rules of the game.

Bentley and I arrived at Miller's Ale House on a Tuesday night, and I was thrilled to have her by my side. We entered the reserved room with the private bar, and there were a couple of dozen people already there, talking and drinking beers. I recognized former players immediately. Everyone was extremely friendly, and most expressed at least mild trepidation about the week ahead. The common denominator was our mutual love of the Braves.

Most of the evening was a blur because of the sheer number of people we met that night. There were sixty players, fifteen former Braves players turned coaches, and assorted training staff from teams in Atlanta, Gwinnett, Mississippi, and Lynchburg. And there was this larger-than-life figure who simply owned the room; Wes and I became instant friends that night. That evening could best be described as finding a family you never knew you had.

I arrived at Champion Stadium the next morning, got off the bus, walked through the tunnels underneath the stadium, entered the clubhouse, and searched for my locker. In it were two jerseys—home white and road blue—with my name and number sewn on, along with a whole bunch of Braves goodies. It was the most incredible feeling putting on that uniform for the very first time.

Greg McMichael outlined what we should expect from the skills evaluation and explained that teams would be drafted behind closed doors. At some point during lunch, he would read aloud the new teams and then post the roster by the clubhouse door. We'd all play in our first game that afternoon. He had rightfully assumed that none of the older guys wanted to squat behind home plate for an inning, much less a whole game, so he added a full-time collegiate catcher to each roster.

The teams were announced, and we were all instructed to report to our respective fields. The ESPN Wide World of Sports Complex consisted of Champion Stadium, surrounded by four full-sized baseball fields. Once we arrived at our field, Greg Olson and Zane Smith, two retired MLB players, introduced themselves, talked about expectations for the week, assigned our positions, and announced the batting order. And just like that, my new teammates and I took the field. I was forty-three years old and about to play in my very first baseball game.

I don't remember the details or even what outfield position I played. All that mattered to me was getting a hit in my very first game. I had so many self-doubts coming in, but the biggest one was that I would go hitless for the week and be the laughingstock of camp. That thought ate at me week after week, which is why I trained so hard. However, my insecurities vanished with a seeing-eye single earlier in the afternoon. By evening, we were all drinking beers, playing ping pong, and telling stories about our opening day games.

Later that night, I ran into a handful of players from another team and their coach, Pete Smith, another former Braves pitcher. We sat around a table sharing stories over a few beers when Pete mentioned that his former teammate, Tom Glavine, had just agreed to come to camp and would serve as a guest coach for a day. He planned to arrive the next night and would spend all day Thursday hanging out in the locker room, watching games, and signing autographs. I told the table about my son Davis, his defection from the Braves to the Mets when Tom left during free agency, and that I had to find a way to get him to Orlando so he could meet his favorite baseball player.

"Figure out a way to get Davis here by tomorrow night, and you guys can join us for dinner," Pete offered.

Bentley had already flown home, and I knew she couldn't fly Davis back down to Orlando on such short notice, so I quickly checked online and found a direct flight on Southwest that landed in time for

Davis to have lunch in the clubhouse. But he would need someone willing to fly down, get him from the airport to the ESPN complex, and then sit in the stands for a couple of days to watch me play baseball. The only person who checked all three of those boxes was my sister, Emily, and she was an immediate yes. I confirmed everything with Bentley, bought the two round-trip tickets, and then called Davis to deliver the news.

"How would you like to skip school for the rest of the week, come to Braves camp, watch your dad play a few games, and, oh yeah, have dinner with Tom Glavine?" I asked.

The only reason this trip was possible was due to a knee injury Davis had suffered three weeks earlier while playing for his middle school basketball team. We'd taken him in for a consult with Dr. Benton Emblom, and he'd recommended that Davis undergo a simple arthroscopic debridement procedure to help reduce his pain and improve movement. The surgery had gone very well, but Davis still had three more weeks of non-contact, non-basketball-related rest to complete, so the timing to meet me in Florida for a few days was perfect.

It was our second game, the bottom of the sixth inning, and we were hanging onto our lead by a very thin thread when Davis and Emily arrived. We started strong, but our college catcher had broken a finger on his throwing hand in the third inning, and the coaches were forced to make battlefield promotions. Our hitting coach, Greg Olson, who played behind the plate in the 1991 World Series against the Twins, needed three guys to eat one inning each. Two of my teammates had done their job in the fourth and fifth innings, and it was my turn to be the backstop in the sixth. We were just three outs away from staying undefeated when Davis walked up to the fence behind home plate.

"Dad! Why are you catching? You've never caught before in your life!" Davis exclaimed.

"Not so loud, bud. Nobody here knows that," I said.

It wasn't a crazy idea. I had caught for both Cade and Davis in the backyard and a handful of times at practice, but never in an actual game. Besides, a former Braves catcher asked me to step up, and I enjoyed a good challenge. My heart was racing, and we brought in one of our best arms to close things out. My only job was to provide a good target and not let any balls get behind me. I recall that it was a quick three-up, three-down inning, and we escaped with our second win.

After packing my gear, I met up with Davis and Emily, who were speaking with Greg McMichael, the Braves' senior director of alumni relations and the man running our camp. We talked about the injury to our catcher, and Greg told us they were already calling some of the local junior colleges to see if they could get another player to the stadium in time for our afternoon game.

"If you can't find someone on that short notice, I'm sure my son would be happy to fill in," I said to Greg. "He's a catcher, too, and plays for his school team."

Davis had just turned fourteen and was coming off a knee injury, but I knew his rehabilitation had gone well, he wouldn't be batting or running the bases, and that he could catch. Our teammate scheduled to start threw hard, but Davis had caught for his brother for a few years, and I figured he could handle it. The other thing to note was that Davis was already 6 feet tall, so it's safe to say Greg assumed he was in high school. That assumption may have been the best use of the "Don't ask, don't tell" policy in Atlanta Braves Fantasy Camp history.

"All right, Davis. We have a couple of hours before the afternoon game. I'm going to keep calling around, but if I can't get a replacement here by the first pitch, I'll inform the coaches that you'll start for your dad's team. You can wear his extra uniform; I'll have a waiver for both of you to sign, and it's only going to be for this one game," Greg explained.

I took Davis into the locker room, where he got to meet my fellow campers and all the coaches. He got to chat with Pete and shared the story of flying to New York for Game 2 of the NLDS to see Tom

Glavine pitch for the Mets. We had lunch in the clubhouse, talked a lot of baseball and a little smack, and relaxed before our next game. Greg McMichael came in about twenty minutes before first pitch and posted the updated list of team names and records. And there we were, in first place: The Pitch Slappers.

"Hey, Hornak. You're starting at catcher," Greg announced.

I don't think anyone had a clue how old Davis really was, nor did they ask; with a possible appearance in the championship game on the line, all anyone could focus on was winning. Both teams were 2-0 going into the game, so our hardest throwing pitcher got the call to start, and little did he know that his backstop for the game was an eighth grader coming off knee surgery. To be fair, Davis thought he was flying in to have dinner with Tom Glavine and never expected to be thrown into a make-or-break game with team title aspirations on the line.

I knew he was nervous, but everyone else figured it out, too, when he dropped the first two fastballs Ray threw. I was in centerfield and could almost hear the groans emanating from the infield, but Davis quickly settled down, and we got out of the inning without any damage.

We were locked in a pitcher's duel for the first five innings, and late in the game, there was a bang-bang play at the plate. Davis got steamrolled but held onto the ball to keep the run from scoring, and we went on to win the game. That victory moved us into sole possession of first place and gave us the tiebreaker over the second-best team. Another one of my all-time favorite photos is the team picture we took with Davis in his catcher's gear after that game.

Even though Davis was only supposed to play in that one game, both coaches and all my teammates wanted him back behind the plate the next morning. He'd earned his place on the team, and I'd just played in a real-life baseball game with my son. As if the day couldn't get any better, we met up with Pete, Tom, and a bunch of the guys for dinner that evening. Neither of us said a lot; we just listened to the guys share some of their favorite stories from their days in the major leagues.

The talk coming out of the locker room the next morning was whether Glavine would take the mound and pitch against any of the campers. He was only two years removed from his official retirement, but his last major league appearance had been on August 14, 2008. It was so cool just having him walk around the field as we were warming up for the game, but then Tom made the decision to pitch one inning for each team.

I had hit well that week and had been moved into the cleanup spot for the Slappers, so I needed someone batting in front of me to get on base so I could get an at-bat against the Braves' legend. Glavine recorded two quick outs, but our best player and resident shortstop, Nick, who batted third, stepped up to the plate and promptly laced a single to center field.

I stepped into the batter's box. The apprehension engulfed me.

"Strike one!"

Tom had grooved a fastball right over the heart of the plate with his first pitch. Based on the first three games of my career, I had decided I was a first-pitch fastball hitter, so I was pretty sure I had just let the best opportunity to get a bat on the ball blow right by me. *That was the one,* I thought. But I'm not even sure I could have swung the bat if I wanted to. My body had frozen.

My buddy, Jeff, had driven in from Tampa, curious to see if all my baseball bucket list talk was true, and he walked up just in time to see me squaring off against the future Hall of Famer. I quickly stepped out of the batter's box to buy myself another moment, took a deep breath, and made up my mind that I was swinging at the next pitch no matter what he threw. I saw Nick take a slight lead from first base, placed my right foot back in the box, and waited.

Tom went into his motion and delivered the ball.

I was expecting another two-seam fastball, his bread-and-butter pitch, but the ball looked different the second it left his hand. I'm not savvy enough to be able to say with 100 percent certainty that it was a curveball, but it was either that or a slider. Somehow, I just knew to wait a beat, load up, and let the ball travel. The baseball looked as big as a grapefruit, and I swung as hard as I could—just like I had planned.

I made solid contact and sprinted down the line. Nick was long gone, and I saw the outfielder running diagonally toward the right field foul pole. Only then did I see the ball carrying toward the outfield wall, and for a moment, I thought it might leave the park. But it landed on the warning track, and I knew I was in the race of my life. Every sprint, every hill, and every mile I'd logged for those three months was used up over the next 270 feet around the basepaths. As I made the final dash toward home, I could see Nick jumping up and down behind the catcher, telling me to get down. So, somehow, instinctively, miraculously, I attempted my first slide to the outside edge of home plate and came in under the tag.

The Pitch Slappers went on to win the 2012 Atlanta Braves Fantasy Camp Championship that year with Davis behind the plate for the rest of the week. Former Braves outfielder Dale Murphy even made an appearance that year and spent a day with all of us campers. The two-time NL MVP was Emily's favorite player, so her week ended on a high note, too.

I loved everything about that week I spent with the Braves faithful, so much that I went back and played four more times in Orlando. In 2017, when Greg McMichael called to see if I wanted to help christen SunTrust Park and play in Atlanta's new major league stadium, I immediately said yes. To put icing on the cake, both Cade and Davis got to play too.

Cade and I squared off twice that week when he was on the mound. He struck me out on three pitches in our first head-to-head battle, but I got revenge a day later with a crisply lined single into right field. As luck would have it, Davis and I were drafted to the same team—him first and me much later—and we won another championship together while Bentley, EB, and Emily watched from the stands. Knowing that I could never top that collective family experience, I officially retired after six "seasons" and three championships.

I always enjoyed baseball, but my love of the game really began when I helped coach the boys in T-ball, Fall Ball, and then again when they played in Cooperstown, New York. We've traveled to spring training games in Florida and Arizona, written tons of letters, stood outside Turner Field waiting for the Dodgers team bus to arrive, met countless players, and got booted from our only A's game in the Oakland Coliseum because Cade jumped over a railing and onto the field to shag a batting practice homerun ball. We missed the Randy Johnson perfect game in Atlanta because it was a school night, but we still have the unused tickets.

We've all played at Rickwood Field here in Birmingham, the oldest ballpark in America, where legends like Ty Cobb, Satchel Paige, Willie Mays, Reggie Jackson, and Jackie Robinson shared the same field. We played that week at SunTrust Park and have been coached by real major leaguers. We've taken road trips together to twenty-eight different cities to catch games, and I was with them for the final out when they were eliminated from the state baseball tournament their senior year of high school. I will cherish those memories and countless others for the rest of my life.

As Brad Pitt's character, Billy Beane, said in the movie *Moneyball,* "How can you not be romantic about baseball?"

I know this was a big chapter focused on baseball, but I want to take you back to the game when Sid Bream scored the winning run in the 1992 NLCS game. It was a powerful moment that impacted me as a Braves fan. And twenty years later, at my first camp, I got to meet Sid in person. He was as humble and genuine a man as you will ever meet. And like all the coaches that year, I asked Sid to sign a baseball for me, which he gladly did. While writing this book, I found the ball he autographed twelve years earlier. He had written me this message:

"In this is love: not that we loved God,
but that He loved us and sent His Son to be the atoning sacrifice for our sins."

—1 John 4:10 MEV

24

ELSTREE 1976

"May the dreams of your past be the reality of your future."

—*Jimi Hendrix*

Bentley, Cade, Davis, and I landed at Heathrow Airport, took the Tube into central London, and hailed a black cab for a ride over to our flat in Piccadilly Circus. Our Airbnb was just blocks from Covent Garden, Leicester Square, and Saint James's Palace, and ridiculously close to everything else. We made the eleven-hour *Planes, Trains, and Automobiles* journey to the BFI London Film Festival to see the world premiere of my very first documentary, *Elstree 1976*, at the Picturehouse Central movie theater that first opened in the West End in 1896. EB wasn't with us because she'd gone to Orlando with a group of students from her high school to participate in Project Week.

After working on *Killing Them Softly*, I decided I wanted to pursue filmmaking, but taking that first step seemed overwhelming. I had one background role and an incredible internship under my belt, but I knew deep down no one would hire me without more on-set work experience. I contemplated enrolling in film school, but with three kids at home and twelve years' worth of college tuition staring me in the face, that idealistic notion seemed like the biggest boneheaded move I could make. So I thought outside the box and came up with a new plan.

I scoured the Kickstarter website for in-progress or upcoming film projects that interested me, and then, instead of just blindly making a financial contribution toward someone else's dream, I reached out directly to the creator of the campaign to get to know them and better understand their project and what they wanted to accomplish. Usually, after a couple of emails or a phone call, I'd gathered enough information to determine if they were someone I wanted to work with. If I felt good about the situation, I'd ask one last simple question.

"Is it possible for me to join you on set and help you make your movie?"

I never got a single no. In fact, most directors gave me an immediate yes because we had already built up a rapport, and only occasionally did I get the proverbial, "Let me talk it over with my team." But even those folks got back to me in a day or two with an affirmative response. While my time on a real Hollywood production gave me clear direction about what I wanted to do, the individual Kickstarter projects would allow me to hone specific skills with other young upstart directors from all over the country.

My first yes was from Jed, a director and writer who had just completed filming his feature-length comedy *Nowhere Girl,* and he invited me to be a part of the editing process at Red Bull in Los Angeles. Next up was Frank, who was working on a web series called *BLACK.* I saw his season one trailer and was amazed at how he'd used hyper-realistic drone shots to cover military movements, and after a long phone call, I knew I wanted to work with him.

Next up was Rory, who had built a niche doing webisodes about funny "Only in LA" moments. I saw her work on YouTube, and she was in the process of mapping out her second season, which included one short that would be filmed in New York City. I asked if my daughter could tag along, so EB and I spent a couple of days sightseeing and filming in Manhattan.

But the best piece of advice that I got from the three filmmakers was from Rory. She told me to make sure that my very first project was something that I was 100 percent passionate about. No exceptions. EB and I discussed it over dinner, and we agreed that it had to be something *Star Wars* related.

How would I even break into that world? I had five film credits to my name and had created an IMDb page, but I knew that wouldn't get me a meeting with George Lucas at Skywalker Ranch to discuss my ideas for his franchise. It all seemed like wishful thinking, but then I stumbled across a pitch on Kickstarter from a young director trying to tell the stories of ten actors who had appeared in the original 1977 classic.

Jon was asking for help to complete his documentary, so I reached out, told him my story, and shared my dream. He suggested I speak with his producer. I emailed Hank, we spoke live, got along swimmingly, and decided we could help each other. I jumped in with both feet, started my own production company, and desperately wanted my first project to fall into the *Star Wars* universe. Hank needed additional funds to complete the film, was still working on rights clearance, and hoped to premiere at a major international film festival.

During our negotiations, I discovered that I already knew six of the ten actors who would appear in their documentary. I didn't know them well, but I had met Dave who played Darth Vader at a fan convention in Indianapolis way back in 2002. In subsequent years, I had met and gotten to know Anthony, Paul, Garrick, Angus, and Jeremy, so I felt completely connected to this project. Hank and I hammered out the details of our agreement and joined forces to bring Jon's documentary to the masses.

The premiere was packed, and the entire production team, along with two of the original actors, John and Derek, were in attendance. We chatted away in the lobby, made introductions, and took photos before we moved into the main theater. There was great energy in the room from the sold-out crowd of around four hundred people.

Bentley, the boys, and I took our seats in the theater. Deep down, I believed that this screening would lead to some amazing opportunities and perhaps change our lives. The right person from Lucasfilm would be in the audience. We'd meet at the bar and chat for hours. They would schedule my interview. I'd get hired onto my first *Star Wars* project, and the rest would be history.

When the house lights went down and the movie began to play, I thought about my dad and how cool it would have been to have him in the theater with us. I always carried some resentment toward him for denying my Hollywood dream, but when I appeared in *Major League II,* he was the first person I called when I got home that night, and the slight bitterness I had vanished in an instant. "I can't wait to see you in a movie," he said.

The premiere was a success, and we celebrated with the cast and crew during the after-party at the Member's Bar inside the theater. It was an evening I'll never forget. And seven months after the London premiere, *Elstree 1976* was officially released in the United States. We received solid press from the *Hollywood Reporter, Rolling Stone,* and *Variety,* and a very nice review from Neil Genzlinger of the *New York Times,* who gave us a fresh review on *Rotten Tomatoes.*

The next morning, the four of us made a trip out to Stonehenge in Wiltshire, England, and spent the rest of the day sightseeing in central London. That night, while shopping in the Mayfair district, we stumbled upon Langdon's Brasserie. Bentley had dined in this classic Anglo-French restaurant when she visited London with friends after graduating high school, and we celebrated Davis and Cade's eighteenth birthday in that same establishment. We capped off the evening at The Argyll Arms, a Victorian pub in Soho that dated back to 1868.

I've been extremely lucky and blessed not only to have lived out my dream to make movies but also to have had the opportunity to work with Bentley and each one of my kids on at least one film or series. However, one project allowed me to connect with my dad in a way I never would have imagined.

In 2022, twenty-four years after my dad's suicide, I produced *SOLDIER*, a short documentary about PTSD and military suicide. Our director, Justin, focused the entire short film on Daniel, a married father of five and former Army sniper with over ten years' experience in Iraq, who unsuccessfully tried to take his own life.

When I talked to Justin about the project, I felt an intense pull to be a part of it, but I wasn't sure what my role would look like. You see, over the years, I'd enjoyed telling a handful of stories about my dad, but they were always funny or relatable things. I never volunteered much about his suicide.

But a strange sequence of events unfolded. *SOLDIER* was accepted into the Sidewalk Film Festival; Justin jumped on a last-minute flight to Birmingham, and we represented the film together. After it screened, we took part in an audience Q&A session, and I stood on a stage and spoke about my dad's suicide in front of a room full of friends and total strangers for the very first time. It was equal parts gut-wrenching and therapeutic, but that day freed me of all the baggage I had carried since he took his own life.

"For the gifts and the calling of God are irrevocable."

—Romans 11:29 NKJV

25

JUST LIKE HEAVEN

"I was standing
You were there
Two worlds collided
And they could never tear us apart."

—Michael Hutchence

B entley and I liked to mark our big anniversary milestones by taking memorable trips. Our general rule was to choose a location neither of us had visited before, allowing us to experience it together for the first time. That was the case when we started planning for our twenty-fifth wedding anniversary. Bentley's health issues seemed like a faded memory. Cade and Davis were doing well in college, and EB was about to begin her senior year of high school. Life was good. We were in a great rhythm as a family, so the biggest question heading into our silver jubilee was where we should go to celebrate.

While studying at Washington and Lee University, Cade had an opportunity to spend a semester abroad in Bayreuth, Germany, located west of the Czech Republic. Bayreuth, the capital of the Upper Franconia region, was a city that neither Bentley nor I had visited, and it gave us the perfect opportunity to see a part of the world that was connected to my Hornak family's lineage. Before we moved Cade into his new life in Germany, the three of us spent time in Munich, the capital of Bavaria. A few days later, we dropped Cade off at the University of Bayreuth, where he would spend the next several months.

Prague is bisected by the Vltava River and nicknamed "the City of a Hundred Spires." This spectacular capital city was founded around the eighth century and is replete with buildings, history, and structures dating back to Baroque, Gothic, and Romanesque times—including the Charles Bridge, which was constructed in 1402, the historic Old Town Square built around the twelfth century, and the Prague Castle founded around 880. This early medieval site was perhaps the most picturesque part of the city and has remained the largest ancient castle in the world.

Bentley and I enjoyed romantic walks around Petřín Hill, Letná Park, and the Waldstein Garden, and we took my favorite photo that week at the Hanavský Pavilion, one of the most impressive Art Nouveau structures that overlooked the city. We crossed over the Charles Bridge, a medieval stone arch spanning the Vltava River, and toured the Old Town Square, where we shopped and saw the oldest functioning astronomical clock in the world. We ate dinner on a converted riverboat and enjoyed a casual ten-minute stroll back to our hotel through the charming streets of the capital city.

To celebrate our twenty-fifth anniversary, we began the day at the St. Vitus Cathedral, a beautiful Gothic church located inside the Prague Castle grounds. I'd arranged for us to attend a private concert at the Lobkowicz Palace that featured members of the Czech Philharmonic Orchestra who played classical music by Bach, Beethoven, and Mozart. We entered the complex through the Royal Gardens, toured more of the castle grounds, strolled through the Garden on the Bastion, watched the extraordinary concert, and exited the complex through the South Gardens, which led us back to the Charles Bridge and an afternoon in the square.

Bentley and I capped off our anniversary with a private dinner inside the luxurious Prague Carlo IV, a Neo-Renaissance palace that had been converted into an exquisite hotel. We reflected on how grateful we were to be together in this exact place and moment in time, how blessed we were that her valve repair was still as good as ever, and how happy we were for each of our children and what they were building for themselves.

Our time in Prague proved to be the most wonderfully relaxed and romantic trip we had taken in recent memory. Everything about the experience was priceless, and our time together served as a reminder that Bentley and I still had so many special places left to explore.

We couldn't wait to begin this next chapter of our lives.

"The man who finds a wife finds a treasure,
and he receives favor from the LORD."

—Proverbs 18:22 NLT

26

NASHVILLE (PART I)

"Friendship means little when it's convenient."

—*Hiroyuki Sanada as Shimazu in* John Wick: Chapter 4

After celebrating our anniversary in the Czech Republic, Bentley and I traveled from Prague to Tennessee to meet up with a large group of friends from our Northern Virginia days. More than half of us who made the journey to Nashville that weekend had moved to other states, so when we wanted to spend time together, we had to be purposeful about it and willing to travel. So, fifteen of us flew into "Music City," ready to hit Broadway and celebrate our friendship. And what a weekend we had.

We texted Chris and Sarah, our old Crestline neighbors who'd moved to Nashville to start their medical careers, and said that even though we'd been on the road for almost two weeks straight, we still wanted to swing by to see them before we went home. So after a brief visit and as we were getting ready to walk out the door, Bentley told Chris, who had completed his residency at Vanderbilt University Medical Center in Otolaryngology, that her left ear hadn't popped since we'd gotten off our transatlantic flight a few days earlier.

Chris was an ENT physician. Because we were at their home, there wasn't much he could do, but he examined Bentley's ear using his otoscope, a small device with a magnifying lens and a light. He also gave her a basic hearing test. Nothing stood out, but he was worried that her ear hadn't popped and that everything on her left side sounded muffled. He suggested she find an ENT in Birmingham, get a more thorough exam and a complete hearing evaluation, and then he casually mentioned that she should get an MRI as soon as possible.

"An MRI—why?" I asked.

"Well, there's less than a 1 percent chance that Bentley has a brain tumor, but I'd want to rule that out right away," he explained.

A week later, Bentley was diagnosed with a vestibular schwannoma, also known as an acoustic neuroma, and I quickly learned that a tumor like that only occurs in roughly 1 in 100,000 people per year. But somehow, some way, she had completely defied the odds again, and now she had a brain tumor. After leaving the doctor's office in Birmingham, I called Chris to get his assessment of the situation.

"What would you do if Sarah received this same diagnosis?" I asked.

"First off, you don't have to make a rash decision because this type of tumor grows very slowly. In fact, she's probably had it for quite some time, and you might not have recognized any of the symptoms," Chris said.

"So, how would you handle it? Where would you go for the best treatment options?" I pressed.

"Vanderbilt has one of the best acoustic neuroma programs in the country. I'd also recommend The House Clinic in Los Angeles," he said.

"It isn't easy to travel long distances for medical care, but we've been going to Cleveland for years. I'm not against making a trip to L.A. to meet with those physicians, but I prefer the idea of being able to drive to Nashville for a consult," I said. "Where would you start?"

"I'd reach out to the Ingram Cancer Center and make an appointment with one of their radiation oncologists," Chris said. "Meet with them first and see what they suggest. It will either be radiation or surgery."

On June 20, 2018, only two months after celebrating our anniversary in Prague, we walked into the Ingram Cancer Center for an appointment with Dr. Albert Attia, an assistant professor of radiation oncology who held a secondary faculty appointment in the Department of Neurosurgery. After he reviewed Bentley's chart and scans, he suggested we meet with Dr. Lola Chambless for a neurosurgery consult. He thought it might be best to surgically remove the tumor right away since it was relatively small, and at her age, she would tolerate the procedure well.

"Don't rule anything out. Just have a conversation with Dr. Chambless," he said.

We weren't diametrically opposed to the brain surgery, but Bentley had some reservations. First, everything about the surgery sounded much bigger and more intense than what she'd previously been through. I wouldn't say Bentley was scared, but I would say she was intimidated by all the "what ifs" of cutting into her skull and digging out a tumor that was near so many critical structures. She was also facing a fifth open-heart surgery in the not-so-distant future. We discussed all the pros and cons of surgery versus radiation during our consult with Dr. Chambless but told her we preferred to move forward with radiation instead.

With that decision made, it was time to focus on how her radiation therapy would proceed. Also working with Dr. Attia was the director of head and neck radiotherapy at Vanderbilt. His job was to determine the total dose of radiation she'd receive and then map out her treatment strategy. Ultimately, he decided her tumor would respond best to fractional radiation, which meant splitting her total radiation dose into smaller doses over a pre-determined number of visits. This method was designed to maximize the effect of radiation on the tumor while reducing the damage to healthy cells.

Early on a Tuesday morning in July, we drove to Nashville and arrived at the Ingram Cancer Center to begin her first day of treatment. Each rigidly scheduled appointment lasted about thirty minutes, although each session only took a few minutes. With all the prep and delivery combined, we were in and out of the hospital in under an hour each day. Everything about the process felt routine, and the team of doctors, nurses, and technologists had each visit down to a science.

One of the unique parts of Bentley's treatment prep was that they created a radiotherapy mask specific to her. The shell was custom-fitted from a special mesh material carefully shaped to the specific contours of her head and neck. The thermoplastic mask ensured that she'd remain perfectly still during the radiation procedure so they could deliver the precise dose directly to her tumor. But Bentley hated putting it on each day and being strapped down to the table.

Chris and Sarah invited us to stay with them for as long as she needed to go back and forth to Vanderbilt. So, after Bentley's first session, we drove to their house and got her settled in the guest room. After a brief visit, I drove three hours back to Birmingham to be at home for EB and the dogs, and that became my daily routine. I'd drive to Vanderbilt for Bentley's treatment session, make sure she was resting comfortably back at our friends' house, and then head back home. It was a grind, but I knew that our friends had her covered if she got sick, the schedule changed, or I was too exhausted to make the six-hour round-trip drive.

On her last day of radiation, Bentley's treatment team held a very moving ceremony in the Ingram Cancer Center. One of the nurses read an inspirational poem about finishing treatment, and Bentley got to ring a brass bell that hung from the wall. Everyone on the team cheered, and they gave Bentley a graduation certificate in honor of the milestone. We had dinner with Chris, Sarah, and their kids that night and drove back to Birmingham the next morning, feeling exuberant that we had dodged yet another bullet.

However, the euphoria didn't last long. We'd been told to expect some side effects after radiation, and Bentley had her fair share. She was constantly fatigued, had headaches, nausea, and dizziness, but she also developed significant memory problems in the weeks that followed her treatment. But all those symptoms would pale compared to what came next. She was easily disoriented, had ringing in her ears, and lost a considerable amount of her balance and vision. Therefore, she couldn't drive. The doctors prescribed outpatient vestibular training and balance therapy, and Bentley went to those sessions at least two days per week.

Over the next six months, Bentley walked a tightrope of improvements and setbacks. Many of her side effects started to dissipate, and she saw marked improvements in her concentration, stability, and vision—so much so that I took her up to an abandoned mall near our house so she could practice driving again. But as happy as she was to get behind the wheel, she was dealing with far bigger complications post-radiation. The ringing in her ears was diagnosed as full-fledged tinnitus, which, medically speaking, was an intermittent or continuous perception of sound when there's no external source. Sadly, a patient must learn to live with this condition because there's no cure. As her tinnitus got louder month after month, it affected her mental well-being. Furthermore, what little hearing she had on her left side gradually waned into nothingness.

Her six-month follow-up with Dr. Attia was a paradox of outcomes. Bentley's MRI showed that the tumor "demonstrated relative stability," but images showed that it still sat in her skull, millimeters away from her brain stem. And through audiology tests, they confirmed that she'd completely lost her hearing on the left side, yet the ringing from her tinnitus continued to grow louder. On the positive side, her balance was back to normal, she was driving again, and she didn't have any other major neurological complaints. That day, there was no celebration, no ringing of the bell—just a lot of doubt about whether choosing radiation over surgery had been the right decision.

"Friends come and friends go,
but a true friend sticks by you like family."

—Proverbs 18:24 MSG

27

THE WAITING ROOM

"The worst pain a man can suffer is to have insight into much and power over nothing."

—*Herodotus*

I'd known since the middle of 2019 that Bentley's repaired heart valve had been leaking more profusely, her cardiac function had deteriorated, and that she needed a fifth open-heart surgery to replace the failing valve. The last repair had bought her ten years with a good quality of life and freedom from anti-coagulation medication, but the timer had run out.

Bentley was more distraught about this surgery because it meant she would need a mechanical valve and a complete replacement of her ascending aorta up to the three vessels that branched off the arch. I couldn't bring her much comfort, but over the next few weeks, she made peace with the idea of another surgery.

Her cardiologist proposed a fall surgery date, but I asked if we could push the procedure out to the spring to avoid traveling to Ohio during the winter months. The doctor approved that request, and we set our sights on early April for the big repair. The timing was perfect for us. Bentley wanted to see another Cavs game, and the trip might allow me to catch an Indian's game at Progressive Field. And we both wanted to take a tour of The Rock & Roll Hall of Fame. I'd hoped that the two games and tour would take Bentley's mind off her pending repair.

Then COVID-19 hit.

Bentley's surgery was scheduled for the first week of April, but the world started shutting down in the middle of March. Cade had finished all his graduation requirements for Washington and Lee, and he'd rented a house with a bunch of his fraternity brothers. But the university shut down a couple of weeks into the pandemic and ordered them to leave. EB was halfway through her second semester at The College of Charleston, but we received a call that gave us a two-hour window to move her out of the dorm. She was home a couple of days later. Davis was the last holdout. He lived by himself in an off-campus apartment in Auburn and never received any orders to flee the city.

Bentley, Cade, EB, and I gathered in Birmingham, stocked our pantry with enough food to last a couple of weeks, and settled in to help "flatten the curve." With this unexpected free time at home, we started binge-watching *Modern Family, Frasier,* and *The Office*—and, of course, the incredible third season of *Ozark.* But two weeks turned into four, and Davis decided to leave his apartment and come back to Birmingham.

This time we spent with the kids was a blessing we never expected. We played board games, worked on puzzles, and shot hoops in the driveway most days. Bentley and I came up with a list of great '80s and '90s movies we felt were mandatory viewing, so each night, we checked off a John Hughes comedy or another Schwarzenegger action flick. We didn't eat out; we were all walking or exercising, and frankly, we were in the middle of a great family reset. However, after a couple of months, things started to crumble. Cade's late May graduation was canceled. Davis and EB's classes had been postponed indefinitely. My inability to travel had let me forget about work for a few weeks, but the question of how I could do my job in this undefined reality consumed my thoughts. To make matters worse, Bentley's health kept declining.

The Cleveland Clinic cut back on the number of surgeries it normally performed to deal with COVID. Bentley's surgery date was bumped from early April to late June, and that adjustment felt reasonable. It gave things time to settle down, and it also gave me time to make our new travel plans for the surgery. The kids were going stir crazy with the isolation and wanted out of the house. It didn't feel like COVID was as rampant in Birmingham as it was in other major cities—or perhaps we'd stuck our heads in the sand—so we let them wander out to see some select friends. Cade and Davis started jamming with their high school teammate and friend at his house, and within a few weeks, they'd written a few songs and jumped into rehearsals. EB, our most social child, had friends over two or three times a week, and they hung out in the backyard by the pool.

However, when the pandemic continued to spread and thousands upon thousands were dead, a new fear took hold of me. I only left the house once a week to get groceries or prescriptions and followed reasonable safety precautions, but our kids didn't do the same, not because they wanted to rebel against us but because they were young and felt bulletproof. I never felt at risk, but Bentley's health had deteriorated so quickly that I knew she was a target for infection. I couldn't risk having the kids bring this contagion home to their mom. So, I played the death card and locked down the house for good. The pushback was mild because I think deep down, the kids had the same concerns. We all saw that Bentley was weaker every day.

She'd gone from walking outside daily to feeling chronically tired. She got short of breath while walking from the bedroom to the kitchen. She had heart palpitations, chest tightness, and was constantly lightheaded. She stopped exercising altogether and stayed in bed for long stretches every day. When she did come out to join us in the family room, she simply wasn't present. Her thinking had slowed because her left ventricle couldn't properly push enough blood out through her aortic valve and into her body without leaking backward into her heart. Her body was starving, and the new fogginess took its toll on her mentally. She couldn't focus on the simplest task, like watching TV.

That summer, I called the cardiology clinic every Monday morning to see where she stood in line, but I already knew the answer. I saw the broadcasts, read every online article, and knew that the news in Cleveland wasn't any better. Many of their procedure rooms had been turned into makeshift COVID ICUs, and I'd received a call that the hospital had modified its protocols and only allowed one open-heart surgery per room per day. But Bentley's body didn't care. She had lost weight, she sweated while resting on the couch, and her breathing was visibly labored. She struggled to catch her breath every hour of every day. She couldn't stand on her own. Eating exhausted her. All we could do was watch and tell her it would be all right.

As Bentley withered away, I felt completely helpless. I gave the Cleveland Clinic staff a daily update and asked for a surgery date. Any date. Any time. I told them they could call me in the middle of the night, and I'd have her at the check-in desk within twelve hours. Without treatment, her aortic valve regurgitation would turn into congestive heart failure in approximately two years—a precursor to death. And she'd already passed the one-year mark since we were told she needed surgery. My thirty years in the medical field, everything I knew about heart disease, and all my contacts didn't matter. I could not help my wife.

I contemplated my options daily, but no amount of bully prowess or sheer determination could get us through the front door of that hospital. I could not "will" her onto the table—not this time. We needed a miracle, and I didn't know what to do.

It was a couple of days before Halloween and almost sixteen months since our last visit to Cleveland. All that waiting. All her suffering. All that despair and the weight of helplessness. And then my phone rang.

"Mr. Hornak," a woman said, "this is surgery scheduling at the Cleveland Clinic. How are you?"

"We've been better," I replied. "Hoping this is a good news call."

"It is. Bentley has been scheduled for surgery on the twenty-third of November. Can you get her here?" she asked.

"Yes! Absolutely," I said as relief washed over me.

"You're the only one who can enter the hospital with her, and you can't stay overnight in the room. You and Bentley must both have a negative COVID test administered within seventy-two hours prior to her admission. We'll send an email with the location of her drive-up testing site and your designated arrival time in Cleveland on Friday, November 20. If Bentley doesn't get tested at the assigned time, she won't be eligible for surgery. Do you understand these requirements, Mr. Hornak?"

"Yes," I answered.

"You'll also need to be tested within seventy-two hours of your arrival and show proof that you don't have COVID."

Cutting her off, I said, "Can't I get tested with my wife?"

"We can't accommodate your testing at the Cleveland Clinic. You'll have to do that before you arrive. If you don't provide the proper proof, you can't enter our facilities. Do you understand these requirements, Mr. Hornak?"

"I do," I said.

"Immediately following her COVID test, bring Bentley to the main campus where she'll complete her pre-operative workup. We'll email you a list of her appointments. You should expect to be here at least a week. Do you have any questions for me?

"I don't," I said.

"We look forward to seeing Bentley on the twentieth," she said and ended the call.

While the whole family wanted to celebrate this news, we knew it was almost four weeks away. Four weeks for Bentley to suffer and for us to watch. We couldn't mess up this opportunity or do anything that might prevent her from getting to the testing site. I was the only one who left the house that month and only for groceries or medication.

These were targeted runs, and I only got what I could carry in my arms, just the essentials. When I got home, I wiped everything down. And while the kids and I never showed any symptoms of COVID, I'm not sure we would have known if Bentley had been exposed.

So, we waited.

About two weeks out, I decided we couldn't risk flying since it meant traveling through three airports and passing thousands of people. I looked at booking a charter flight, but the expense was pro-hibitive. Our only other alternative was to drive, but that was also a terrible solution. Bentley was constantly fatigued, had chest pains, and her body was sore all over. Driving meant bouncing around in the back of the car on a rough interstate for eleven hours, but it was the best of all the bad options.

To minimize potential contact during the trip from Birmingham to Cleveland, we decided to leave at 9:00 p.m. on November 19 and drive straight through. I had our 2008 Chevy Suburban serviced at a local gas station, removed the rear seats, bought an air mattress at Walmart, and booked a hotel room about three blocks from the hospital.

And we waited.

On that Thursday evening, we said prayers with the kids in the front yard and pulled out of our driveway. Bentley lay lengthwise on the makeshift bed I'd cobbled together in the back of the Suburban. It wouldn't win any awards, but I knew our plan gave us the highest probability of success.

"Wait on the LORD;
Be of good courage,
And He shall strengthen your heart;
Wait, I say, on the LORD!"

—Psalms 27:14 NKJV

28

CLEVELAND (PART II)

"What I've come to find out is that no matter what happens, the storm eventually ends."

—*Kobe Bryant*

Five minutes after we pulled out of the driveway, the reality of our circumstances and the unknown road ahead hit me like a ton of bricks. I'd packed two candy bars to eat along the way but had nervously devoured both before we were outside the Birmingham city limits. I'd packed a large bottle of water, but I was too afraid to drink it and risk an extra stop for a bathroom break. Every hour or so, I took a tiny sip. Bentley slept, so I couldn't play music, and I chomped through my entire pack of gum before we ever crossed into Kentucky. Everything about this trip felt otherworldly, and the drive was excruciatingly long.

We made one gas stop outside Cincinnati on the 712-mile drive and arrived in Cleveland about forty minutes before the scheduled COVID test. We parked on the side of the road about two blocks away from the testing facility. I helped Bentley move up to the front passenger seat, we said a prayer for a negative COVID test, and we sat with the engine idling. We put on our N95 masks, pulled into the near-barren parking lot at the exact time we were told, and slowly drove the Suburban toward the tables under a large tent. Everyone wore blue protective gowns from head to toe, full plastic face shields, and surgical gloves. They looked like a group of actors on an apocalyptic movie set. I inched up and rolled down my window.

"Name," the nurse said.

"Bentley Hornak. She's the patient. On the passenger side," I answered.

Without hesitation, another nurse approached the right side of the vehicle, verified Bentley's name and date of birth, and performed the thoroughly invasive nose swab, which made me recoil.

"Mrs. Hornak, the results will be sent to your provider within forty-eight hours. Do you know where to go next?" she asked.

"We do. Thank you," Bentley said as we drove to the main parking deck next to the hospital.

The Cleveland Clinic is an incredible facility. It's modern, clean, and always bustling. But today it looked like a ghost town. As we walked in, a wave of nervousness rushed over me again. Yes, I had a negative COVID test with me, but I felt like I was approaching an East German checkpoint with contraband in my bag. They verified who we were, asked a ton of questions, took our temperatures, and verified my COVID test results from Birmingham.

They drew Bentley's blood for her lab work and gave her an EKG and chest X-ray. She also had to get anesthesia clearance. Our last stop was an office visit with her cardiac surgeon, the same physician who'd performed her repair in 2009. They chatted briefly and had a mutual connection based on their love of horses, but this meeting was to explain the plans for Monday morning.

Dr. Pettersson expected to replace Bentley's aortic valve with a new mechanical version that he referred to as the "black diamond." He would most likely need to replace her ascending aorta, the large artery that carries blood away from the heart to the rest of the body. He also said he'd clean up any other issues in need of repair after he opened her up and got a good look inside.

I knew with all my heart that Bentley was in excellent hands with Dr. Pettersson, and I felt enormous peace. She and I agreed that we were in the right hospital with the best doctor. Still, Bentley was the one going under the knife, which brings with it a different kind of anxiety, especially for someone who'd had repeated operations for close to fifty years.

We drove to the hotel, checked in under very similar conditions to those of the hospital, and I took her straight to the room. I unloaded the Suburban and drove it back to the main garage at the hospital, where it would remain for the rest of our stay. Even with Thanksgiving approaching, the near-vacant hotel had kept its restaurant open with a skeleton crew. I didn't need to locate a grocery or convenience store or do any shopping, so we lay low in the hotel for the entire weekend. Yes, we were waiting again, but the finish line was in sight.

During our forty-eight hours of downtime, Bentley told me how difficult and painful the drive had been. Every start and stop, every bump in the road, and every sharp curve generated force that pressed into her body from all directions. As carefully as I'd tried to drive, she'd been in constant pain.

Bentley never complains—and I mean *never* complains. So, when she told me she couldn't bear the thought of bouncing around on that air mattress for eleven hours on the way home with her newly wired sternum, I got to work. I put a plan in place, so we'd never have to drive that Suburban home.

Our Suburban was thirteen years old, and it had seen better days. Have you ever had a kid throw up in your car? We did—multiple times. Ever transported dogs or cats that whizzed or defecated to a veterinarian clinic in your car? We did—countless times. We tried to get all the smells out but couldn't. We soaked those spots in Nature's Miracle, got the Suburban detailed multiple times, bought a porta-ble carpet and upholstery cleaner, and tried everything to remove the collection of foul odors. And when none of those things worked, I got a box cutter and sliced out all the carpet that had been in the splash zones. Still, it smelled rank. So that morning, with my wife's blessing, I called her brother. He knew where we were and why we were there, and he was caught a little off guard.

"Hey, man. Everything all right?" Dave quickly asked.

"Everything's good," I said. "Hey, I have a question for you."

"Sure. Fire away," he said.

"Does John still need a car? I know he was trying to save up to get one," I asked.

"Yeah, but he hasn't been able to afford anything yet. All the cars he's looked at are so expensive," Dave said.

"Can you ask him if he wants our truck?" I asked. "It has 150,000 miles on it and is beat up pretty bad, and it smells like a pack of wild dogs got a bout of food poisoning."

Since John was our nephew, I was willing to give him the Suburban for free, but to his credit and perhaps some prodding from his dad, we agreed it needed to cost something. I gave him the family discount, and we reached a gentlemen's agreement to make the transfer under one condition: he had to get to Cleveland and pick it up the next day. That Sunday, I handed John the keys, and with them, our only logical way home.

At the crack of dawn on the Monday before Thanksgiving, the sky was dark, there was a chill in the air, and the streets were deserted. The hospital's courtesy shuttle ran on a loop between a few of the nearby hotels, and it stopped in front of the main entrance of the Cleveland Clinic. We walked through the main doors, passed through Checkpoint Charlie, signed in at the cardiothoracic desk around 4:15 a.m., and spent the next two hours getting ready for surgery number five. The transport staff came to Bentley's room and helped her onto the gurney. They let me walk with her, and at 6:25 a.m., we stopped in front of a sign that summed up the exact reason we chose this hospital and Dr. Pettersson eleven years earlier:

"Through These Portals Pass the World's Greatest Cardiothoracic and Vascular Surgical Teams."

These men and women had practiced excellence for so long, and I was at complete peace when Bentley passed through the double doors and into the operating room.

I went back to the main lobby and sat in almost complete isolation. Bentley had given me a list of her friends from the neighborhood, church, and Bible studies and asked me to give them regular updates throughout the day. I texted the kids, her mom, my sister, our extended family, and a handful of close friends. I used Facebook to keep everyone else updated. It was the same drill as in 2009; except this time, I asked this eclectic collection of friends, co-workers, and neighbors to pray for her and the surgical team.

I'd been checking emails, responding to a barrage of texts, liking all the social media comments, and had spoken with each of the kids. So, I was a little taken aback when I got a text that the surgery was over. It felt too quick. Something must have gone wrong. But when I met with Dr. Pettersson fifteen minutes later, he told me Bentley had done great, there were no surprises, the surgery was a success, and that her new valve should be good for the next twenty years. While we were talking, she'd been whisked out of the OR to the ICU, where she'd remain for the next twenty-four hours.

One more thing about Bentley, especially as it relates to the ICU—she absolutely hates being intubated—a procedure that involves inserting a tube down her throat and into the airway to help her breathe. Like clockwork, when she started to rouse up, she looked me dead in the eye and pointed her finger at the tube. She wanted it out, but they had to leave it in until they were confident that she could breathe on her own. Thus began the dance of seeing who I could upset less: the doctors, the staff, or my wife.

Bentley's recovery was remarkable. During that first walk with her the next morning, I thought, *This girl is crushing it.* Just like she wanted that tube pulled out the day before, she wanted out of the hospital so we could be home for Thanksgiving. But I knew a Turkey Day surprise wasn't in the cards.

One of the downsides of receiving a mechanical valve is that the patient needs a blood thinner like Coumadin to keep the leaflets patent and functioning properly. Leaflets are a key component within any valve that controls the flow of blood to ensure one-way circulation through the heart and out into the body. Keeping these small, pivoting doors patent means to keep them free of debris like blood clots. Coumadin, or other similar versions of this drug, creates one of two scenarios. If the levels are too high, the blood clots too slowly, which could lead to excessive bruising or uncontrollable bleeding. If the levels are too low, the blood clots too quickly, and the patient is at risk of developing dangerous blood clots, which could cause a stroke. In Bentley's case, excessive clotting could harm the leaflets and prevent the valve from functioning properly. The drug designed to keep her new valve ticking was the same one that could cause her to stroke or bleed out.

Finding balance amidst this tension is necessary for the patient to live a normal life. And that process takes time, which was good for me because we didn't have a way to get home. While Bentley was resting or sleeping, I checked all available flights out of Cleveland. Due to mass cancellations caused by COVID, there were limited options, and all of them required a connection through Atlanta.

Remember her flight home in 2009, when we raced through the airport in that aisle chair? That experience was so terrible that I knew we couldn't do it again. I had a very short list of people I knew with access to a private plane, but the costs associated with booking on such short notice were astronomical. And even if I had the money, I had no idea when she'd be released or if there'd be a charter service available on that day.

So, what were we waiting on? Bentley had to have a consistent INR—international normalized ratio—a blood test that measures how quickly blood clots. A doctor uses the INR results to determine the correct dose of Coumadin. Since every patient is different and there is no right dose of the drug, every new mechanical heart patient must go through this initial trial-and-error period. The good news was that each day that passed got us closer to hitting the right number. But the bad news was that one day the hospitalist would walk in and say, "We got it! You're free to go home."

After being told we were one or two days away from validating the correct dose and stabilizing Bentley's INR, I got a call from an old friend that I never expected. I was sure he was calling to see how she was doing, but he took me by complete surprise.

"How's Bentley? he asked.

"She's doing really well," I said. "The valve is fantastic, her heart function has never been better, she's eating and walking the halls, and frankly, we're ready to get out of this place."

"What's the holdup? Why can't she leave?" he asked.

"They're trying to balance the new medication, and they won't let her leave until they do," I said. "She has to stay until they get it right."

"Well," he said, "my wife and I want to do something for the two of you. We have a plane on standby to fly you directly from Cleveland back to Birmingham. Whenever they let you leave, it will be there for you," he said.

I was in complete disbelief. This was so beyond generous, beyond anything I could have possibly imagined, that I told him I couldn't accept it. That we would find a way home without it. That it was surely too expensive a gift. That there was no way I could ever repay them for this unbelievable gesture.

He simply said, "Let us do this for you and Bentley."

I left the hotel and went back to the hospital, where I told Bentley everything.

"How could we possibly accept this?" I asked her.

"This isn't your gift to control," she said. "They wouldn't offer it if they couldn't do it, and you'll forever taint their generosity if you don't accept it graciously."

I called my friend back, told him how overwhelmed we were, and accepted his offer for the flight. Two days later, Bentley got clearance to check out the next morning. I stopped by the main desk to see how to arrange a car to take us to the downtown regional airport. The lady asked me for my wife's name, and when I told her, she said that Dr. Pettersson had already arranged for a limousine to take us wherever we needed to go. I was dumbfounded by this second generous act of kindness.

Early the next morning, Bentley and I made the fifteen-minute drive from the hospital to the Cleveland Burke Lakefront Airport in style. Two hours later, we landed at the private jet terminal at the Birmingham International Airport, where Cade, Davis, and EB picked us up for the short drive home, where we were met by our closest friends and neighbors.

"Consider it pure joy, my brothers and sisters, whenever you face trials of many kinds, because you know that the testing of your faith produces perseverance. Let perseverance finish its work so that you may be mature and complete, not lacking anything."

—James 1:2-4 NIV

29

STILL WATERS

"There's something out there waiting for us—and it ain't no man."
—*Sonny Landham as Billy in* Predator

We should have been able to relax a little bit. Bentley's post-op recovery had been incredible, and she was determined to stop taking her pain medication and get out of bed. In record time, she was walking up and down our street two or three times a day, which made it appear like she'd recovered from her fifth open-heart surgery.

But on the inside, Bentley wasn't doing well at all. The mechanical valve thumped so loudly that she felt like it would burst out of her chest at any moment. And there was no way to muffle her tinnitus. She described it as a constant, high-pitch siren and ranked the volume as an eight on a scale of one to ten. She couldn't sleep. The mental fatigue had become unbearable, and she'd slipped into a depression. Yes, she was alive, but what was her quality of life?

Then I started to question God. Why the debilitating tinnitus? Why the tumor that could survive radiation? Why the mental suffering? Why the waiting? Why the chronic insomnia? And why the possibility of a massive, skull-based surgery? I'd been so confident that the cardiac repair would fix everything, but instead, all we did was swap one major problem for two new ones. Our situation felt hopeless, like everything we did made matters so much worse.

While the final weeks before her surgery had been terrible, it was nothing compared to the next fifteen months. She was discharged from the Cleveland Clinic in December 2020, and she did everything the doctors recommended to expedite her physical recovery. Her heart valve and ascending aorta had been repaired, her cardiac output had never been better, and her radiated, slow-growing brain tumor was still sitting there, like a lone buoy bobbing in the middle of a lake. Medically speaking, she was fixed to the best of everyone's ability, but she was miserable inside her newly repaired body. And there was no escape.

I continued to read countless articles about tinnitus, but they all drew the same conclusion: there was no cure. And depending on the severity, it came with its own set of nightmares, like emotional stress, anxiety, and insomnia, and it could lead to depression or even suicide.

When I asked Bentley what I could do to help, she said, "Pray for me."

In May, we were still living with the reality of Bentley's failed radiation and her persistent brain tumor. I learned that only about 3 percent of patients treated for a vestibular schwannoma with fractional stereotactic radiation failed that type of treatment and required any sort of salvage operation. Yet, she was in that statistical minority again and back at Vanderbilt for yet another workup, which was beyond disheartening.

That morning, she underwent another MRI, had a baseline audiogram test, and met with Dr. David Haynes for a follow-up consult. He said Bentley's tumor was still lurking near the brain stem, but it hadn't grown larger, and he didn't consider it an imminent threat. In fact, she could probably wait a year for her next scan unless there was a significant change to her health or she became more symptomatic. She already had hearing loss, tinnitus, headaches, and some balance issues.

He wanted us to watch for any tingling, weakness, or facial numbness on the left side of her face. Based on his assessment, there was no need to meet with the neurosurgeon on this visit, so we canceled that appointment and were thrilled that there was nothing else to do until the next May.

I regularly prayed for Bentley's tinnitus to go away—sometimes a little and sometimes a lot. I prayed for a reduction from an eight to a five. I prayed for it to go away completely. I prayed that a wonder drug would be developed to kill this phantom menace. After a while, I prayed for the suffering to stop. I didn't curse God, but I certainly couldn't comprehend why someone so faithful to Him and His son Jesus should suffer in this way. To be honest, I thought it was my fault, that I simply didn't know the correct way to pray or how to properly ask God for something this big. I hadn't heard an audible voice. I hadn't seen a vision. And Bentley certainly wasn't getting any better. In fact, her overall health continued to get worse.

One Sunday afternoon in August, Bentley gave me a brief synopsis of a book she was reading called *A Message from God* by Retha and Aldo McPherson. She had probably suggested fifty or so books over the course of our marriage that she thought I might enjoy, and until that day, I'd never read a single page of any of them.

I'm not a jerk. And I do read. I just don't read books. In fact, the last book I remembered reading was *My Losing Season* by Pat Conroy. And before that? As a kid, I'd read *My Side of the Mountain* by Jean George, followed by *Lord of the Flies*, and then *Star Wars*. Before heading off to The Citadel, I read *The Lords of Discipline*, also by Conroy. That's it. That was my list. I'd only read five books cover to cover in my entire life, so what I did next took both of us by surprise.

Perhaps I decided to read *A Message from God* because I was searching for answers after Bentley's last evaluation. Maybe I was sympathetic to her because of how she described the words of a child who'd talked to his mother about his encounter with Jesus. Maybe I was just so desperate that day that I agreed to read book number six. Maybe I got a nudge from God. Whatever it was, I made quick work of the book. But there was a single half-page of text that stood out to me—thirteen sentences in the entire book.

This young boy, Aldo, was in a car wreck with his entire family and was seriously injured with severe brain trauma. After slipping into a coma, he had a supernatural experience and met God. Through his mother, he told the story of being with Jesus and seeing a crowd of people standing on a golden bridge trying to get into Heaven. They were crying and covered in "clothes of mud," but they couldn't enter because "they weren't ready," Aldo said. They were muddy, he said, because they didn't know Jesus.

I don't dream, and I've never had a vision, but I did ask God to show me a sign. From my love of films, my mind tends to see things through a movie-making lens. I'm always looking at angles and backdrops or picturing a scene, so I'm not 100 percent sure what happened next. I know it wasn't a dream. All I can say is that one night in September, as I was slowly nodding off on the couch, I saw something.

I was standing on that golden bridge, maybe one hundred yards outside the gates of Heaven. And the bridge was packed with people. Nobody was moving. We were crammed in like sardines, and I didn't recognize a soul. But on the other side of the gate, I saw Bentley. Although there weren't as many people on her side, she stood out so prominently that I knew it was her. I started waving, but she couldn't see me, and I'm not sure she was looking for me. I kept waving and trying to push forward, but I couldn't get past the wall of faceless people all dressed in grey clothes. I looked down and saw that I, too, was wearing grey, and I blended in with everyone else on the bridge. It could have been mud, but I don't recall the sensation of being dirty or wet. I was just grey. And then it ended. I was still on the couch.

I still don't know how to process what I saw. But I couldn't unsee the separation between Bentley and me. I felt it. I immediately told her about what I'd seen and chalked it up to having recently read the book

A Message from God. Then I tried to intellectualize it and surmised that I'd visualized that chapter and turned it into a scene in my head.

Earlier that week, Bentley told me she wanted to get baptized. Normally, my gut reactions to things I hadn't planned were never good. I'd get angry or refuse to participate because it wasn't my plan, so Bentley had been hesitant to tell me that she'd been planning this for some time. She was going with or without my support. The second the words came out of her mouth, I looked at her and said I wanted to get baptized, too. I'd flaked out on so many things in the past that I'm not sure she believed me, but I reached out to the church via email and received a call from Ross Hendricks, one of the pastors. We talked about Jesus and the reasons I wanted to be baptized.

That weekend, on October 9, 2021, at The Gathering Place Church in Moody, Alabama, Bentley and I were baptized in front of family, friends, and complete strangers. She went first, and I felt something happening inside of me. I was overjoyed for my wife and teared up. I was next, and the only thing I distinctly remember after rising out of the water was hearing Davis shout, "Way to go, Dad!"

Later that month, at a casual dinner with friends, and having mustered up enough courage, I shared that I'd read *A Message from God.* I gave them the synopsis of the book and said that I'd seen myself standing with thousands of other grey people on that golden bridge. I believed that because Bentley couldn't see me, it might have been a sign that I needed to take some kind of action, which had most likely played a part in my getting baptized earlier that month. I told the other couples that since that Sunday morning two weeks earlier, I'd had a nagging feeling that I was supposed to help other people get off that bridge, too. That night, I talked about God for the first time in public.

A few days later, Bentley told me she had felt a strange twitching on her left cheek and wanted me to look at it, but upon closer examination, I couldn't see anything, so neither of us was overly concerned. Around that same time, my daughter gave me a copy of *Jesus Calling,* a daily devotional written by Sarah Young. EB said that she'd started reading it in college and thought I might enjoy the straightforward message every day. Within a week, we started reading it together as a family before we went to bed. A couple of weeks later, a friend told me about a Christian historical drama called *The Chosen*, a television series co-written and directed by Dallas Jenkins. The show first aired in 2019, so the first two seasons were already released. We binge-watched it as a family, and I instantly felt connected to the show.

That November, a new thought popped into my head. It was definitely not a dream and certainly not a vision—just a thought. *What would happen if I were standing before God and He said, "What did you think of My book?"* I've winged answers on the fly before, but I had no idea how to respond to this. I remained still and wondered where this thought had come from.

That's so weird, I thought. But His follow-up question was even clearer and more direct.

"I've only written one. Did you read it?"

I felt pursued by something I couldn't fully comprehend. I wasn't sure what to do, but I knew I had to act, so I downloaded the Bible App on my iPhone and started reading the Bible that day.

> "What do you think? If a man owns a hundred sheep,
> and one of them wanders away, will he not leave the ninety-nine
> on the hills and go to look for the one that wandered off?
> And if he finds it, truly I tell you, he is happier about that one sheep
> than about the ninety-nine that did not wander off.
> In the same way, your Father in heaven is not willing
> that any of these little ones should perish."
>
> —Matthew 18:12-14 NIV

30

CHRISTMAS COAL

*"When you come out of a storm,
you won't be the same person that walked in.
That's what the storm is all about."*

—Haruki Murakami

It was just another normal Saturday morning when I proposed the idea of a family photo shoot. Bentley and the kids always resisted because they hated the process, but they also admitted that they loved the results. So that December day, we all jumped in my truck and headed downtown to the old John's City Diner. The building has an exterior wall with a painted mural that reads "It's Nice to Have You in Birmingham." The slogan dates to the 1950s and was one of the more iconic spots for photographers for many years. And now, it would be the backdrop for our Christmas card.

I made quick work of the setup, and speed was important because at any moment, my family might say, "That's plenty of pictures" or, "I think you got what you needed." Instead, about halfway through the process, Bentley quietly walked over and told me that her face felt funny, like she had a never-ending tingle. I saw noticeable drooping just below her left eye and immediately knew something was wrong. Bentley had instantly become symptomatic, and my mind started to race a million miles a minute. *What is happening? Is this what Dr. Haynes told us to watch for? How did it happen so fast? It was supposed to be a slow-growing tumor, right?*

I went into full panic mode and knew I had to call the three physicians who had the most detailed knowledge of Bentley's history and current situation. I immediately called Dr. David Haynes at Vanderbilt, but it was a Saturday, so I didn't reach him right away. His answering service informed me that he wasn't on call, and another physician would need to speak with me first to determine what was happening. I also had the cell number for our primary care physician, Dr. Raymond Browne, who'd seen us for years but had stepped into a more vital role concerning Bentley's care since she'd received her aortic mechanical valve in 2020. He'd often told me to call if there was ever an emergency. My third call was to our old neighbor, longtime friend, and ENT physician in Nashville, Dr. Chris Mantle. I trusted these three implicitly and knew they'd either pick up the phone on the spot or call me back as quickly as they could.

They each fired questions at me in quick succession: When did it start? Which side of the face? Rapid onset or slower progression? Did I notice any other symptoms during the event? Had she had any degree of recovery? Can you send me some photos?

Both Bentley and I knew there was a problem, but the rapid onset of symptoms was what threw us for a loop. With such a slow-growing tumor, an acute event such as this was incredibly unlikely, and I couldn't get a unified diagnosis from my three trusted doctors. Of course, none of them were able to examine her in that moment, so all we could do was share the details, make educated guesses based on the available information, and act quickly to preserve as much of her facial function as possible.

Their answers were all over the place. Maybe it was Bell's Palsy or Ramsay Hunt. Perhaps it was shingles or another stroke. Given her medical history, all of these were possibilities, which could make it harder to treat her. Concerned that every second we waited would cause more permanent paralysis, we had to do something, so Dr. Browne prescribed a combination corticosteroid and antiviral regimen. I picked up both meds, and Bentley took her first dose less than an hour after the symptoms emerged. Within two hours, they started to dissipate.

With the drugs on board and doing their job, I needed to get Bentley back to Nashville. That Monday morning, about forty-five hours after her acute facial paralysis event, I spoke with an ENT nurse from Vanderbilt, explained the events of Saturday morning, her subsequent prescription written by our primary care physician, and stressed the urgency to get her a scan and consult as quickly as possible. I promised the nurse that I'd have Bentley at the hospital with as little as three hours' notice. But the earliest they could get her in was the middle of January.

FOR YEARS, BENTLEY HAD ASKED ME to go to church events or Encounter nights. She wanted me to tag along to a service focused on experiencing God's presence so I might get to know Him in a deeper way. I often went kicking and screaming to an occasional Sunday morning service, so I don't know why she thought I'd be willing to attend a four-hour Encounter night. I'll give her credit; she never stopped trying, but I always had an excuse. My tried-and-true reason was, "I'm just too busy," and that usually did the trick. And, honestly, I didn't want to be around that many church people—especially on a Friday night. Like always, Bentley said there was a speaker I might like who was coming to Birmingham in January, and she asked me to join her. I was certainly changing, but I hadn't swum out to the deep end yet. But I felt something inside me say, *Don't tell her no.*

It was my first Encounter night. We started with praise and worship music, and then the speaker took the stage. Only seconds in, I heard the following as plain as day:

"Jesus didn't die for good guys to be a little bit better."

For a moment, it felt like I was the only person in the room. I looked at Bentley and wondered if she'd heard the same thing. She had. My entire "this is how you get to Heaven" thesis had been built on the simple fact that, at my core, I was a good guy. I didn't need religion or a church to tell me that. I already had a track record of good deeds, a couple of coaching awards on my shelf, and felt secure in whatever future was waiting for me in the afterlife. But now, a total stranger had used my lifelong tagline against me. *Was he talking to me? It sure felt like it. Am I not going to Heaven?* I didn't know how to process any of that in the moment. I needed answers.

Later that month, we went back to Vanderbilt to check off some big boxes before Bentley's brain tumor surgery. We had another consult with Dr. Haynes, a preoperative evaluation and anesthesia meeting with the High-Risk Surgical Encounter (HiRiSE) team to discuss allergies, intubation risks, medications, and surgical preparation steps, and Bentley had her blood drawn.

We were supposed to meet with the other half of our surgical team, Dr. Lola Chambless, but she was tied up in surgery. Her office said that they'd schedule a conference call within the next week. But when that call came, it was much different than we expected.

"Bentley, can you and your husband be in Nashville on February 8?" Dr. Chambless asked.

"We already have another trip scheduled," Bentley said. "We're driving to Charleston to see our daughter at school before my surgery, but maybe we could stop in Nashville on our way."

"We can't do this over the phone. We must meet in person," the doctor stated.

Apparently, we had to meet before the surgery because, as Bentley's neurosurgeon, the doctor thought there were too many things we needed to discuss and agree to beforehand. I naturally assumed that this concern stemmed from setting the timeline for Bentley to stop taking her Coumadin before the surgery. She would be required to take Lovenox shots twice a day, every day, to keep her heart valve functioning properly. The difference between her daily tablet and the two shots was the speed at which her body would process the drug. Lovenox would exit her body faster, while reducing and hopefully preventing any brain bleeds during surgery. But I was only half right and not prepared for what came next.

"We know Bentley was struck by an acute event that severely damaged her seventh cranial nerve and resulted in a considerable amount of left side facial paralysis," Dr. Chambless said. "That nerve has already been stretched by the tumor and was damaged during your original radiation treatments more than four years ago. Basically, you have a very compromised facial nerve, and none of us are exactly sure how it will react or hold up during the surgery."

"But what does that mean? You're not sure how it will hold up?" I asked.

"After radiation, the facial nerve becomes sticky. That's not an issue if the tumor is destroyed, but in her case, it could mean that the nerve is stuck to the tumor, which will make it much harder for Dr. Haynes and me to separate the two," Dr. Chambless stated.

"But you can get it all?" Bentley asked.

"Probably not. If parts of the nerve are too sticky and don't easily separate, then we'll have to leave some tumor behind. We'll get as much as we can, and since it's a slow-growing tumor, we're very hopeful for a good outcome. But there are some real risks we need to discuss," she said.

"Like . . ." I asked.

"Like significant facial paralysis. You already have some right now, Bentley, and it will get worse—maybe a lot worse. If we try to take too much tumor, then we risk severing the nerve. If that happens, you'll have more significant issues. It's going to be a delicate balancing act," she said.

Nothing about that conversation felt good. It was all terrible—very dire, in fact. Our world was crumbling around us, and we needed some kind of silver lining.

"Do you have to shave my head?" Bentley asked.

"Actually, we won't need to shave a ton, just the area around the incision behind your left ear," Dr. Chambless stated. "When you recover from this and head home, no one will be able to see the scar."

The news, along with the possible complications, was tough to digest. It was much later than expected, and we still had more than an eight-hour drive to South Carolina to see EB.

We had a wonderfully long weekend in Charleston, but there was a certain heaviness to it, like this might be the last time Bentley and EB would ever spend time together. Although the dread constantly circled us, we all chose not to discuss the matter. Back in Birmingham, we joined a group of friends at a general healing service at a nearby church.

After that service and about a week before Bentley's surgery, I caught up with a very good friend of mine, and he shared some excellent spiritual advice with me. Lance and his wife were in a firestorm and had been constantly praying for their daughter following an automobile accident. From the moment she was hurt, through her first surgery, and then during the days and weeks in the hospital, he'd shared updates with friends and family. He asked for specific prayers for his daughter and what she was facing the rest of that day. It was his "be specific" format that intrigued me. He told me to remove the complexity of the brain surgery and share what Bentley was facing each day. Giving people a roadmap regarding what to pray for was extremely helpful. After that, so many people came to me and said, "Thank you for directing my prayers where they were most helpful for your wife." I even got a few responses from a handful of friends who said, "I've never prayed before, but you told me exactly what to say."

"And Peter answered Him and said,
'Lord, if it is You, command me to come to You on the water.'
So He said, 'Come.' And when Peter had come down out of the boat,
he walked on the water to go to Jesus.
But when he saw that the wind *was* boisterous, he was afraid,
and beginning to sink, he cried out, saying, 'Lord, save me!'
And immediately Jesus stretched out *His* hand and caught him,
and said to him, 'O you of little faith, why did you doubt?'
And when they got into the boat, the wind ceased.
Then those who were in the boat came and worshiped Him, saying,
'Truly You are the Son of God.'"

—Matthew 14:28-33 NKJV

31

NASHVILLE (PART II)

"Every great story deserves a great ending."
—*Christopher Nolan*

It had been almost five years since Bentley was first diagnosed with an acoustic neuroma brain tumor. She'd failed her radiation treatment, completely lost the hearing on her left side, was stricken with severe tinnitus, suffered through COVID, received a mechanical heart valve, and survived an acute attack that had paralyzed the left side of her face and affected her eye, cheek, and mouth. Yet, after all the symptoms, procedures, complications, and smothering fears, her fighting spirit persisted.

Drs. Haynes and Chambless walked into the pre-op area to conduct their final run through before surgery—the surgery Bentley had dreaded since hearing the words, "You have a brain tumor."

Before being transported to the operating room, she told the doctors, "I just want it out."

The doctors had trained for this moment their whole lives, and it was finally time for Bentley's surgery. I kissed her on the forehead and left the room. As I walked down the hall to find the boys, I thought of one of my favorite lines in the movie *The Lord of the Rings: The Return of the King* when Gandalf spoke to Pippen on the eve of war and said, "We come to it at last, the great battle of our time."

EB, who was finishing her final semester at the College of Charleston and working two internships while holding down a full-time job with the RiverDogs, couldn't be in Nashville for the surgery. Cade and Davis were in the patient waiting area, and I told them we were going to relocate. I didn't like being holed up with all the other families because it's too distracting, and time moves at a snail's pace. We found a private nook on the second floor, down the hall from the waiting room. I was wearing a thin, black fleece that I'd purchased in the gift shop at the Cleveland Clinic back in 2020—for luck. My hospital pager was in one pocket and my cell phone in the other. I like routines, but this day was already different. We were waiting for our good friend and old neighbor to make an appearance. This was the first time anyone had ever sat with me during one of Bentley's procedures or surgeries.

Chris arrived an hour later and said that he'd cleared his schedule and would be with us the whole day. He'd been the very first person to examine Bentley when we returned from Prague when she couldn't get her ear to pop; he was the one who suggested she get an MRI, and he had introduced us to Dr. Haynes. Not only had he been a friend for nearly twenty years, he'd also single-handedly shepherded Bentley through the labyrinth of medical care for the past five years. I couldn't help but reflect on all the joyful connections between Bentley and me, our longtime friends Chris and Sarah, our kids, and their kids—juxtaposed with the fact that his mentor was now operating on my wife. As the old saying goes, "There are no coincidences."

The four of us sat and talked for a couple of hours, but we all started to get a little restless. I'd only received one text from the nurse, and that was when the procedure had started. I relayed that information to our family, close friends, and the list of people who were praying over Bentley's surgery. According to the time estimate they'd told me, I only needed to be patient for another ten hours. But that's an impossible task for me on most days, and this wasn't a normal day. I was restless. I told Chris and the boys I needed to walk around to ditch some nervous energy. It was still early in the morning. I wasn't really hungry, but the Panera Bread in the hospital was open, so I stopped in for a bowl of their mac and cheese. I ordered, got my food, and ate it in about ten minutes. Only nine hours and forty-five minutes left to go.

As I wandered around the hospital, I stumbled upon the chapel on the first floor. The sign said it was open twenty-four hours a day, seven days a week, but as many times as we'd been at Vanderbilt, I'd never walked in until then. It was completely empty and eerily quiet. When the door shut behind me, I couldn't hear any of the hustle and bustle of the main lobby. I walked with slow reverence and went to the front, where I saw three books placed side by side on a pedestal in front of the altar. One was the Bible, one was a Hebrew Bible, and the third was the Quran. I'd only recently begun reading the New International Version of the Bible, so my curiosity was piqued. I leafed through each book for a few minutes until I saw the words "For with God nothing shall be impossible," a short scripture taken from Luke 1:37. I sat down in a pew on the second row, kneeled, and began to pray.

The rest of the day was just as tortoise-like as those first few hours. Chris showed Cade and Davis around the hospital and the surrounding area. I bought my first *USA Today* in years and went back to the same Panera Bread for a second helping of mac and cheese. This is what I always did whenever Bentley was in surgery. I sent texts and emails, read the newspaper, aimlessly roamed the halls, and ate the same exact meal in the same exact restaurant multiple times until she was out of surgery. It's like my baseball hitting ritual before stepping into the batter's box.

However, as I'd experienced many times in my life, even the worst days eventually come to an end. After eleven hours, I got a text from the nurse. She said that the surgery was over, and I needed to report to the waiting room for an important update. The text didn't say, "Your wife is alive. It's all good. Wait in the tiny room for the doctors to come in and give you an amazing update," so I sprinted through the lobby and up the flight of stairs. As I approached the waiting room, I was filled with worry. I slowed to a half jog as I walked through the sliding glass doors and approached the patient liaison desk. I told the attendant my name. She looked at her screen and said to go to the private room in the back left corner.

"It will be about ten minutes," she said. "Both surgeons are coming."

My heart sank. That statement had bad news written all over it, and my concern skyrocketed. I didn't know where Chris or the boys were, so I messaged them and said that the doctors were on their way. I'd learned a lot about Bentley's brain tumor over the last five years, but I also had access to a trusted friend who had assisted on these types of procedures. I needed his years of experience and expertise to help interpret anything that might fly over my head. A few minutes later, with Chris at my side, both surgeons walked into the tiny room.

"She tolerated the surgery well. We were able to cut out most of the tumor. We didn't encounter any major surprises, and there was no major blood loss. She's resting comfortably in the ICU," Dr. Chambless said.

"You told us you wouldn't be able to get all the tumor. What percentage was left behind?" I asked.

"As expected, the facial nerve was very sticky from the radiation therapy, and at times, it was very difficult to separate the nerve from the tumor. But we cut out everything we could and then went back and scraped as much residual tumor from the nerve as possible without damaging it any further. I'd say we were able to excise 90 to 95 percent, which we're very pleased with," she said.

"Since the tumor is, by its nature, such a slow grower," Dr. Haynes added, "we aren't overly concerned about the amount left behind, but we'll definitely want to look at it again in six months and then every year after that if the scans look good."

"What about Bentley's acute event back in December? Is there any way to determine what happened to her that day?" Chris asked.

"We're still not exactly sure," Dr. Haynes said. "What we saw was a cyst-like structure that was attached to the tumor. We think, but we're not 100 percent sure, that Bentley's new anticoagulation medication for her mechanical heart valve may have thinned the blood in such a way that it started leaking into and filling that undetectable cyst, which caused it to expand rapidly. We think that event stretched her facial nerve in such a way that it caused temporary paralysis. That's our working hypothesis right now."

"What about her facial paralysis? How does she look?" I asked.

"We won't lie to you. It's not good," said Dr. Haynes. "As you know, she came in with a degree of paralysis before we began the operation. She has an extremely weak facial nerve, and it's caused considerable drooping in and around her eye, her cheek, and all the way down to her mouth and chin. It's significant and noticeable, but we've seen worse."

"Dr. Chambless, in our meeting a few weeks ago, you said there would be healing over time? What are we talking about based on what you saw?" I asked.

"As a general rule of thumb, we tell our patients that the facial nerve heals at a rate of 1 mm per day, every day, for roughly the next fourteen months. And then at some point, the brain will shut down the healing process," she said.

"It doesn't keep healing?" I asked. Chris looked at me and shook his head no.

"It doesn't," said Dr. Haynes. "And it's not an exact science. It heals at such a slow rate that you'll think nothing is happening. You must be patient with this process. There's no way for us to tell you how much healing she'll experience."

I profusely thanked the surgeons for getting Bentley through the surgery and off the table, and I thanked them a second time for everything they'd done to get her to this point. She was alive, most of the tumor had been removed, and she would need a lot of time to heal.

Chris and I left the room and shared the most important facts with Cade and Davis. I called EB to let her know that her mom had crushed it as a patient again, and then I began digging out from under the avalanche of waiting messages.

An hour after we met with the doctors, I finally got permission to enter the Neurological Intensive Care Unit (Neuro ICU), picked up my badge, and made my way to Bentley's room. The long walk past all the patient rooms made me realize that she wasn't the only one who was dealing with a major calamity. I quietly entered her room and was slightly taken aback because it looked like Bentley was hooked up to every possible machine. She wasn't awake and didn't move when I entered, so I sat in the only seat available to me: the large patient recliner on the other side of the room. A steady stream of nurses came in and out through the sliding glass door, each with a specific job to do. There finally came a moment when I had a chance to approach Bentley and look at her face. The paralysis the doctors described was real and significant, but not as pronounced as I'd pictured. I said a prayer thanking God that she was alive and for all He had done.

Around 3:00 a.m., a little less than twenty-four hours since our day had begun, she groggily woke up and looked around the room. I immediately walked over and took her hand.

"Can you talk?" I asked.

She nodded her head yes.

"How do you feel?" I asked.

"Like I've been hit by a truck," she said.

"How does your head feel?" I asked.

"It hurts. How big is the scar?" she asked.

I leaned in close to the area behind her left ear and did my best not to touch anything. "It's not as big as I thought. And it looks like Dr. Chambless didn't shave a ton of hair."

She gave me a slight smile, and that's when I noticed the significant downward pull at the left corner of her mouth. Then she said something that I never expected to hear.

"The screaming has stopped."

Bentley had never uttered the word "screaming" before—not once in all those years. When someone asked her what the tinnitus sounded like, she tried to mimic a high-pitched screeching sound, which I felt was almost intolerable to hear even in short bursts, but it was her only way to try to describe the constant clamor that dominated her life. I couldn't stand to hear Bentley make that sound for only a few seconds and couldn't imagine living with that noise buried deep in my head every waking moment of every day. And yet, she'd survived the sustained bombardment of shrieks for over four years.

Bentley went right back to sleep after speaking those words. So, while she napped, I sat back down in my chair and googled "tinnitus and screaming." I found page after page of medical websites, self-help links, and medication that guaranteed to eliminate the condition with a magic formula in as little as thirty days. But a few pages in, I came across a link to a book titled *23 Minutes in Hell* by Bill Wiese. The book chronicled his firsthand encounter after being taken to Hell during an out-of-body experience. He said he'd woken up in a cell, saw demons and a lake of fire, smelled foul, putrid odors, witnessed unimaginable torment, and then he described the constant shrieking and deafening screams of agony—screams of untold terror.

Bentley rested until the neuro team came to check on her around 6:30 a.m. The group of young doctors checked her vitals, looked at her incision, asked a bunch of questions, talked to the nurses, and then quickly moved on to the next room. At 7:00 a.m., the nurses began their shift change, so it was a busy environment with a lot happening in a short amount of time. Such is the life of a patient and their family members in the ICU. When things settled back down, I had a chance to talk to Bentley again. I mentally ran through my series of questions, then asked the only one I cared about.

"How's your tinnitus?" I asked.

"The screaming has stopped," she said.

She slowly nodded off again, and I went back to my chair to do more research about how this could have possibly happened. Two more times that day, when we were alone, I asked her the same series of questions.

"How do you feel? How's your incision? How's your tinnitus?"

"I feel loopy and nauseous. My scar itches. The screaming has stopped," Bentley said.

By dinner time, less than twenty-four hours after leaving the operating room, she was much more lucid, and we had our first real conversation as she tried to eat a few bites of food and chase it with some Sprite.

"How do you feel?" I asked.

"Really nauseous, like I've been punched in the head—and I'm disoriented," she said.

"Well, that was from all the anesthesia you had yesterday. You were under for close to eleven hours," I said. "How was the surgery? Do you remember anything?"

"I remember being wheeled into the operating room," she said, "and it was so much bigger than any of the other rooms I've been in for heart surgery. I saw lots of people and all these robotic arms in the room. It felt like I was on a car factory floor, ready to be dismantled. Then a nurse came over and said they were going to start IV lines in both of my feet, which I'd never heard of before. It sounded cool, but I also thought, *That's going to hurt.* And then one of the doctors came over and explained how they would clamp my head into place, and I said, 'Please knock me out before you do any of these things.'"

"Did they knock you out right away?" I asked.

"Well, this was the most incredible part," Bentley said. "The anesthesiologist came next to me and said they were going to put me to sleep. I saw two nurses near my feet, a couple of people started to strap me to the operating room table, and then another person positioned my head inside this big clamp. A massive wave of anxiety started to come over me, and I was like, *Yep, this is happening*. I started to feel scared.

"And then I saw Jesus standing at the end of my bed. He was bigger than anything else in the room; His head was touching the ceiling, and it was such a beautiful thing to see. He was a translucent silhouette. He was at the foot of my bed, and He was like a giant. He overpowered the room. And in that moment, He gave me a lot of comfort," Bentley said.

"I'm not even sure what to ask you right now," I said. "Was it like your second surgery—like being with the angels?"

"No, it was more of a feeling and something I saw. My time flying with the angels was an experience," Bentley said.

Before I could ask my next question, she told me the second most incredible thing of that night. "The screaming has stopped," she repeated for the fifth time.

"You said that a couple of times in the middle of the night, and then again this morning. What do you mean it's stopped?" I asked.

"It's gone. It stopped. It's so eerily quiet now. It's peaceful. I went into surgery, and there was constant screaming, like usual, and then I woke up to absolute silence. It was like going from one extreme to another, and I couldn't believe it," she said.

During those eleven hours on the table, something completely altered Bentley's life, and there was no medical explanation. We'd prayed so many times for God or Jesus to intervene and heal this maddening condition, and while she was asleep on the surgical table, her debilitating tinnitus had vanished. The only explanation was that Jesus had healed her.

The next morning, Cade and Davis both needed to get back to Birmingham for work, and Bentley's biggest goal was to get out of bed and walk with her boys. With the aid of the nurses and the support of her sons, she got out of bed and shuffled through the ICU with her walker. I'd seen Bentley do some amazing things, but witnessing her sheer desire to walk with Cade and Davis was as inspirational as it gets.

We had a FaceTime call with EB to celebrate all the miracles of the past forty-eight hours, and over the next few days, Bentley remained in the hospital and kept getting stronger. We walked laps around the ICU several times a day. She was getting her appetite back; I made twice-daily runs to Panera Bread, and we got to see both Dr. Chambless and Dr. Haynes as they checked on her progress. During one of those visits, they noticed that her left eyelid didn't close all the way, which meant she needed a minor procedure.

So, we met with Dr. Priyesh Patel, another member of the surgery team who specialized in facial plastic and reconstructive surgery. To correct the problem, he made an incision in her left upper eyelid and implanted a gold weight just under the skin. This weight, along with gravity, would help close her eye when she blinked. It would help protect her cornea and improve the appearance of her eyelid. The downside was a possible change in vision over time. Bentley said it was one of the least favorite procedures she'd ever had, but Dr. Patel was great at reducing her anxiety with his wit, humor, and skill.

Bentley loved the visits from Dr. Haynes, who stopped in to check on her each afternoon. And on the evening before she was released, we had one of our more poignant conversations when we told him that her chronic tinnitus had miraculously vanished. I don't know if that news prompted him to draw any spiritual conclusions that day, but I'd like to think the door was opened for further discussions. I thanked him again for taking such good care of my wife and said we'd see him in four weeks for her follow-up.

Bentley was discharged on March 3, and we spent that first night at Chris and Sarah's house, hanging out with their kids and eating ice cream. I reflected on the day twenty-one years earlier when two young medical students moved into the house across the street from us in Birmingham. After all the years, schooling, training, weddings, kids, and the difficult times that life had brought, we were all together in one big room that night without a worry in the world.

There are no coincidences, I thought to myself again. I realized that God had a bigger and better plan. He put the right people in our path at the right time. All according to His will.

> "So be truly glad. There is wonderful joy ahead,
> even though you must endure many trials for a little while.
> These trials will show that your faith is genuine.
> It is being tested as fire tests and purifies gold –
> though your faith is far more precious than mere gold.
> So when your faith remains strong through many trials,
> it will bring you much praise and glory and honor
> on the day when Jesus Christ is revealed to the whole world."
>
> —1 Peter 1:6-7 NLT

32

GOD'S PLANS

"I think a man does what he can, until his destiny is revealed."

—*Tom Cruise as Nathan Algren in* The Last Samurai

The first- and second-round games of the 2023 NCAA men's basketball tournament were held in Birmingham on March 16 and 18 at Legacy Arena. Back in 1991, with a small basketball-centric subset of our Virginia friends, we'd started a tradition to travel to a host city to see either the Thursday or Friday block of opening round games. Our first trip had been a short drive to the Cole Field House on the University of Maryland campus, and after that, we always picked a city, entered the ticket lottery, hoped we got some great matchups, and had fun spending time together.

Birmingham hadn't hosted any of the tournament games in fifteen years, but with the arrival of the Birmingham Squadron (the G-League affiliate of the New Orleans Pelicans), our group of friends was swayed to meet up in Alabama. We had enough beds in our house to accommodate everyone, so we invited them all. Some would drive in from Atlanta; another couple came from Cape Girardeau, Missouri, and three longstanding members of our hoops crew would make their way down from Virginia. Since two others couldn't make it, the empty seats were quickly filled by Cade and Davis.

Because our basketball weekend had been planned months earlier, Bentley's unexpected brain surgery wasn't considered a risk the day tickets went on sale. She'd been discharged on March 3, and the games in Birmingham tipped off thirteen days later. All our friends were up to date on her surgery and recovery, but most of them felt it would be too difficult for her to host that many people so soon after her "skull had been cracked open." But she wouldn't let anyone squirm out of the trip and let everyone know that she was fine to host. So, less than two weeks after leaving the hospital, almost everyone made it in to see Bentley and enjoy some basketball.

We were on such a high after seeing all our Virginia friends, but that feeling of euphoria quickly waned. Bentley still felt the side effects from eleven hours of anesthesia, ate very little except for Ben & Jerry's ice cream, and had constant bouts of nausea. The steroids wreaked havoc on her sleep schedule, and even after flushing those pills down the toilet, she still couldn't get more than a couple hours of sleep per night. So, only weeks after getting out of the hospital, it seemed she'd merely traded her chronic tinnitus for new cases of insomnia and depression.

Another fun event that we'd planned months before Bentley's surgery was to spend my birthday weekend in Charleston. EB was scheduled to graduate in May, and one of the local events that we hadn't yet checked off our list was the Cooper River Bridge Run. It felt mildly criminal that EB had lived in Charleston for over three years, and we'd never participated in the annual 10K race. So, Cade, Davis, EB, and I, with only minimal training under our belts, managed to make it over the Ravenel Bridge and complete the 6.2-mile course in non-record time. We were greeted at the finish line by two family friends while Bentley stayed back at the hotel and waited for our moderately jubilant return. That night, we celebrated my fifty-sixth birthday at one of Bentley's favorite bistros, Fast & French, for an early dinner, then walked to Carmella's Café for dessert. On Sunday morning, we all attended the 11:00 a.m. service at Saint Michael's Church on Broad Street. And to my absolute surprise, Bentley had arranged for us to renew our wedding vows with the minister at the conclusion of their normal schedule, with Cade, Davis, and EB as witnesses.

At only 1 mm a day, we hadn't observed any noticeable healing since Bentley's surgery. I often stared at her face for two or three minutes and could only see a single twitch near her eye or a slight movement above her cheek. It was excruciatingly slow for me, so I couldn't imagine how she felt. Without seeing any changes in real time, I started taking a close-up photo of her face every week. By the end of the first month, I swiped through the four images in quick succession, and the microscopic changes started to reveal themselves. And day by day, we all grew in our spirituality. Most nights, we'd take turns reading *Jesus Calling* and leading the family in prayer. Each time we'd end with the same prayer: for Jesus to put His hands on Bentley, to heal her head, her heart, her incisions, and her facial nerve.

That May, my sister, Emily, joined us for EB's graduation from The College of Charleston in front of Randolph Hall for the quintessential Southern ceremony in the Cistern Yard. Under the massive oak trees and Spanish moss, EB walked across the stage in a traditional white dress while carrying a bouquet of red roses. After a casual sunset stroll down King Street, we toasted her hard work at Poogan's Porch, a Victorian townhouse turned iconic culinary establishment that served incredible Lowcountry cuisine. It was a fitting end to the day's festivities and her four years in Charleston.

Over the summer, we still didn't see a ton of healing, so we went back to Vanderbilt in August with moderate expectations. We already knew that remnants of the active tumor had been intentionally left behind, so there weren't any surprises when we met with Dr. Haynes for Bentley's consult. She said she was still suffering from insomnia and continued fighting bouts of depression. As he examined her, it was obvious that she still had trouble closing her left eye. She said that the weight had continued to alter her vision. Conversely, what pleased the doctor the most was the evenness of her facial tone, especially around her eye and cheek, and the fact that he could see some nerve activity under direct observation. It had only been six months since her surgery; he told us to be patient.

Between August and November, I noticed considerable changes to Bentley's face. Her eye and mouth didn't droop quite as much, and the nerve below her cheek often twitched, which meant there was activity under the surface. And I could see tiny vibrations just below her eye in an area called the infraorbital margin. The 1 mm per day prognosis was real and had started to pick up steam. Bentley was eating again and getting a few hours of sleep at night, albeit for inconsistent, short stretches. She was feeling better physically, and she was excited about the potential for more improvements. And the best news was that she still had about seven more months to heal.

After settling into our lives in Mountain Brook, our community outside of Birmingham, we made Saint Luke's Episcopal Church our permanent church home, in large part because of Reverend Rich Webster. His ability to blend spiritual truth with our real-world existence, wrapped in solid storytelling, resonated with me. Occasionally, we attended the Sunday morning service at Cathedral Church of the Advent to listen to the teachings of my old friend and Citadel classmate, Reverend Craig Smalley. Once I decided to dive deeper into the Word, he was the first person I approached to ask questions about God, Jesus, the Holy Spirit, and the Bible. And while Bentley had visited a multitude of churches in Birmingham over the years, we heard about yet another church in the area when a stranger came to our house to pray over Bentley's tinnitus.

We didn't know Matt Wilson, and he didn't know us, but he'd heard that Bentley needed healing and that she wanted someone to pray over her. At the time, I couldn't understand why he'd do such a thing and thought he might have an angle, but as I got to know him over a dozen lunches and from worshiping together, I realized how much he loved the Lord and wanted to help people—even total strangers.

It was difficult to comprehend that people not only felt called to pray but also enjoyed ministering to and laying hands on others. And every time it happened, it felt more normal. Before Bentley's brain surgery, another pastor and a friend visited us to pray and offer communion to our family when it was impossible for her to attend church in person. And the prayers poured in from so many in our congregation. My old friend and Citadel teammate Mark Brown and his wife held a prayer call with us two days before Bentley checked into the hospital. She was prayed over by her friend, Jahan Berns, ministry teams, at weekend retreats, and multiple Encounter nights. Yes, more strangers prayed over her. And the one person who'd been praying for Bentley the longest was her mom.

We continued to read *Jesus Calling* and prayed together each evening, attended Sunday services, often at two different churches, and re-watched episodes of *The Chosen*. I was just weeks away from completing my read of the entire Bible. Cade was also moving fast in his walk, was active in two men's groups, and told us that he'd decided to give up his life for Christ. So, on Sunday, November 12, 2023, Cade was baptized at The Gathering Place Church. And we were further blessed when Davis and EB felt called in the moment, chose Jesus, and were baptized in the Holy Spirit that same morning. I cried in the back of the room, knowing that my three children had just been saved for all of eternity.

All five of us had accepted Jesus Christ as our Lord and Savior, had been baptized, and were saved. And it was time to rest—or so we thought. A new work opportunity popped up for Davis in Raleigh, North Carolina. One of his former fraternity brothers lived in that area and invited Davis to crash with him for a few months to make sure he liked the job, his boss, and the city. Cade, who'd been an assistant basketball coach for three years, wanted to pivot and found a new opportunity in sales. EB, who had completed college internships with the Charleston RiverDogs and Atlanta Hawks, got her first paid job working for the Birmingham Squadron.

Bentley approached her one-year anniversary with a sense of accomplishment and excitement for the future. Things were as close to normal as they'd been in five years, so we ordered a brochure from Viking River Cruises and started planning a trip from Amsterdam to Budapest along the Danube River. I accepted a new job with a French robotics organization, and we felt so good about where things were headed that we rescued another German Shepherd dog. Bentley's health had taken massive leaps forward, the kids were all working and happy, our first two dogs got along with the new puppy, and it felt good to be back at the helm of my battleship.

Four weeks later, Davis told us that he'd rented an apartment and was going to make a go of it in Raleigh. Bentley and I knew there were far more opportunities for him to work in commercial real estate in the Research Triangle than there were for him in Birmingham, but we still felt caught off guard by the news. He said he'd be home in two weeks to pack up all his things. And before we'd even processed that news, EB received her dream job offer with the Charlotte Hornets that came with only one stipulation—she had to start pronto. That night, Bentley and I sat on the couch and tried to comprehend what had just happened. We didn't have one child flying the coop; we had two moving to another state within the span of two weeks. It felt surreal, and we teetered back and forth between excitement and grief. Everything that Bentley and I had wanted, which had finally come together only six weeks earlier, had just been torn to shreds.

We still hadn't come to terms with the news of the double move when Davis called the next day to ask about a few pieces of furniture that he liked that he thought would come in handy in his new apartment. Our sadness mounted, not because he was asking for a handful of items, but because none of this was part of our plan. We loved our kids, would do anything for them, and genuinely enjoyed each other's company. Whether it was walking the dogs, seeing a concert, road tripping to a Braves game or a weekend in the Big Apple, watching a movie together, or just going to church as a family—we loved our time together. Bentley and I had been thrown for a loop and struggled mightily those first few days to process it all. But there's a scene near the end of *The Matrix*, when Morpheus aptly tells Neo, "There's a difference between knowing the path and walking the path."

Over the next twenty-four hours, we started to see things in a different light. Wanting Davis and EB to stay here was part of *our* plan, not what God had intended for their lives. We knew we had to let go, not only of our children but also of all our stuff, and that led to one of those rare epiphany moments. How could we be expected to follow Jesus if we held onto the past and all our possessions? How could we properly acknowledge God's mercy and many blessings over our entire family if we were unwilling to make sacrifices? Did we honor Him by digging in our heels and praying that things wouldn't change? Of course not. The only way to acknowledge God's plans was to let go and let Jesus take over. Once we made that decision, He went to work.

Bentley and I sat down with the kids and said that if we truly wanted to walk this new path with Christ, we needed to let go of a lot of things. And that process would begin with everything in the house. That didn't fully register with them at first, so we laid out some ground rules. Every single item in our home was available and could be selected. In the first stage, they placed a sticker on the items they wanted. If two or more of them wanted the same piece, it would trigger a discussion. Perhaps there was some sentimental motivation or perceived value that had caused them to select that specific item. Whatever the reason, we tried to find a solution before the draft. We stipulated to them that whatever Bentley or I were still using or were personal in nature would remain with us in our home but would be held in a virtual escrow to be picked up at some point in the future when we no longer needed them.

Next, we had to decide who would pick first. Historically, our most successful format was to do a snake draft. That meant Cade would go first, then Davis, followed by EB, who would make two selections, and then it would come back to Davis, end on Cade, and start over again. With those formalities out of the way, we could get down to business. The items that only one of the kids wanted automatically became their property. Anything that had two or more stickers would be available in the draft. The kids spent the next thirty minutes making their picks, and no feelings seemed to be hurt. The biggest surprise was what *wasn't* selected. A lot of things that were important to Bentley or me held no value for the kids.

On Sunday morning, we loaded the U-Haul, and Davis hit the road on the eight-hour drive to Raleigh. Two weeks later, we did it all over again with EB. She and I made the trip to Charlotte together, and I helped her get settled in her apartment. When I got back home, everything was different. The top floor was a wasteland; there were holes in the walls where pictures had hung, and the dogs were lying on the bare hardwood floors of barren, lifeless rooms. Everything felt off. Neither of us wanted to call the painters or run to the store to start replacing things, so we lived in the emptiness.

However, that wasn't truly living. Jesus hadn't done all these amazing things so we could mope around our half-empty house feeling sorry for ourselves. I remembered hearing Pastor Philip Anthony Mitchell say, "Sometimes He has to stop you so that He can complete you." That insight allowed us to talk some more, and by the next weekend, we had our second epiphany. It was an open and honest conversation about what we wanted our future to look like, where we wanted to be, and what we wanted to do. We both wanted more Jesus and less stuff weighing us down.

"Are you saying what I think you're saying?" I asked.

"I think so," Bentley said. "Are we selling the house?"

"I think so," I said. "Let me make a few calls."

I talked to my friend John about the market and tax implications. Next, we received a call from our friend, neighbor, and realtor, who informed us that we had only a short window to get the house prepped and on the market for the spring selling season. I told her to sit tight while I called my sister.

Ten years earlier, when I'd started planning the future for our kids, I purchased a small, three-bedroom rental house in our same neighborhood. It had access to an outstanding public school system, and the plan was that whichever child got married and had a baby first could buy the house from me at a discounted family rate. And while we waited for that plan to hatch, I turned it into a rental property to make a little extra money. It was occupied for the first three years but had been vacant for a couple of months when my sister Emily had asked if she could rent it for a year. She'd been trying to buy a place of her own but hadn't found anything she liked. So, she became our renter, and now, seven years later, I called her with an idea.

"With Davis and EB in North Carolina, Bentley and I are going to downsize. We want less to manage, and she'd prefer a one-story house because she doesn't want to go up and down stairs. Have you thought about moving?" I carefully prodded.

I connected her with our realtor, and they started looking at properties. After a punishing string of dead deals, Emily had all but given up hope of finding a home she loved. The realtor said there was a townhouse about to hit the market that Emily had to see, but she was a little concerned about scheduling a viewing since none of the other options had panned out. I asked Emily to look at it and said that if it wasn't what she wanted or the offer wasn't accepted, we could take a break, and I'd figure something else out. But God had a plan. Emily loved the townhouse and purchased it. Bentley and I moved into our old rental, fixed up our current house, and sold it to a wonderful family on the second day after it went on the market.

When the house sold, we donated anything that didn't fit into our new place. Clothes and furniture went first. I donated around twenty collectible *Star Wars* items that were sold at a charity auction. We completed a car swap with Bentley's brother, bought a truck that could transport our three dogs, and I donated my old Range Rover to

Vehicles for Veterans. The entire move, with construction crews working at both houses was completed in eleven days. There's no way I could have pulled this off by myself. Everything lined up perfectly—every deadline, permit, and work crew. God had started this process ten years earlier when our offer for the rental unit was accepted. And for some odd reason, I'd kept the recorded voice message from Bentley all those years ago when she said, "Babe, we got the house." My plan had been to try to dictate where one of our kids would live. God's plan was to provide a new beginning for Bentley and me.

Socrates once said, "The unexamined life is not worth living," so I began re-reading the Bible, watched old Billy Graham Crusades on YouTube, and downloaded *The Chosen* app, which gave us access to the historical television drama and four seasons of Bible Roundtables (a series of discussions that piggyback off each episode of the show). These were hosted by Dallas Jenkins, the creator and director of *The Chosen,* and offered biblical and historical context from a Catholic priest, a Jewish rabbi, and an Evangelical scholar. I appreciated the diverse perspectives and absorbed everything I could. I poured over countless devotionals, visited the Museum of the Bible in Washington, DC, and had in-depth God conversations with friends and family—people I'd had relationships with from ten to fifty years—about faith, miracles, baptism, and Jesus.

After coming to terms with the notion that my good deeds wouldn't get me into Heaven, other doubts had crept into my mind: there's no hope for me; I'm so late to the game, and what value could I possibly bring to His table? But on the weekend that Cade, Davis, and EB were baptized, I realized that through my words and actions, I had a profound influence on the people closest to me. On the day when Davis married Kathryn, whom we love very much, I felt a constant nudge to say a few brief words to all the guests at the reception. *Be bold. Don't mince words.* As I wished the new couple blessings over their marriage and future together, I shared something I heard Pastor Matt Scott ask during one of his sermons at The Gathering Place Church, and I posed it to the group that night.

"What's your billion-year plan when it comes to Jesus and your eternal future?"

That question had hit me hard. I spent thirty years paying off a house, socking money away in my 401(k), planning vacations, and making sure my kids could go to a good school, but I stood on the sidelines when it came to God. While I had been wading comfortably in the shallow end of the pool for the past few months, I knew I'd just treaded out into the deep end. I had to decide. It's a choice every single person must make. No one can do it for you. You must accept Him or reject Him. The beautiful thing is that choosing Jesus is available to all. But how do you do this? Where do you start? You say, "I'm too far gone. I've sinned so much. I'm not worthy of God's mercy." Near the end of Davis and Kathryn's wedding, my cousin Katie and I were talking about Jesus when she asked me point-blank, "What do I have to do?"

At that moment, I didn't feel equipped to give her an answer. Shoot, I had just talked about God and eternity in front of more than one hundred people without so much as a plan, but here's what I would tell her now and why I can't wait until I see her again. I thought back to when I saw myself standing on the bridge just outside the gates of Heaven. My first reaction was that I didn't want to be separated from Bentley. But the more I read and studied God's Word, I realized that I didn't have any type of relationship with Jesus. The Bible is clear that there is only one way to Heaven. You must put your faith in Jesus Christ, who came to this earth, lived the life of a man, was crucified, died on the cross, and was buried. On the third day, God raised Him from the dead. And since I wasn't sure how or where to begin, I relied on the only spiritual voice I remembered from my childhood, Billy Graham. I'd spent hours listening to his many sermons, and in one of them, he outlined what I needed to do to have a relationship with Jesus.

First, I had to admit I was a sinner. Then I had to ask for forgiveness for everything I'd done. This wasn't an easy step and required much self-reflection and atonement to those whom I'd hurt. But that wasn't enough because I also had to be willing to turn away from my sins. Then I had to believe that Christ died on the cross for me and that He rose again from the dead. And lastly, through prayer, I had to invite Jesus Christ to come in and control my life through the gift of the Holy Spirit. Our sin is what separates us from God, but Jesus died for all our sins—past, present, and future. He took our place on that cross and suffered terribly so we could have eternal life.

However, what Billy Graham said happens next is truly amazing. He spoke about the books that God keeps, where under everyone's name are all the sins they've ever committed. All the bad thoughts and all the terrible deeds are recorded and will confront every person at their judgment. But when you come to Christ, repent, follow Him, and take up the cross daily, Jesus blots out everything written about you in that book, and He writes your name in another book called the Lamb's Book of Life. During Reverend Graham's crusade, he asked the crowd, "Do you know if your name is written in that book? If you aren't sure, then do something about it. Take action! The scripture says if your name is not written in the Book of Life, you will not enter Heaven."

As you read this right now, you might be saying to yourself, *I go to church, I read the Bible, I give money to charity, I coach a youth team, I helped my spouse and children through some difficult times,* or *I'm a good person.* You cannot reason your way to Christ. There's no amount of money you can give or good works you can perform that will allow you to enter God's Heavenly Kingdom. The only way to Heaven is by the grace and mercy of God. We are all sinners. We all deserve judgment and Hell, but because of what Jesus Christ did for us on the cross, we can be saved.

I've come to the cross. I've received Christ. He's in my heart now by the presence of the Holy Spirit. He's forgiven my sins. I am a child of God. I have been saved.

Let's examine that last sentence from a worldly perspective. I've shared many amazing, crazy, dumb, funny, and harrowing stories about my past and life with Bentley and the kids. It's now painfully obvious to me that God was looking out for me long before I came to know Him. For starters, He watched over the nine-year-old me as I sat alone in the theater. He walked beside me while I hiked the Appalachian Trail and all the days I was alone in the wilderness, and He disciplined me in the Charleston County Courthouse as any good father would, for the purpose of correction and growth.

Speaking of discipline, He orchestrated it for me to go to The Citadel and gave me the strength to survive some of the toughest days of my life. He kept me from being taken to jail in Columbia, South Carolina. He was with me in Spain, the United Kingdom, and countless other places, and protected me more times than I care to remember or have written about in this book. He was a witness to all my excessive drinking, boorish behavior, and foolish recklessness. He kept me from killing myself or someone else, but He also grew tired of my defiance and determined that my life needed to radically change that night on the 14th Street Bridge. I could have lost my marriage, my job, and my freedom, but He gave me a warning shot to wake me up. Denzel Washington may have summed it up best: "I've been protected. I've been directed. I've been corrected."

He blessed me in my marriage to Bentley, lovingly supported her through the birth of Cade and Davis, and gave me the toughness I needed to get through my dad's suicide and endure the dark days that followed. He was in the room with Bentley during her first three open-heart surgeries and both pregnancies. He pulled my ring out of the Pacific Ocean, saved EB from a more horrific injury in Paris, and surrounded all five of us the day we raced my BMW on the Talladega Superspeedway. He watched over and protected Bentley through four strokes, open heart surgeries number four and five, radiation, and brain surgery. How do I know He was there? He made His angels visible to Bentley when she was seven. Jesus stood at the foot of her bed when she was fifty-three. He saved me from killing myself countless times. But most importantly, He showed me I was on the outside of His Kingdom looking in. He's always been there. It's what this book is about.

However, He's also blessed our marriage and trusted us to nurture Cade, Davis, and EB. He guided us through good times and bad as we parented the kids. He's introduced us to lifelong friends and placed us in a strong spiritual community. He's rewarded us with so many opportunities and dream-fulfilling experiences, like Bentley racing on the Autobahn or getting her first Porsche or me playing baseball with the Braves or producing my *Star Wars* documentary. He's repeatedly made us uncomfortable, but in a good way. He's helped our family navigate countless challenges and changes, many that seemed too monumental to overcome. But He's also remained faithful. Guiding us. Nudging us. Leading us to the narrow gate—the only way to an eternal future.

Jesus doesn't say life will be easy. In fact, it's just the opposite. In John 16:33, He states, "I have told you these things, so that in me you may have peace. In this world, you will have trouble. But take heart! I have overcome the world."

I know I've received the gift of the Holy Spirit and that my eternal future and that of my family is secure. That knowledge is worth more to me than anything I could possess in this world. So, what are we called to do with this gift? Simple, we are to share the good news of Jesus and eternal life. In the book of Corinthians, the Apostle Paul tells us that God, through the Holy Spirit, will do the heavy lifting. He will plant the seed of faith in the unbeliever's heart. It's not our job to save people, but to share what we know with our co-workers, family, friends, neighbors, and even complete strangers.

Once you have been saved, there's work to do. What has Jesus called all His followers to do? To love God, love others, and make disciples. The first thing I do each morning is open the Bible app on my phone. Whatever time I need to get up to start my day, I set my alarm to go off forty-five minutes earlier. It's a habit now, but it wasn't easy in the beginning. I supplement my daily readings with devotional plans and am currently re-reading the Bible in a way that combines Old Testament and New Testament stories into one cohesive manner. Bentley and I either physically attend or watch a church service online every week. She plays worship music consistently, and we still read *Jesus Calling* each night before bed. We attend small group gatherings and have participated in church workshops, and I do my very best to strike up a Jesus conversation with anyone I run into. I've talked about God on two flights, with neighbors, relatives, old friends, and even co-workers. When I'm asked about Bentley, I purposely use words like blessings and miracles to see what kind of response I get. If it's a positive reaction, I just let God take over.

I have fasted from everything except water multiple times since my baptism. The first time, I fasted for ten days leading up to Bentley's brain surgery. I broke that fast when Reverand David Hall and our friend, Sandy Porter, came to our home to deliver communion to Bentley. I've completed seven-day fasts for my wife and children, asking God for specific breakthroughs. I'll admit that I've even had a few false starts, usually on the third day because that's when the hunger pangs are at their worst. In Matthew 26:41, Jesus said, "Watch and pray so that you will not fall into temptation. The spirit is willing, but the flesh is weak."

So, if you are in Christ, you've been made sufficient to preach the gospel. In fact, we are called to go out and spread the good news. If we are to be followers of God, we must know His Word, be obedient and grateful, forgive, show mercy, and give generously. I read scripture each morning, strive to walk a path like Jesus every day, and give God thanks in all things, good or bad. I've apologized to countless people for any wrongdoings I might have committed and forgiven everyone I can think of whom I've held a grudge against. Why did I do that? Because Jesus has forgiven me for far more egregious things, and He has changed my life forever. I do not dwell in the past. I live for today and trust in God's plans for my future.

I changed how I act toward other people, but more importantly, how I react to people when I'm in a stressful situation. I now bring my prayers to God and know that whatever happens is His will, so I'm at constant peace with the outcome—even when I'm in the midst of a storm. Lastly, not only do I tithe, but it also feels good to give more freely. I've come to realize that I'm merely a steward of what God has given me. I'm accountable for what I do with these gifts, and understand that generosity is encouraged in the Bible. In 2 Corinthians 9:7, it reads, "Each of you should give what you have decided in your heart to give, not reluctantly or under compulsion, for God loves a cheerful giver."

In the book of Galatians, Paul adds to this list when he writes about the fruit of the Spirit: love, joy, peace, patience, kindness, goodness, faithfulness, gentleness, and self-control. When we allow the Holy Spirit to shape us, He transforms the ways we think and act. My heart is more focused on Him, and I'm less angry and more forgiving. I try to listen more, especially when it comes to Bentley or our children. I have peace knowing that God has a plan for each one of them, so I'm more cautious when interjecting my opinion. It's not my ship to steer, and that gives me the freedom to pray for them in a very different way. I simply hope that my will—or more importantly, their will—aligns with His. I've shifted many of my pursuits, reshuffled priorities, and have a new sense of purpose to speak to others about Christ. God did not intend for me to be self-sufficient or live out my days on an island, so I'm listening to Him and striving to become the person He created me to be.

Another significant change is that I can no longer take the Lord's name in vain. Blasphemy means expressing something disrespectful or evil about God. I wouldn't tolerate it if someone cursed my children at the park or in a gym, so why wouldn't I react in the same manner for Him? In Philippians, Paul wrote, "God exalted Him to the highest place and gave Him the name that is above every name, that at the name of Jesus every knee should bow."

So, I must ask myself, would I be comfortable sitting next to Jesus at dinner, in a movie, or at a party, and simply laugh it off when someone uses His name in a derogatory manner? Of course not. It's because I now see the world differently. I see Him differently. God doesn't save us and then leave us unchanged. If you've truly been saved, your old life is gone, and a new one has begun.

I've heard it said that the best time to meet God is when you meet God. If you haven't encountered Him yet, I pray it happens soon. I want for you what was so freely given to me: an eternal future. This is the story of how Jesus saved me and how I finally recognized that *He* was always with me.

"Many are the plans in a person's heart,
but it is the LORD'S purpose that prevails."

—Proverbs 19:21 NIV

EPILOGUE

"Be patient and tough; someday this pain will be useful to you."

—*Ovid*

This chapter wasn't supposed to exist.

In July 2024, we went back to Vanderbilt for Bentley's eighteen-month post-surgical checkup. It had been a long, arduous road since we first learned about her brain tumor six years earlier, but she was about to cross the finish line. This day was supposed to be a formality because everything had looked so good during our last visit with Dr. Haynes. He was so impressed with her recovery after seeing her six months earlier that he'd scheduled a consult to have the gold weight removed from her left eyelid. But first things first—we had to swing by radiology and get a final MRI.

Usually, if we had some downtime between Bentley's tests and an appointment with Dr. Haynes, we'd grab breakfast at the Pancake Pantry. It was only four blocks from the doctor's office, and the food was beyond delicious. Occasionally, we sat in silence after an appointment to absorb what we just heard. Sometimes, we had poignant, gut-wrenching conversations, and other times, like today, we talked about how lucky we were to have found Vanderbilt and all its amazing physicians.

It was a five-minute walk back to Dr. Haynes' office, and we waited for him to bring us the good news. Without missing a beat, he walked into the room with a smile on his face and said the MRI looked great. Now we could find out whether Bentley was doing well enough to have the gold weight removed. The doctor verified her excellent nerve function, her ability to open and close her eyelid, and her strong facial tone. For the first time in a long time, Bentley had a clean bill of health. Dr. Haynes had to call the plastic surgeon, so we waited for him to arrive and confirm that the weight could come out.

Dr. Haynes sat in the exam chair on Bentley's deaf and problematic left side, and I sat across from him next to her healthy ear. We were casually chatting when he asked to switch seats with me.

"I just want to take a quick look," he said.

This was a little weird because in all our visits, he'd never examined her right ear. Nothing had shown up on her previous MRI or CT scans, and she didn't have any hearing loss in that ear. He swung the otomicroscope from her left side over to the right and examined her good ear, then immediately pushed his chair back and took off his glasses.

"What's wrong?" I asked, but I already knew by the look on his face that something was off.

"There's a new mass. A cholesteatoma in your middle ear," he said.

We sat in stunned silence.

"It's a benign growth," he said, "but it will damage your middle ear and the surrounding structures. You could have dizziness or facial paralysis on the right side, and if left untreated, you'll lose your hearing in this ear, too," he said. It was a gut punch of epic proportions.

Didn't we just leave this party?

I thought there was no possible way that Bentley could have another mass and need another surgery, but that's exactly what we now face. We all went from being on cloud nine to discussing the possibility of Bentley having permanent deafness in thirty short seconds. And it all played out in the time it took the surgeon to walk from his office to the exam room.

Dr. Haynes quickly arranged for a departmental CT, and the scan confirmed what he'd seen in his examination. The tumor was small, so the MRI didn't pick it up

"I don't want to risk operating on your only good ear, but if I don't, you'll be completely deaf in a few months," Dr. Haynes said. "We have no choice."

Bentley and I looked at each other for a few seconds, then agreed to schedule the surgery without ever saying a word. We just nodded to each other. This wasn't what we prayed for or the outcome we expected, and it appeared to hit Dr. Haynes the hardest. But Bentley looked at him and said, "It will be OK."

The news was devastating, yet Bentley was calm and supportive of him, like a peace had washed over her. For over four years, we'd prayed separately, together, and in groups for her tinnitus to go away, and when she woke up after her brain surgery, those prayers had been answered. God provided the miracle.

Following that brain surgery, we prayed every day that Bentley's nerve function would be restored and that her facial paralysis would be healed. At only 1 mm per day of healing, the outcome wasn't immediate. We had to rely on faith. And she'd been blessed with enough millimeters over enough days that we realized those prayers had been answered, too. God provided the miracle.

In the weeks leading up to today's appointment, we'd prayed for the tumor to be destroyed, a clean MRI, and an amazing checkup—for her left side. And those prayers had been answered. God provided the miracle.

Yet, after all these miracles, Bentley had to face another surgery. They scheduled her for a tympanomastoidectomy, which is a really long word for saying that they needed to remove the diseased tissue from Bentley's middle ear and mastoid bone. He said it couldn't wait, that he would add her to the schedule as quickly as possible and would message us when the surgery was confirmed.

Over the next seventy-two hours, I asked myself a lot of questions. Why was this happening again? How much can one person endure? Why didn't it show up on the scans? Could we have prevented it? Why did Dr. Haynes look in her right ear? Was it a God nudge? Because if that's what happened, it would be another miracle. After much reflection and in my search for answers, I've realized that I don't have any. I never did. I was never in control. Jesus has been carrying Bentley her whole life. And I got to be a witness.

We now sit and wait for the surgery date and what's to come, but we have peace and a sense of calm that says everything will be OK. Do I worry about her? Yes. Am I fearful about what life will look like in the future? Yes. Does it make me sad that she may never hear her children's voices again? Yes. Yes, to all these things, but I'm not living in fear anymore. I'm not paralyzed by all the what-ifs and catastrophic thinking. I know that God has her and that Jesus Christ died on the cross so she may be made whole one day. I pray that it's in this life, but I know it's a certainty in the next one.

"You intended to harm me, but God intended it for good
to accomplish what is now being done, the saving of many lives."

—Genesis 50:20 NIV

"At one time, we too were foolish, disobedient, deceived, and enslaved by all kinds of passions and pleasures. We lived in malice and envy, being hated and hating one another. But when the kindness and love of God our Savior appeared, he saved us, not because of righteous things we had done, but because of his mercy. He saved us through the washing of rebirth and renewal by the Holy Spirit, whom he poured out on us generously through Jesus Christ our Savior, so that, having been justified by his grace, we might become heirs having the hope of eternal life."

—Titus 3:3-7 NIV

ACKNOWLEDGMENTS

First, I want to thank Nancy Erickson, my book coach and publisher at Stonebrook Publishing. From our very first conversation, she put me at ease. In the span of those thirty minutes, I went from being vehemently opposed to writing my story to knowing it was something I had to pursue. She showed me grace even when I missed multiple deadlines to turn in my manuscript. She listened, challenged me when I needed it most, and frankly made me a better writer than I thought possible. Without Nancy's encouragement and support, I don't know that I ever would have written this book.

Next, I'd like to thank Dr. Lori Rosenthal for her help in identifying the right scriptures for this book. I was new to the Word and unsure where to start, but she had an amazing ability to guide me to the best passages to close a chapter. She also made excellent recommendations for verses that I ultimately used in my text. Lori toughed it out when I gave her first drafts of chapters or sections completely out of sequence, and maybe most importantly, she listened patiently when I struggled to cohesively bridge the secular and spiritual worlds.

I want to offer my sincere thanks to Sid Bream for writing the foreword to this book. I was a new follower of Christ and had only spoken to a handful of men about my transformation. However, after finding the baseball he signed for me, I kept getting this nudge to reach out to him specifically and share my story. The second I heard Sid's voice, I knew I'd called the right person. He listened and asked questions; we talked about God, his walk, my walk, caught up on life, and he agreed to read this manuscript. I am so thankful that baseball allowed our paths to cross so many years ago and blessed that such a strong man of faith is part of my story about Jesus.

Two more people I would like to thank are Reverend Rich Webster and Jahan Berns, both of whom I hold in high regard for their uprightness and love of God. I was lost for so long, but I trusted you both as stewards of His Word and always listened intently to your messages. From the very beginning of this process, I specifically wanted your opinions and feedback. You both took time to speak with me, to better understand my background, never judged, were reassuring and kind, and I thank you for that gift.

To Cade, Davis, and EB, who have brought so much joy to my life. What an amazing honor and absolute privilege it is that God selected me to be your dad. I've enjoyed every minute of fatherhood and the lifetime of incredible memories you've provided. I look forward to seeing you grow as individuals in your walk with Jesus, and I pray that I might be a source of guidance and strength for each of you and your families in the years to come. I love you all dearly, and I look forward to spending eternity with you in Heaven.

They say it's never a good idea to single out one of your kids, but I'm going to do it here. Cade was a massive help to me throughout the entire writing process. I bounced ideas off him; he gave me advice on story structure, guided me as I honed my writing style, and helped me work around a few of my biggest writing roadblocks. However, Cade's greatest assist was the day I wanted to throw in the towel and give up. I just couldn't do it anymore. He was calm and encouraging and suggested that we pray about it. Thank you, bud. I couldn't have done this without you.

And to my wife Bentley, thank you for never giving up on me. I pushed back on all your efforts to bring Jesus into my life for almost thirty years, but you didn't waver. Now I have a relationship with Him. My life has been forever changed—all because of you. I thank God for you every day. You are the greatest gift in my life. How blessed the kids are to have you as their mom and a pillar of strength in their lives. They look up to you as a beacon of mental toughness and unwavering courage through your faith in God. Your limitless love and lifetime of persistence with all of us have resulted in generational blessings being bestowed upon our entire family. I will strive to be more kind, loving, and especially patient. Thank you for everything you do, both seen and unseen. I love you more than you will ever know.

It's impossible for me to properly acknowledge everyone who has impacted my life, given me incredible source material, joined me on some of the more outlandish adventures, worked with me, played on teams I coached, stood by my side through thick and thin, helped me in the early days of my walk with Christ, or listened to me talk about this book, without inadvertently leaving people out. Including everyone was my original intent—so much so that my first draft read more like an opus and came in well north of four hundred pages. As you might imagine, having long lists of names in the body of the text, placing fifteen characters in a scene, or creating lengthy end-of-chapter acknowledgments hindered the message. Careful editing took over, multiple chapters were cut, condensed, and rearranged to tell a more cohesive story. After all, I wrote this book to illustrate the eternal impact that accepting Jesus has had on my life and that of my family. So, here's where I'll sign off. If He could do it for me, I know He can do it for you. All you have to do is ask.

ABOUT THE AUTHOR

Robert Hornak is a graduate of The Citadel, sales professional, husband, dad, coach, filmmaker, and follower of Jesus Christ. After running track at the Military College of South Carolina, Robert embarked on a career in the medical device space. He married his wife Bentley in 1993, and they have three children, Cade, Davis, and EB. He coached soccer for five years in Alexandria, Virginia, before eventually coaching his twin boys' and daughter's basketball and soccer teams in Birmingham, Alabama. Robert founded his production company, Verax Films, in 2013 and has produced nine shorts, documentaries, and feature-length films. He was saved by Jesus and baptized in the Holy Spirit at fifty-four years old. His story is depicted in these pages.